COURSE CORRECTIONS
One Man's Unlikely Journey

LARRY J. NEVELS

iUniverse, Inc.
Bloomington

Course Corrections
One Man's Unlikely Journey

Copyright © 2011 Larry J. Nevels

iUniverse books may be ordered through booksellers or by contacting:

iUniverse
1663 Liberty Drive
Bloomington, IN 47403
www.iuniverse.com
1-800-Authors (1-800-288-4677)

ISBN: 978-1-4620-1636-5 (sc)
ISBN: 978-1-4620-1637-2 (hc)
ISBN: 978-1-4620-1638-9 (e)

Library of Congress Control Number: 2011906886

Printed in the United States of America

iUniverse rev. date: 06/22/2011

This book is dedicated to the three wonderful women in my life…wife Linda and daughters Lauren and Stacey as well as all the angels who have guided me through good times and bad.

Preface -

I was the runt of the first litter, the youngest of four born between late 1941 and 1945. Though she wasn't from the south, while we were growing up our mother would occasionally serve some pretty fine fried chicken. My older siblings made it a ritual to convince me, if I ate the wings, when I grew up, I would be able to fly. For a few years at least, I fell for the ruse which, of course, saved the thighs and breasts for them. Ironically, as it turned out, they were right. Between the ages of 22 and 42 I did a lot of flying as a pilot in the Navy flying mostly multi-engine aircraft over the vast expanses of the Pacific, Indian Ocean, Atlantic, North Sea, and the Mediterranean (Med).

In the early days of my flying career I did quite a bit of DR (dead-reckoning) flying. That is, the estimation of a direction to fly to reach a destination based on a last known position, calculating the effects of in-flight factors such as wind direction and speed, barometric altitude, magnetic heading, airspeed and other conditions. Some refer to it as a semi-scientific wag, or even a wild-ass guess, but pilots and seamen have been using these techniques long before I came along.

Back in the sixties and seventies we would make the flight from Danang or Cam Ranh Bay, South Viet Nam flying out over the South China Sea to Cubi Point Naval Air Station in the Philippines. The distance was about 950 miles and, depending on conditions, took us about four to four and a half hours. We flew on a heading using electronic means until we were too far out to pick up a signal. At 7,000 feet and with our dated equipment that did not take long. We then used

DR techniques for the next several hours until we could pick up a signal in the Philippines that we could follow to our destination.

With training and experience one would get pretty handy using this type of navigation. Later in my career, and in larger aircraft, I would fly much longer distances where there were minimal navigation aids, in places such as the Southern Indian Ocean to Diego Garcia. (Despite its Hispanic sounding name it is owned by the British). Or to Cocos Island, the northern most Australian owned island in the Indian Ocean.

Occasionally, we could take a sun line in the day or shoot a star or two at night. Sometimes, there would be an island or other land mass from which we could determine an exact position and make a *course correction* and get back on track to our destination. The simple rule of thumb was, the more accurate you could determine where you were, *the better you could make a course correction to where you wanted to go.* About one third of my life was flying in the Navy, while two-thirds has been periodically making similar corrections in my personal life.

For many of us, life itself is just a wag, but, there are times when we have the opportunity to determine our precise location. Sometimes we realize we are off track and, if we are smart, we correct to get back on course.

Of course, if you don't know where you are going, it really doesn't matter which direction you fly. For a great part of my personal life I just flew the path of least resistance and landed in some interesting places. But, often I found myself in more than a few very lousy situations. Over time, I wearied at the uncertainty and the realization that my life had become a perpetual WAG.

It was then that I made it my intentional quest to discover exactly where I wanted to go. In the midst of setting out on that quest I was reminded of the wisdom in the trivial comment, *"Life is not a destination, it is a journey."* More accurately, *"Life is a perpetual series of mysterious destinations with the wonders of the journey in between."*

As I started out on my new mission, the logical question was where to begin? Contemplating that, it occurred to me that to know where you are you must understand where you began and the forces, factors and events that brought you to this particular place at this particular time.

So, I began the effort to recall the steps, the turns, the stumbles, the heights, the depths, the smiles and the tears along my path that led me to where I am today. I wanted to understand it all so I just started writing, and writing. This is a journey of the heart and a somewhat dynamic quest to understand ones soul.

I suppose it is impossible to relate a life completely and accurately. Memories can be fickle, and uncertain, and subject to interpretation. The more so as time has lapsed. With that said, I have tried to resist embellishing memories, or *Sea Stories*, and have limited my descriptions to the facts, as I remember them. I have used other sources to verify certain fuzzy events including speaking with many of the people involved and consulting other reputable sources. Try as I might to avoid it, memories and facts may have inadvertently collided. Where possible, I have tried to err on the side of fact. If you remember events described herein differently, *God bless you.*

There are portions of this that are painful to relive and in the interest of protecting others, there are some events I have declined to include. One of my literary heroes, W Somerset Maugham, wrote that his classic, *"Of Human Bondage,"* was *cathartic* for him. In his story, the hero had a club foot. Maugham's albatross was a stutter.

I also had to deal with an embarrassing stutter when I was young. As a result, I didn't talk unless it was absolutely necessary. Demosthenes, considered the greatest orator of ancient Greece, suffered from a speech impediment and he worked at a series of self-designed exercises to overcome it. Legend says he placed a couple river stones in his mouth for years to improve his diction. I heard this story when I was young and, not having any rivers close by, I substituted marbles. Occasionally, one or two would fall out but I just smiled and said, *"Oops, I lost my marbles again."* I think I swallowed one, but it came out in the end.

Like Maugham, writing has been cathartic for me, and like Demosthenes, I overcame my stammering to become a DJ at several different radio stations and obtained a minor in speech at college. While I have stuttered very little since my youth, even today, I cannot speak to a group without the fear of stammering.

At the time of this writing, I am in the autumn of my life. I do not remember the past 65 years as a novel or even a long running movie. It is rather a series of short stories, vignettes, perhaps even photographic snippets of time. If I knew I was going to write a book I probably would have taken better notes along the way; but then, maybe not. You may notice as you read this, I do bounce around a bit so fasten your seatbelts, keep all arms and legs inside the car at all times and I hope you enjoy the ride.

While producing this work this may have been cathartic, no amount of writing can fully remove the scars of our youth and our lives. But, I have learned to look the devil straight in the eye while I'm picking his pocket for my soul. When I wake in the morning that evil man cringes and says, "Crap, here he comes again." He may eventually cause the ravishing of my body but he will never steal the sweetness of my soul!

IT WAS IN 1945 that I was born. For over half of that year our country was at war, but on the 15th of August Japan surrendered and WW-II was finally over; though the official surrender-signing was a little later.

Technically, I suppose, I came along a little early to be designated a *Baby Boomer*. Still, the microwave oven and the slinky were invented that year, along with nuclear weapons. The world would forever be a different place, but, I doubt my coming had much to do with that.

Thinking back to when you were young, it is sometimes hard to put things in proper order. What happened and in what sequence can get muddled over the years. While I was a huge fan of Bill 'Hopalong' Cassidy, or 'Hoppy' as he was referred to in those days, from where I sit today he was not my "First Hero." Still, he was right up there.

My mother wanted me to like Roy Rogers and I did, but he just wasn't 'Hoppy' to me. She couldn't believe I was disappointed when I got a two-holster set of Roy Rogers's guns for my fourth birthday in 1949. It's hard to hide your disappointment when you are only four, but I did try. I mean, they were really cool guns; they just weren't the black Hoppy version of my dreams.

No, my first hero was Tommy Hamilton. Tommy lived next door to us on 522 W. 168th St. in Gardena, California. It seems odd, I cannot remember what I had for breakfast this morning but I remember that address from over 60 years ago.

My first memory of Tommy was probably from 1949. I was four, my two sisters were five and six and my older brother was seven. Someone once told me, *"You never know when the first one is coming, but all the rest are nine months apart."* That pretty much described the four that made up the first litter of kids in my family. By the time my mother was 22, she had these four children tugging at her apron.

The four of us were playing cowboys and Indians and I was the designated Indian. Seems the older three caught me and decided there should be a *hangin'*. A rope was dangling from a tree and I was lifted onto a chair or a barrel (that detail is a bit fuzzy). Well, the barrel/chair slipped and left me dangling there. My slightly older siblings evidently panicked and ran off. The next thing I remember I was in the arms of Tommy Hamilton. Tommy would have been about 19 at the time but seemed a giant of a man to me.

Did this little episode really happen? My siblings do not recall the event, but then, they were the culprits with the most to lose if they were caught, and dangling from a tree with a rope around your neck tends to brand an event on your mind. For me, it is etched in my memory as visible as any other memory I have, recent or distant. Growing up, and even now, I cannot wear a tie unless it is very loose, and every relationship I have ever had will attest to my drastic reflex when my neck is touched.

My father, Joseph William Nevels (JW), was a strange man who wrestled with so many demons over his lifetime that he's hard to describe. I have no fond memories of the man at all during my childhood. My earliest memory was waking one night after I had been sick and I badly needed to go to the bathroom. I was probably three, maybe just turned four.

My brother and I slept in the living room in one of those beds that folded into the wall during the day. They were called Murphy Beds, named for the inventor William Murphy who patented the design in 1916.

I was sleeping in one of those full body pajamas, probably with a flap in the back. Evidently, I made too much noise making my way to the bathroom in the dark and awoke my father. He came out of his bedroom screaming, *"What are you doing out of bed?"*

"I have to poop," I sheepishly explained.

He picked me up and took me back to the living room, threw me in the bed, and yelled, *"Don't get up again!"* I still hadn't 'pooped' but I was too terrified to say anything or get out of bed again. I did eventually go to sleep but awoke in the morning with soiled PJ's.

I pretended to be asleep until my father had left, my siblings had gone to school and my mother returned from working her graveyard shift and had gone to sleep. I tried to hide my PJ's, but finding a place to secret-away a pair of crap-laden sleepwear in a small house is harder than you might think, especially for a three year old.

Not too much time had passed before my next memory of my father occurred. It was in the summer when I became carsick while riding in the backseat of a 1940's era car as he smoked a cigar. His anger was uncontrollable when I said I thought I was going to throw-up. Eventually, I stuck my head out the back window and lost my cookies while he puffed away. He laughed at first, and then he was overcome with anger when he realized the back of the car had been soiled.

I have always referred to him as 'JW' or, if forced, I would refer to him as 'father' since, while I was biologically attached to the man, he never seemed like a *dad* to me.

Then there was my next memory of Tommy Hamilton, probably within a year of the first encounter.

It was a typical pleasant California afternoon. My father was involved in a rare fatherly task of teaching my oldest sister how to ride a bicycle. Nancy was not catching on to the whole thing fast enough for him and it turned into a very loud, one way, shouting event. I know I had not yet turned five so Nancy was probably seven. The shouting must have caught my attention because I remember going outside to view the commotion. Our *father* got so angry at Nancy and the angrier he became, the more nervous she was with the whole endeavor. "Counter-productive" and "patience" were not terms he understood. That was when one of his demons took control and he began hitting Nancy for not meeting his timetable for learning to ride the bike. I remember crying for Nancy, because, there just wasn't anything else a four year old could do.

Just then, almost like Superman, my hero, Tommy Hamilton, showed up and got between Nancy and our father in the middle of the street in front of our house. Tommy screamed at my father that if he ever saw him hit Nancy again he would kill him. Born in 1930, Tommy was about 20 at the time. I calculate our father was about 26. Like most cowards who beat kids, our father backed off when confronted by another man and quickly retreated into the house, with us in tow.

It was Christmas Eve at the end of that same year. We had a small tree but there was nothing under it. We went to bed that night hoping that Santa Claus would bring us something. I know I wanted a black 'Hopalong' Cassidy holster set. Sorry Mom.

We awoke the next morning, as millions of kids across the world did, with great anticipation for what might await us on Christmas morning. To our wonder and amazement there were many gifts under our tree. How had Santa managed to do that without waking one of us, we marveled? We four kids dared not touch anything until we were told we could. A short time later our mother showed up but our father never appeared. We were apprehensive to touch anything without him being there, until our mother told us we could open our presents.

I was too young to read much beyond my name, but there was some confusion over whose gifts were for whom. You see, the names on the presents did not reflect anyone in our household. Could Santa have made a mistake? My mother opened each present a tiny bit and when she saw what it was she would give it to one of us with only a feeble, "*This one is for you.*" We were too excited by the moment to be troubled by the inconsistencies and gleefully opened our Christmas gifts.

One of my presents was a teddy bear and another was a gumball machine with plastic coins you could insert into a slot, turn the dial, and get a gumball. I admit I cannot remember what anyone else received but I do recall before the day was out, we were sent to pack and left the house.

We went to a small one room garage apartment with an outside stairway as the only entrance. All I knew about the owner was that his name was Jacob, and we referred to that outside stairway as *Jacob's Ladder*. We did not go back home to 522 W. 168th street for some time, at least a few weeks, probably longer.

There came a knock on the door at the top of Jacob's ladder, and three men came in. I remember at least two were in suits and the third may have been a policeman, but I am not sure. I sensed something was amiss and picked up my teddy bear and found a safe place in a far corner of the room. The men began taking my brother and sister's Christmas gifts. I figured out that it would soon be my turn, so I left my teddy bear in the corner, picked up the gumball machine that was still half full of gumballs, and handed it to one of the men. I then went back to my corner, picked up my teddy bear, trying desperately to make myself as small and inconspicuous as possible.

It looked as if the men were about to leave when one in a suit come over to me in the corner and held out his hand. I just looked him in the eye and held tight to my teddy bear.

My mother came over and said, *"Give the man your bear."* I think I paused a moment and my mother firmly said, *"Larry!"* I handed the man my bear. The men quickly left and we were in a room at the top of Jacob's ladder totally confused and befuddled at what had just happened. I remember thinking we must have done something terribly wrong to cause the men to come in and take our Christmas away. My brother and sisters were crying while I just sat in the corner, too dazed to cry or do anything.

A few days later we climbed down Jacob's ladder for the last time and returned to 522 W. 168th St. We did not see our father for some time. Eventually, he returned and my remaining memories of him from that time were of us going into some wooded areas to collect mushrooms. Another time, we were sitting on the side of the road in our car while he and our mother sold socks to anyone passing by.

Later that year, our father disappeared again, but that was such the norm for us that we did not consider it unusual. To tell the truth, it was more pleasant when he wasn't around.

Then came the day when my mother said we were going on a trip. The five of us climbed into the car and headed north to Sacramento. I spent much of the trip with crayons and a coloring book. We stopped and spent the night in the car on the side of the road on the way north. Our mother made baloney sandwiches for supper. It was summer and it was hot, very hot, especially in Sacramento.

We drove to a place where my mother told us we were going to see our father. I left my crayons in the glove box of the car. We walked through several gates and eventually into a room behind a heavy screen, or, perhaps it was glass. He was wearing a straw hat and wore some sort of uniform. That's about all I remember about the visit, except when we returned to the car, I went to retrieve my crayons only to find these puddles of colored wax on the bottom of the glove box. Sacramento is *hot* in the summer.

We returned to 522 W. 168th St. and settled into a modest routine. Since my birthday was in October, I had not started school yet. Our mother found a job at the Firestone Tire & Rubber factory, similar to one she had during WW-II in Ohio. She worked *the graveyard shift,* which sounded spooky to me. The four of us were left to our own devices all night. She would come home in the morning and sleep all day while my sisters and brother were at school. I learned quickly to be quiet since my mother was not in a good mood if I woke her during the day.

The Korean War broke out and Tommy Hamilton went off to war. I don't know if he joined the Army or was drafted. Before he left, Mr. and Mrs. Hamilton, Tommy's parents, asked if he could store his car in our garage while he was overseas. Since our father was *away* and our mother worked nights it was evidently an easy decision.

There was this one particular evening that is clearly etched into my mind. Our mother was at work; I had just turned five, Carole was seven, Nancy was eight and Don was nine. The four of us were *home-alone*, so to speak, when we came across some wax Santa Claus candles in the garage. We played with them for awhile and, eventually, could not resist the temptation to light them. Sometime, later that evening, we took them back to the garage and went back in to play or read or color.

We had this fishbowl shaped TV and sometime during the evening it went dead, along with all the lights. That was not an uncommon occurrence in that house. We had these round screw-in circuit breakers that would often pop and shut things down. The solution had always been to replace the glass circuit breakers, if we had any spares. This particular night we had no spares but, we had learned that you can put a penny in the circuit breaker socket, screw in the old one, and it would work just fine. So, that is what we did. Remember, these were four kids ages five to nine, playing with a live CB box, and stuffing pennies behind them. Looking back, the chances of someone being electrocuted were very high. God watches over kids and crazy people.

On this night, all our efforts were to no avail. We began to look around and noticed a light outside and discovered the garage was engulfed in flames. Somebody, Carole I think, ran next door and woke-up Mr. & Mrs. Hamilton, who called the fire department. By the time they got there the garage was hopelessly in flames and they barely saved the house with just some minor fire damage to the back porch that contained the fuse box.

I remember standing in the driveway, with extreme sadness, as the men fought the fire. I knew Tommy Hamilton's car was totally destroyed. I also remembered that my brother Don's rocking horse,

6

which I was supposed to inherit someday, was in there as well. But it was my hero's car that saddened me most.

The four of us kids never said a word about the candles or the pennies in the circuit box. The firemen concluded the whole event was caused by faulty wiring. Our mother was convinced that our father had hired someone to kill us, and shortly afterwards we were shipped off to the first of many foster homes. Much later I was told that my father was convinced that our mother had turned him in to the police and evidently vowed "*to get her/us*" as he was led away after his guilty verdict.

I doubt our mother had any choice about the foster homes. Leaving four kids so young home-alone was frowned upon in California, even in 1950.

It wasn't until several years later that I heard more of these stories, part of which I had surmised. Our father had broken into someone's home on Christmas Eve, stole their presents, put them under our tree and fled back to his mother's home in Pennsylvania. When he returned he was arrested and given a light sentence since the gifts had been recovered. However, sometime later he had been at one of Gardena, California's infamous gambling halls and lost all the money he had. Convinced the man had cheated him, he hid on the floorboard of the man's car, knocked him in the head with a wrench, and took all his money. He might have gotten away with it, except, while he was crouched down in the back of the man's car, his wallet fell out of his pocket. I never said the man was bright.

Since this was his second offense, and it was considered armed robbery, he was sentenced to about 10 years in Folsom Prison; yep, the same one ole Johnny Cash sang about.

Sometime after the fire and before we went off to foster homes, an Army staff car pulled up in front of Mr. and Mrs. Hamilton's home on 168th St. My hero and friend, Tommy Hamilton had been killed in battle in Korea on September 26, 1951.

"*I don't remember if I cried; the day I learned my hero died. But something touched me deep inside, the day my hero died.*"

Many years later, in 1968 I think, after I had graduated from college and just before I went into the Navy I went back to 168th street with my sister Carole. Mr. Hamilton had died, but Mrs. Hamilton was still there. She shared a letter she had received a few weeks after she was notified of Tommy's death. It was from Tommy and he seemed to know what was about to happen. He wrote, *"Mom, this may be my last letter to you. Things are not going well here and we are going out on patrol in a few moments. If I don't make it back please know that I love you and Dad with all my heart......"* He wrote a couple more lines and signed it, *"Your Loving Son, Tommy".*

She also gave me his obituary from a local newspaper:

Thomas A. Hamilton
Born 1930, Private, U.S. Army
Killed in Action, September 26, 1951 in Korea. Private Hamilton was a member of the 8th Cavalry Regiment, 1st Cavalry Division. He was Killed- in-Action while fighting the enemy in North Korea on September 26, 1951. Private Hamilton was awarded the Purple Heart, the Combat Infantryman's Badge, the Korean Service Medal, the United Nations Service Medal, the National Defense Service Medal, the Korean Presidential Unit Citation and the Republic of Korea War Service Medal.

As I read this, it seemed such a sanitary way to sum up the life of a 21 year old young man who served and died for his country. There is no mention that a couple years earlier he saved my life, that he humiliated a child abuser, that he had dreams and plans. I know, rationally thinking, who knew? But every person has a story and every story deserves to be told.

Yes, Tommy was my first hero and throughout college, and my 20 plus year naval career, he was my inspiration.

~~~

There is a scene at the end of the movie *"Saving Private Ryan"* where, after many years, Ryan returns to a WW-II military cemetery in France with his children and grandchildren. As a young soldier in WW-II, Ryan was the last surviving son in his family. The Tom Hanks character was sent with a platoon of men to bring him back from the front lines.

Ryan locates the stone with the name of the Army Captain (Tom Hanks) who was sent to bring him home. The Hanks character had been mortally wounded and his last words to Ryan were, *"Lead a good life."*

As the much older Ryan kneels towards the grave marker, his wife comes up behind him. He turns to her and asks, *"Have I led a good life?"* Not knowing the reason for the question, she honestly responds, *"Yes, of course."* The elder Ryan, still kneeling before the grave, turns and touches the stone marker.

~~~

"Tommy, it's been 60+ years since you saved my life. I've tried to lead a good life for both of us. I hope you approve."

— 2 —

IT SEEMS ODD, somewhat speculative even, looking back and searching for a moment when life changed forever.

It was 1997; my new wife and my daughter Lauren and I were on a trip to California for a vacation and to introduce them to my mother. Though technically Lauren had met her grandmother, she was too young to remember, and I wanted her to have a chance to know her because I suspected the ravages of time were most likely soon to make that improbable.

Many years of experience had taught me that my mother had this internal clock that must have been attached to something akin to C-4 explosives. For about 4-6 hours she could be the most charming and loveable mother and grandmother anyone could imagine. Then, the sand in some ancient timepiece would run out and she would morph into someone almost unrecognizable. Except for the timing, it was sudden and unpredictable, like a Mrs. Hyde had suddenly possessed her body.

My wife and my daughter had never seen this, and I was determined to continue that for as long as possible. I intentionally timed our arrival so that our departure would be easy, just before that specific, predictable time. My reason for leaving was that we were off to Disneyland, three hours to the North. But, my plan was almost derailed when Mother announced how much she would like to go with us to the Magic Kingdom.

The visit was going well and I was tempted to agree to her proposal, but years of experience had taught me not to fall into that trap.

10

There was about an hour left in our visit when I asked to speak to her privately. Lauren and Linda went for a walk, and I reminded my mother about a story she had told me many years earlier about when she was young. She loved to talk about those times. It seemed to be the only subject that kept her calm, when things started to go awry.

I asked her some specific questions about the time when she was young and her eyes would smile as she relived many stories. The truth is, I was trying to make some sense of many things and, the more she spoke, the clearer things became to me.

In grappling to understand subsequent events, it is always difficult and perhaps impossible to correctly connect the dots, but as she spoke to me, some things started to make a little sense. That itself provided some clarity to much of the odd and bizarre behavior that seemed to control her at times.

This is what I learned…

She was born Dorothy Ann Comer in 1923, in the town of Turtle Creek, Pennsylvania, the second daughter of Joe and Rachel Comer. All told, she was an above average student in school and quite the looker. Her junior year in high school she had her eyes on Robert Taylor, a senior. Dorothy Ann was determined when it came to boys and once she put her sites on Robert, he didn't stand a chance. Towards the end of her junior year, his senior year, Robert invited her to a senior party. Her mother, Rachel, at first said *no,* but relented to the insistence of Dorothy that they were just going to a friend's house for a "small graduation party".

Robert picked up Dorothy and lit out for a roadhouse just over the county line towards Pittsburg where he knew they would not check her age. The roadhouse was packed with seniors about to graduate from high school and college students from Pittsburg looking for cheap booze and loud music. There were tables & chairs surrounding a dance floor that became increasingly crowded as the evening wore on. Above each table was a light bulb in a socket dangling on the end of a wire that provided the light for the room.

Dorothy was happy to finally be on a date with Robert and felt all grown-up, being one of the few underclassmen in the joint. Though the drinks were watered down, as the night wore on, they began to have an impact on the kids. There was a small combo that tried to play the

Big Band Sound. It probably sounded better and better as the night wore on.

Later in the evening, when everyone was *feelin' good,* Robert asked Dorothy to dance but she thought the floor was too crowded. Robert then climbed on the table beside the dance floor and invited others to join him. Dorothy just couldn't bring herself to climb onto the increasingly crowded table top. There was a group of college kids that walked by and began shaking the table. The kids on the sides stepped off while the college kids shook the table even more. People were clamoring to get off the table but Robert kept smiling at Dorothy, determined to be the last man standing. Dorothy tried to get the college boys to stop shaking the table, but to no avail. They were as determined to bring Robert down as he was to stay up there.

Finally they gave the table a quick push and Robert lost his balance. As he started to fall backwards he grabbed the wire light fixture to help him catch his balance. In an instance, sparks were flying and Robert was in a death grip with the hot electrical wire. He hung there shaking, unable to free himself from the wire. Dorothy reached out to him, but she was pulled away by others, a move that probably saved her life.

Eventually, but sadly too late, someone found a board and knocked Robert free of the electrical trap he had been in, and he fell to the floor with a thud. There was a sickening smell of burning flesh from Roberts's hands and he wasn't breathing. No one, including Dorothy, knew what to do. People ran screaming from the road house, trying to get away before the authorities arrived. It was almost an hour before help finally showed up for Robert. For Dorothy, her beau was dead at the hands of *"those damn college kids,"* an incident that would impact her life for decades to come.

Dorothy completed her senior year, not doing as well academically as she had in the previous years. She had lost interest in school and her plans for higher education disappeared after that night at the roadhouse. She got a job and began hanging out at bars and roadhouses, not drinking to excess at first, but enough to make her vulnerable. At age 17 she met and married Joseph William Nevels and over the first 5 years of marriage had four kids, me being the fourth. She would eventually have seven children, one of which was stillborn. She was definitely fertile territory and it seemed that just being downwind of that stuff would lead to another pregnancy.

Dorothy and Joe Nevels moved to Cleveland, Ohio, where Don was the first born, just four days after Pearl Harbor was attacked. This was followed in predictable succession by Nancy, who was born in Monroe, Michigan & 10 months later Carol, who was born in Bakersfield, Calif. Dorothy would drop a baby, take a few days off and leave the kids with either her mother, Rachel Comer, or Joseph's widowed mother.

During the war years, in between having babies, Dorothy worked at the Firestone Tire plant in Ohio and other odd jobs. Despite being a prolific producer of babies, she was ill prepared for motherhood, and the war was a convenient way to be sacrificing for the countries effort.

Joseph William's contribution to the war effort has always remained a little fuzzier. In later years he claimed he was discharged in California because he had so many kids but my mother maintained he was kicked out with a *Less than Honorable* discharge for *unspecified reasons*. In later years, I remember she made the charge that he insisted she have more babies in order to get a deferment.

It could not have been long after Carol was born in Bakersfield, California that they moved back to Monroe, Michigan where I came along in 1945, just a couple months after the war ended. In later years, I liked to point out the Japanese started the war when they found out Don was coming and quit when they realized I was on the way.

I could tell my mother was becoming tense and though I had many more questions I would have liked to ask, I knew it was time for us to leave. She mentioned one more time about going to Disneyland with us but I knew in my heart and head that that would not end well. I felt terrible for her, but there just was no alternative.

For her entire life, my mother was a captive to her past, including that incident decades before in a roadhouse outside Pittsburg. Even though all six of her surviving children became college graduates she held a deep resentment for those *"Hoity-toity college kids"* until the day she died.

As she spoke, I couldn't help but wonder, are these events reasons, excuses or just points in time where subtle decisions are made that define our future? In the end, regardless of the event, it all comes down to choices. An ambling mind may easily fall victim to circumstance, while a focused person can choose to maintain their direction by refusing to allow isolated events to control their future.

Many people become prisoners to their past and become mired

in self-pity and anger over some obscure thing. The longer they hold on, the harder it is to let it go. Too often, it can become a cancerous memory that permeates an entire life, ruins relationships, and keeps people from enjoying the happiness that was theirs, and remains all along, right there on the tips of their fingers.

But this memory, and other events, and her inability to let it go, prevented her from a life of joy and celebration as each of her children graduated from college. I know she did not attend any of my graduations and I suspect she avoided my sibling's celebrations as well. It may have been logistically impossible for her to attend, but I do not recall any cards or letters expressing pride or even congratulations. I can't help but think that, for some people, memories of events can condemn them to lives of misery. The insidious part to all this is that some people wear these events like a perverted badge of honor, and cling to their memories and their miseries as an entitlement.

—————————————————————————————— 3 –

DESPITE BEING MY father, I know very little about Joseph William Nevels. What little I did learn from my mother was likely slanted by her tainted view of the man. Many years later his sister, my Aunt Helen, spoke of him much more favorably.

I have made it a major tenant of my mine to judge people on my own experience with a person, and not someone else's. With that in mind I make judgments about my father based on what I know to be true and not based on someone else's perception. I know he was born in Pennsylvania in 1921.

Evidently his father, my grandfather, also Joseph Nevels was from an aristocratic family in Hungary. He fell in love with a peasant girl named Mari Molnor who was born on August 13th 1895. Mari's father was Joseph Molnar and mother Rosali Mata Molnar.

An aristocrat and a peasant girl coming together was out of the question in the late 19th century and early 20th century in Hungary so my grandfather and his brother came to America to make their fortune and start anew. They came through Ellis Island where he reported his name as Joseph Nevelos. It was recorded, however, as Joseph Nevels and, as was the custom of the time, the spelling of the name became permanent.

Joseph Nevelos-Nevels incessantly pined for his true love, Mari, back in Hungary and, after saving enough money, he returned to his homeland and brought Mari Molner to America. Since they could not marry in Hungary, they were either married by the Captain aboard the ship or they claimed to be married and entered America as husband

and wife. It seems the nicety of a marriage certificate was rare in those days. An application for social security my grandmother filled out in the 1930's, indicated they arrived in this country as husband and wife.

Joseph tried to reconnect with his brother but he no longer resided in upstate New York and left no forwarding address; he never heard from him again. People who knew him indicated he went to Kentucky or West Virginia to work in the coal mines there. Joseph found a job in the coal mines of western Pennsylvania where he was noted to be comparatively higher educated than the average coal miner of the time. He spent a short time in the mines and, rather quickly, was promoted to a mid-management position.

My father rarely talked about his father. One time he mentioned him as being strict and demanding and hinted at him being abusive.

Not much more was told to me about my grandfather except my grandmother told me about a miners' strike that occurred sometime in the late 1930's. Apparently my grandfather, Joseph Nevels, was at the mine one evening, a shot from a disgruntled miner rang out, and my grandfather was killed.

My mother insisted that was not the true story and that my father had several times confessed to her that he shot my grand-father during the strike and my grandmother vouched for her son and insisted he was home at the time of the shooting. Since all the players in this tragedy are all gone on to their own judgments, we will never know the truth of the matter. Just as well, I suppose.

My grandmother stayed on their farm in Perryopolis, Pennsylvania, which we visited a few times over the years, and where she cared for me from time to time. She was a fundamentalist Catholic which, I observed, was not much different from my other Grandmother, Rachel Comer, who was a fundamentalist Baptist. I know, some of you may see that as a contradiction, but their similarities far outweighed their differences.

While Mari Molner Nevelos-Nevels was somewhat distant and lacked the fun sense of humor of Rachel Comer I have fond memories of them both.

I was, without a doubt, closest to Grandma Comer, our mother's mother. Off-and-on over the years, she lived with us, and at least once I lived with her. She used to tell the story that, while taking care of me, I would run in the front door, through the small house and out the back door all the time screaming, *"I'm hungry, I'm hungry."* Evidently, I made several cycles of this until she fixed one of those baloney sandwiches that seem to permeate that side of the family.

Grandma Comer was a big woman; at least that is the way she seemed. Our mother was petite by comparison. But, man-oh-man, could Grandma Comer laugh. Every memory and every picture I ever saw of her was with this huge belly-laugh-look on her face. She was the happiest person I have ever met. I suspect I inherited much of my sense of humor from Grandma Comer. Lord knows there wasn't much on the other side of the family. There was only once that I remember her without a smile.

It seems there was this terrible flood in Gardena California in the early 1950's and the five of us thought it would be great fun to go out and play in the water. Yes, I said the 5 of us. Grandma Comer had another daughter besides our mother, Aunt Joan, who was born in 1939 or maybe it was 1940. She was pretty close in age to Don who was born in 1941.

I recall going to the flooded streets just north of 168ᵗʰ St. and making these rafts of wood and watching my older brother go sailing down, what was just moments earlier, a busy street. We are talking some serious flooding. I wanted so badly to get on the raft but my brother refused, so I ran in waist deep water trying, to keep up. Nancy and Carole were there as well and we all came home totally soaked, just as our mother arrived from work. She was furious and we all were on the receiving end of a huge belt, reserved for just such occasions. Since Aunt Joan was the oldest, our mother felt that she should have stopped those neighborhood yacht races and made it known to Grandma Comer that Joan should have been chastised much more than she was.

"What do you want me to do?" Grandma Comer responded to my mother, "Kill her?"

I never knew my grandfather, Joe Comer, except it was noted that Aunt Joan and my mother had different dads. There were stories that he was an alcoholic and a wife abuser. I do know he died in 1960 from complications of alcoholism. He had one other daughter besides my mother, my Aunt Thelma, and two sons, Uncle Dick and the youngest, Uncle Joe. I understand both sons died from alcohol related illnesses.

I think it was Uncle Joe who lived with us a few months in Southern California. I remember going to watch auto races with him in the late

1940's or early 50's, that were more demolition-derbies than races. I also remember the night he was so in need of alcohol he drank a bottle of shoe polish along with a bottle of vanilla. I don't think either one of those products contains alcohol these days.

Many years later, my sister Carole and I made a trip to Lake City, Arkansas where my Aunt Joan lived with her family along with Grandma Comer. Grandma actually lived in a second small house on the property. I knew this might very well be the last time I would see my grandmother; she was up in years and I was going into the Navy. My grandmother had very few possessions but that never affected her pride or personality. The nicest item she had was this pyrex baking dish. She pulled it out and handed it to me.

"Larry," she began, "I probably won't be around when you get married and I want you to have this as a wedding gift." My natural inclination was to refuse the gift since she had so little and was giving to me the best she had, but I remembered the words that were read to me several years earlier…*"And you receivers … and you are all receivers… assume no weight of gratitude, lest you lay a yoke upon yourself and upon he who gives…for to be mindful of your debt is to doubt the generosity of he who has given."* More about that later.

I accepted her gift but got a little misty-eyed as she beamed with joy at her ability to give me something. I have been humbled in my life, many times, but seldom so humbled as I felt the moment my grandmother gave to me her very best.

4

AFTER THE FIRE that destroyed Tommy Hamilton's car, my two older sisters Nancy and Carole went to one foster home, while my oldest brother Don and I, were sent together to another. At age five, the very idea of a foster home was terrifying. While I do surmise the intentions of our foster parents were genuine, I had no idea who they were and I did not understand why we had to leave our home on 522 W. 168th St. I remember thinking it must have been punishment for the fire. Certainly we had done something terribly wrong.

I don't think we were in the first home for very long. About all I remember is our "foster parents" seemed much younger than my mother and father. I know Don was in school but, being born in October, I had not yet started first grade. For some reason, I wondered off one afternoon and on my way back I passed a gas station. There was this Pepsi bottle sitting there and I proceeded to take a big drink. *It was awful!* I ran home and tried to rinse my mouth out with water. My foster mother realized something was wrong and when I told her what had happened we went back to the service station and discovered the bottle was filled with gasoline. They rushed me to the emergency room of the nearest hospital where they wound this tube down my throat and proceeded to pump-out my stomach.

My last memory of those foster parents was that they evidently got into trouble for taking me to the closest hospital, which was not the county hospital to which they were instructed to take us.

Shortly after that event, Don and I were off to another foster home in Redondo Beach, California. These "parents" were much older than the previous ones. They lived on a goat farm along with the father of one of them, who lived in a small house adjacent to us and continuously smoked.

We must have lived there for about a year or more. While there, I started the first grade at George Washington Elementary School in Redondo Beach. On my first day of school, my teacher asked us to spell our names. I very proudly wrote, 'Larry Nevels' and to my surprise was corrected by my teacher who said, "No, your last name is spelled N-e-v-i-l-s. I insisted she was wrong and it was spelled N-e-v-e-l-s. Evidently, I was rather insistent, some might say stubborn, and she made me stay after school that first day and tried to get me to write it her way on the blackboard several times. I kept writing my name the way I believed to be correct so she called my foster parents to come and get me.

While we waited for them to arrive, an elderly Hispanic man came in selling strawberries, with the teacher buying a full case that contained several baskets of the fruit. When my foster parents arrived they explained that little Larry was right. It seems the state of California had mistakenly informed the school my name was spelled with an "i." The teacher apologized to me and gave me a basket of strawberries, which was quickly confiscated by my foster mother.

The goat farm was a great place for three boys. It seems that in addition to my brother and me there was another foster child living there when we arrived. I don't think he was too pleased by our arrival and he was always telling on us about one thing or another. Don and I did not like him very much.

The three of us dug this cave in the back of a rise in the barnyard that was not visible from the house. We conspired to expropriate a can of fruit cocktail from the house to have a "feast" in our cave. All three of us boys enjoyed the fruit but the third kid turned us in to the couple as having stolen the can. I don't know if we defended ourselves or not but I do remember getting several whacks from a razor strap while 'the traitor' looked on and smiled.

We must have stayed in that home for what seemed like an eternity, but was probably about a year. Then there was the day the three of use confiscated a pack of cigarettes from the elderly man who smoked so much. Don was in the fourth or fifth grade & offered to teach me how to smoke. So we got a pack from the old man's house and met in our cave. Don tried to teach me the right way to smoke but I just kept blowing, not inhaling.

The Saturday after our attempt at smoking, while Don was away playing baseball, I was called into the house by my foster father. In the living room there was a carton of cigarettes and a box of cigars in the middle of the floor. The other kid had squealed on us again.

The man made me start smoking and told me Don would join me when he returned home. A short time later, Don arrived and was ushered into the living room. We were told we had to smoke the entire carton of cigarettes and the box of cigars. As when I was younger, the very smell of a cigar made me sick. The man said that if we threw-up before getting to the bathroom he would toss in another pack of cigarettes.

As best I can recall we went through the entire pile of tobacco. I suppose we were the first kids on our block in Redondo Beach to have emphysema. While I don't recommend that approach I must point out that neither Don nor I smoke and, as far as I know, never have since that sadistic Saturday on the goat farm in Redondo Beach, California.

I always wanted to eat lunch at school but my foster parents insisted I walk home for lunch and every day. There was this guy, Arthur Godfrey, on the radio who always played the ukulele and sang, not very well, five-year-old music critic that I was.

There was a particular lunch that remains clear in my memory. I arrived home to fried liver as the main entrée for lunch, a dish which I could not eat without gagging. They told me I would have to stay at the table until I ate my serving of liver. Well, minutes turned into hours and I sat there all afternoon and into the early evening looking at that really awful stuff. When dinner was ready I was told to go to my room without eating; a small price to pay to avoid that gross internal organ.

Needless to say, Don and I hated our time in these state-run foster homes. Looking back, I appreciate the fact that people would step up and help kids in need but I have to wonder if their motivation was really for the kids or for the monthly payment they received for each child. It's the cynic in me, I suppose.

There was no sadness the day the California state social worker came to pick us up and take us home to our mother. Our foster-parents were probably as anxious to see us go as we were to leave.

Our mother had married this beer truck driver named Bud, a name which always seemed ironic to me, considering there was this huge "Budweiser" sign on the side of his truck. Over the next eleven years I would find myself in many informal foster homes but that day we left Redondo Beach was the last state-sponsored foster home I would see. I was ecstatic to be going home to 522 W. 168th St., even though our stay there would be brief.

5

OUR NEW STEP-FATHER was Nolas Leeroy, but he, understandably, preferred the moniker "Bud." Originally from Clarksville, Arkansas, he had been drawn to California, just as thousands of others were, though he evidently was not fond of life on the west coast.

"Mom! He's a redneck from Arkansas who drives a beer truck. What could possibly go wrong?"

Now don't get me wrong, I met scores of wonderful people in Arkansas and some of my fondest memories are of my time there. But red flags are red flags. Ignore them at your own peril.

Sometime, while we were in foster homes, our mother divorced our father as he was serving the first few of a 10-year sentence. Our father's threats and the fire probably influenced our mother to accept the idea of a move to Arkansas. Whatever the reason, it got me out of that foster home and I was happy.

Our mother sold the house on W. 168th St. and bought herself a *new-used car*, an early '50's station wagon. Bud drove his truck while our mother drove the station wagon, with us four kids, across the Southwest desert on the old Route 66 heading east to Arkansas. I remember stopping at an inspection station and being told by the police we could not continue without a canvas water bag attached to the front of the car. It seems too many cars had overheated crossing the desert and the authorities required everyone to carry emergency water. This was before the interstate system had been completed and gas stations were few and far between.

When one did come across a station on Route 66, there were almost always Indians selling turquoise jewelry and bows and arrows to young boys like me, though I never got one. There were roadside motels where each unit looked like an Indian tee-pee, but we never stopped in any of those. Our new step-father was a long-haul trucker and insisted we drive as far and as long as possible. Our mother bought bread, mayo and baloney and made sandwiches for breakfast, lunch and dinner. I know we ate at least one meal at a truck-stop restaurant when we stopped for gas. Our mother ordered hot roast beef sandwiches with mashed potatoes and some sort of unrecognizable vegetable for each of us. These sandwiches consisted of a slice of white bread on a plate with a few slices of roast beef that was covered with hot brown gravy. Not too bad, actually, but it has been many years since I have seen that entrée on a menu.

I do remember stopping at some sort of campground late one night as we kids slept in the car. The next morning we awoke and discovered a small creek flowing by our camp and Bud out there with fishing pole in hand. He didn't catch anything but it was fun to feel like we were really camping.

Sometimes one or two of us got to ride in the truck with Bud which was pretty cool, especially if we could pull the air horn on top of the truck.

We arrived in Clarksville late at night and went directly to the home of Grandma and Grandpa Towe, Bud's parents. Grandma Towe was totally blind but that did not seem to slow her down much in and around her house. She knew the house by heart and navigated around so well I suspected she was not really blind. But she was, she just had the entire house memorized. We got in trouble if we moved even a chair out of its proper place.

She had the tallest beds I had ever seen with huge feather comforters where a little kid like me could easily get lost. She was early to rise and we all woke to bacon and pancakes on the breakfast table. She had a cool Water-pump in the back porch and we were always fighting to be the ones to get the water for our new *grandma*. There was a jar of water beside the pump that was used to '*prime*' the pump. If you used the prime and didn't refill the jar you got into lots of trouble.

Rather quickly we bought a house on Poplar Avenue, a few blocks from the Towe's. Our new house was only *new* to us and seemed like such a huge place, compared to the places we had lived in 'till then; but it probably wasn't.

There is such a size misperception when you are young. Many years later I went back to 522 W. 168th street and the huge house I remembered seemed to have been a victim of *"Honey, I Shrunk the House."*

At our Arkansas home, there was a stone smokehouse in the back that we used to store canned goods; it was also the designated storm shelter, a necessity in that part of Arkansas. There was also 'the little house' a short distance away where Don and I slept. It was a small wood-frame house consisting of a living area, a bedroom and a small bathroom. We liked it, since we could come and go without being noticed.

My new step-grandfather gave me a dog, a black and white collie he had named Dugan. Dugan and I became friends and we went everywhere together. Though I was just in the second or third grade, he and I would wander into the woods behind our property. There was a trickle of a spring back there and it was such an adventure. I felt like an explorer, as I imagined Indians had roamed these very woods and maybe, just maybe, there were some still there. We would always find our way home in time for supper. I learned that they did not have 'lunch' in the south in those days, it was called dinner and the evening meal was supper.

It was May 6, 1954. That was the day that Roger Bannister became the first person to run a sub four-minute mile. His time was three minutes, 59.4 seconds. It was the talk of the whole school since many had said a sub-four minute mile was humanly impossible. The whole world, and I was no exception, took an entirely different view as to what was impossible…but more of this later.

At age 13, Don got a paper route delivering The Little Rock Gazette, *'The First Newspaper West of the Mississippi'*, or so it stated on the front page. When I turned ten, Don divided up his route and gave me half. We would get up at 4:00 a.m., ride our bikes downtown, fold newspapers and go to a local bakery that was just taking hot glazed donuts out from the oven. They were especially tasty on a cool morning and even better in the winter.

Clarksville was quintessential small town America and a great place for kids, especially boys, to grow up. We wandered around everywhere on our bikes. With a quarter you could go to a movie, get popcorn and a drink. On Tuesday night, Don and I would sneak out at midnight when they would show horror films of giant ants or spiders or some creature that developed in the middle of some nuclear test site in Arizona or Nevada. The movies were pretty corny but riding those bikes home in the dark at two in the morning after a horror movie was not for the faint of heart. We would sleep a couple hours, until four o'clock, and we were back at it with the donuts and the newspapers.

The community had a swimming pool where we all spent most of our summer days. Between the chlorine in the water and the sun I was tan and a tow-head blond all summer – (*'tow' being derived from a mid-English word for flax or straw. Essentially it means having hair the color of straw (light yellow.)*)

On the way home after swimming we would stop by the Sunnyside Café where they sold hamburgers for a dime. I don't think I have ever have had a better hamburger since. That was when I learned, *"Things are just not as good as they used to be, but then again, maybe they never were."*

It was 1955-56. Elvis had just burst onto the music scene. Son-of-the-south that he was, I suppose his popularity was greater in these Southern states at first, but his fame spread like wildfire throughout the nation and the world in a very short time. My sisters were in middle-school and wore the dutiful poodle skirts with frilled petti-coats and pink and blue sweaters. It was the movie *Grease*, only we were living it.

I secretly loved the new Rock-n-Roll music, but it had to remain a secret since our country church thought, like many at the time, that it was the music of the devil.

As idyllic as it was for us kids, neither of our parents seemed able to stand success. Booze, fighting and affairs burst the happy couple's bubble. Bud loved his alcohol, and his long haul trucking must have left him lonely for he had *friends* in many places. Our mother wasn't an innocent bystander and the predictable fights, accusations and late night treks out of town became the norm. It was not unusual to spend the night with our mother and five kids sleeping in the car or in some very small, very cheap, roadside motor court.

By now, there were the four of us from the first litter plus Lee. Our mother was pregnant again and, in the still of a deep dark night, we were all loaded into the station wagon with some meager belongings and headed west…back to California.

We found a place to live there, our mother got a job and we enrolled in school. Craig was born, which meant our mother had six kids to support. I think our mother kept in contact with Bud, for child support I suppose, but most of our essentials were provided by government assistance.

We had been there for a few months when a knock at the door was answered, and there stood two policemen and Bud. It seems he got a judge in Arkansas to issue a court-order that gave him custody of his son, Lee.

With much wailing and gnashing of teeth from our mother the policemen took Lee, gave him to Bud, and they all left. Lee was maybe two, and that night, he and Bud left California for Arkansas.

Over the next few weeks our mother was informed that an Arkansas court order was not valid in California and, that the forceful taking of Lee amounted to kidnapping, with the police as accomplices.

George Putnam was a television newsman and commentator in Southern California for over 50 years until he died in 2008. His show specialized in somewhat scandalous stories, though tame by today's standards. Somehow, our mother got her story about Lee being 'kidnapped' in front of Putnam, and he began a series of stories about her and similar instances. Facing a lawsuit, the LA authorities settled with our mother for an unspecified amount of cash and six train tickets from LA to Clarksville. I think they were happy to have us out of the state.

So, we all packed up again and headed east, back to Arkansas, on the train. The trek had many stops along the way and took several days. We arrived in Clarksville and proceeded back to our home on Poplar St.

Ours was not the 'Last Train to Clarksville,' but the line has been discontinued and the old station is now the Chamber of Commerce. Being in Arkansas again we got back into that routine rather quickly. It is amazing the resiliency of children.

By now it was 1957-58, things were going crazy in Arkansas and throughout the South. In 1954 the Supreme Court had ruled in favor of desegregation and the Governor of Arkansas, Orval Faubus, had deployed the Arkansas National Guard to prevent integration of Little

Rock schools. President Eisenhower then sent in the 101st Airborne Division, and nationalized the Guard to enforce the Supreme Court decision.

Our little country church had a young minister who was in the National Guard and was sent to Little Rock for several weeks that fall.

This was a time before professional preachers, in the smaller towns at least. Our preacher would preach on Sundays and Wednesday evenings and worked in a local rock quarry the rest of the time. Can't help but think sometimes, that was a better way to do things.

On most Sundays, the entire congregation would head down to the river after church for lunch of fried chicken and all the fixing's that were provided by the congregation. If necessary, they would have a baptism in the river. Afterwards, we kids spent the afternoon swimming with a few of the adults watching over us. I couldn't help but think that was the way it was in Jesus' time, minus the chicken; but then, maybe not.

It was before I could swim very well, and as I walked out into the river I stepped into a hole and flailed around under the water until I could scramble to get back to the shore. I looked around, a bit embarrassed, to see if anyone had noticed. As I got out of the water, a man sitting on the shore said, "I had my eye on you the whole time. I would have come in to get you but you seemed to make it OK by yourself."

I never considered us poor, but we did stand in line for government surplus cheese, milk and certain dry goods. I got a pair of shoes *almost* every fall, which I noted was more than others at school had gotten. Many of my classmates came to school barefoot, all year around.

Sallis Elementary School had three classes, grades first and second, third and fourth, and fifth and sixth. There was a cafeteria where some of the poorer mothers worked so their kids could get a free lunch. For many, I think it was the only meal they had all day. Lunch was a nickel, seven cents if you wanted milk. I didn't always have lunch money, but the ladies always motioned us in anyway.

Back home we learned to can all sorts of vegetables and kill chickens, and can them as well. My brother and I were sent out to pick *polk-salad* that grew wild along the roads in Arkansas. Picking and washing the stuff in large tubs was a very itchy job, but when it was cooked, preferably with a little salt pork, it wasn't bad, a bit like spinach.

In the early fall each year these giant auto-transport trucks would come to towns all over America with huge tarps covering their cars. On the same day, all across the land, the tarps would be removed to reveal the latest model of cars to come out of Detroit. The dealerships gave away free pop and hot dogs, and the drama was intense when they finally removed the tarps.

Cars were different in those days. Every year, each make of car was unique, and sometimes spectacular in its design, with their flashy hood ornaments and outrageous fins on the back. Today, cars are bland by comparison and they all look alike. But back then, they had rocket-looking designs that inspired the imagination of us all. Among the boys in school, half were Chevy fans and the other half liked the Fords. We all had a glossary of reasons why ours was the best.

Ah, the 1950's…the cars were cool, the music was wild, the clothes were unique…it was a magical time.

—— 6 –

CLARKSVILLE, ARKANSAS CLAIMS to be the *"Home of the Alberta Peach."* In the early summer Bud would haul peaches from Clarksville through the Ozark Mountains to the markets in Joplin Missouri. Occasionally, my brother Don and I would tag along on these trips. Traveling through the Ozarks, especially at night, could be dangerous in those days. There were mountain men who considered those roads 'their territory.' I remember getting stopped late one night by a group of men with rifles. Bud got out of the truck ordering us to stay put, "no matter what happens." I don't know if Bud spoke their language or paid them off, but when he returned to the truck he seemed a bit shaken as we made our way through to Joplin.

Towards the end of our time in Arkansas we all loaded into the car and headed out to the outskirts of the town of Dardanelle. The state invited everyone to the groundbreaking of a new dam that, ten years later, would create Lake Dardanelle, a 34,000 acre lake on the Arkansas River. After the ceremony they had free fried chicken, lots of potato salad and all the ice cream you could eat. You may have noticed, eating in the South almost always included fried chicken.

In the midst of the magic of growing up there was constant turmoil at home. Bud loved the ladies and his beer, especially when he was on the road. Our mother followed him several times and caught him red-handed in a cheap motel with some floozy.

Pretty soon, all six of us kids were jammed into our car heading west, back to California.

We kids and my mother lived in a small house on the corner of Orange Avenue and Abbot Road in Compton California. Because of the threat that Bud would return to get one, or both, of his boys, we had to live in secrecy. It wasn't "witness protection" but our mother treated it as such, and we were threatened to within an inch of our lives if we told anybody anything.

I was ten years old and doing well in school, making mostly A's without much effort. Our mother was rarely home but came around enough to check in on us now and then. I think we all began to accept this as normal. I know I did.

Sometime after that famous mile run by Roger Banister, I came down with swelling in my joints, pain while walking and was diagnosed with rheumatic fever. The doctor restricted me to the house virtually 24/7/365 and I took penicillin tablets every day. In addition to the swollen joints, I overheard my doctor tell my mother that there was something seriously wrong with my heart.

Supposedly, if I walked to school I would die, if I played with the kids I would die, if I did anything I would die, so I just stayed home doing nothing. Every few days, a home-teacher would show up to pick up my completed school work and give me more assignments. She had the personality of the bottom of my shoe so she was little respite from my miserably boring life. I completed each assignment in about an hour, read the few books she would bring, which were awful and put a capital 'B' in the word boring. They wouldn't let me go to the library to pick out books, evidently, because I would die.

There was a dairy across the street that sold milk products and other items. If I came across any change around the house I would leave my prison, go across Abbot Road and buy an orange Popsicle. It was the highlight of my miserable day and, *wow, I didn't die!* If I couldn't find change I would walk up and down Abbot Road collecting enough pop bottles to turn in for the deposit and buy myself that orange Popsicle.

At the end of the school year we moved to another house farther up Orange Avenue at the corner of Michigan Avenue. We didn't have enough money for the penicillin or the doctor visits, so all that just sort of arbitrarily ended. Soon, it seems everyone just forgot about my rheumatic fever and I certainly never brought it up. When the next

31

school year started I just went to school and the subject was never again addressed…and, I didn't die.

In high school I played football, basketball and ran track…in college I played football and ran track. After college I joined the Navy and became a Navy pilot. Each year for 20 years, sometimes twice a year, I had physicals and they made exhaustive checks of my heart each time. Since rheumatic fever is a congenital thing, my only conclusion would have to be either I had a miraculous recovery or I never had rheumatic fever. Could go either way!

Being back in a real school, things were decidedly going better, but at home, I was miserable. It would probably take a dozen child psychologists to figure out why I did what I did next, but here it is.

We had no father, my mother was seldom home, my older brothers and sisters had their own lives and I was, well, alone. I saw a show on TV where a kid went swimming on the beach and soon thereafter came down with some illness. I had no idea what the illness was but, all I could see was, the kid all of a sudden got all this attention.

So, in the middle of the night I left the house and walked from Orange Avenue down to the Los Angeles River. Those of you not familiar with that waterway need to know it was not Tom Sawyer's Mississippi type of river. It was/is really just a large drainage system to avoid the type of floods that we encountered in Gardena a few years earlier. It was total concrete, bottom and both sides, with a gently flowing, usually constant trickle, in the middle. When L.A. had its annual rain storms it would become a massive torrent.

I went down to the "L. A. River" and sat in the middle of the trickling stream for several hours. It was summer and it actually felt pretty good but I never got sick. Considering what flows in that *river,* I was probably very lucky.

After that failed, I decided to disappear. Having really no place to go, I climbed into the attic when no one was around and quietly stayed there whenever anyone was home. I was careful that no one see me go up or come down. This went on for what seems to have been several weeks. I was sure someone would eventually miss me and start looking for me but, they never did, so I gave up my exile in the attic.

Towards the end of that summer I found a stray puppy in the neighborhood. Well, it was probably not a true puppy, but it was young enough. I pretended to search for the owner, but inside hoped no one would come forward, and they never did. It was a comparatively happy time for me since I had a buddy that played with me and was delighted when I came home. Things were looking up. School started and I just decided to go with the thought, *"If I die, I die"*; couldn't have been much worse than the loneliness I felt at home. I was not about to spend another year with Miss Personality bringing my school work to me.

I was doing well in school and I reveled at being around kids my own age. Plus, I had my dog, Dugan II, to greet me with adoring attention when I came home. Life was good again.

There came a day at school when we were given an announcement about a coming *Father-Son Banquet*.

"Well, this is awkward," I thought. After everyone had submitted their responses except me, my teacher asked why I hadn't turned my form in. I made some lame excuse about my father being out of town, but he had it figured out. He asked me if *he* could go to the banquet with me. I agreed and said it would be OK with my mother. I felt special for a couple of hours, as every child should feel.

It was one evening, a few months into that school year. It was well after dark and Dugan and I decided to go for a walk, as was our custom every night before he joined me in my bed. I did not have a leash and we just casually walked the sidewalk until he "did his business." As we walked along in the dark, unnoticed to me, there was another dog on the opposite side of the street. I momentarily noticed Dugan's ears stand straight up but before I realized what was happening he was darting across the street. As he did, a car came from behind and hit Dugan II.

The car slowed for a split second and then sped on. I ran and picked up my dog. I could feel his heart was beating at a tremendous rate but it began to slow and within a very few moments it had stopped altogether. I sat there in the dark, on the curb, crying, with my broken dog in my arms. I hoped his suffering was small.

This was the second dog of mine that I had seen struck by a car and die in front of me but it wasn't any easier. There was no mother inside our house to go to for comfort. My brothers and sisters were there, but they would not understand, so I just sat there holding my lifeless dog in the coolness of a California evening. After what seemed a very long time I put him in a box behind the house and went inside. No one said a thing to me, as I undressed and went to bed. '*Tomorrow*,' I thought, '*I will find a place to bury my friend.*'

I got through the next day and buried my dog in a field not too far away. No one ever asked about Dugan II; it was as if he had never existed. I began spiraling down into a serious funk; I guess it was depression but, at that time, I couldn't spell it and didn't even know what it meant. My mother, when she was around, would constantly say, "*My nerves are shot,*" and I supposed the feeling I was having had something to do with '*shot nerves.*'

I went to school but was not engaged; I never raised my hand to answer a question anymore, which, evidently, was unusual. I took a few tests and did poorly which was also unusual. The teacher made me stay after school and asked what was wrong with me. At first I was silent, but he was persistent and it all came out in a gush of tears how I had killed my dog by not having a leash the night we went for a walk. My teacher made me talk about it and convinced me it was not my fault and, while I was glad to have someone to talk to, I was still in a funk. My teacher took me home after school and I thanked him for the ride.

A few days later, at school, my teacher asked me to ask my mother if I could go home with him after school the next day for a short while. I told him I would ask, but I knew there was no one home who cared one way or another. My mother was not home that night, but still the next day I told him my mother said it was OK, and off we went. In today's world I suppose he would have been suspected of some nefarious intent. but back in the 1950's that just didn't seem to enter into the equation.

He lived rather far from Orange Avenue and I enjoyed the ride. We arrived at his house which, compared to mine, was a mansion. Even compared to any house in our neighborhood, this was a very nice place. His wife met us at the door and asked me if I wanted a coke and I said, "*Yes, please.*"

We sat in his living room and he explained that he had told his neighbor about me and what had happened to my dog. He then explained that his neighbor's dog recently had five puppies and four had been sold. He said she wanted to give me the fifth puppy. I was too confused to say anything; no one had ever done such a thing for me. I assumed I had to pay for the dog, and that must have come across as he said, "You understand, she wants to *give you the puppy.*"

34

We walked to the house next door and he rang the bell. A beautiful woman came to the door and invited us in.

My teacher introduced me to the woman by saying, "Larry, this is Mrs. Burke." She had a big smile on her face and I instantly liked her, as she escorted us through the house to the back yard. There was a large dog, a registered German Sheppard I was told, with a small puppy close to her. The mother dog came right up to me and licked my face as I went to my knees to pet the puppy.

"I think he likes you," said Mrs. Burke. This puppy was the most beautiful animal I had ever seen. "He is registered and I can give you the papers if you want," she said.

I had no idea what she was talking about, and I barely heard her, as the puppy and I rolled together in the grass. I was astounded that this beautiful woman wanted to give me this puppy; there must be more to this, it can't be true. The puppy and I played in the yard as Mrs. Burke gathered up a travel cage and some other items in a bag.

"This is the puppy's bowl for food, his collar and a leash. Be sure to use the leash when you take him out of the house."

I surmised she was told what happened to my other dog. "Oh, I will," I said, "*I promise.*"

"I know you will take good care of him," she said with a huge smile on her face. I wanted to hug her but I didn't know if that was allowed, so I just thanked her as best I could. As we left, I thought she was crying and I assumed she was sad to be saying goodbye to her puppy, but looking back I suspect there was more. I'll bet she was just as excited for me to get that dog as I was to get him.

My teacher, my new dog and I walked back to his house. As we walked he asked me, "Do you know who that was?"

I simply said, "Mrs. Burke."

He said, "Yes, but her full name is Billie Burke. Does that name sound familiar?" I just looked at him with an obvious confused look thinking I should recognize the name, but I didn't.

He said, "She played Glinda, the Good Witch of the North in the movie, "The Wizard of Oz."

Now, the movie, 'The Wizard of Oz', came out about 15 years earlier in 1939, and was probably lying dormant in some vault. There were no videos or CD's in those days and it may have played once a year or so on TV around Christmas, if you happened to be lucky enough to see it. I had seen it at least once, maybe twice on TV and I did remember the Good Witch, the Wicked Witch and of course those flying monkeys.

To be honest, I was 11 years old and I was just so excited about my new puppy. While I heard what he said, my focus was on my new friend. My teacher took me home and as he dropped me off he handed me a paper. "This is his registration paper; it won't mean much to you now, but look here what it says, "*Signed over to Larry Nevels by Billie Burke.*"

I did remember the beautiful lady who gave me my friend and people would ask, "Where did you get such a fine dog?"

Well, honestly, I couldn't remember her name so I would say, "From Glinda, the Good Witch of the North." People would look at me like I was crazy, but I didn't care. I had a new best friend and that was all that mattered.

In that instant, on that day, my young life turned another corner. I had a buddy and I was determined to take care of him, no matter what. We always walked with his leash and I inwardly vowed to avoid previous mistakes. I had made a minor course correction.

After Tommy Hamilton, Glinda was another angel I remember in my life. All these many years later, whenever I see "The Wizard of Oz" on TV, I watch as Billie Burke, the good witch of the north comes to help Dorothy and I remember how that beautiful lady came into my life, and I smile as I think about my buddy.

— 7 —

SOMETIME BEFORE HIS 10-year sentence was up, my father was released from Folsom Prison and went to work for Campbell's Soup Company in Sacramento. When I was 11, and living in Southern California, I came down with appendicitis. My mother contacted my father and explained she didn't have the money for my surgery. Because of the danger of my appendix rupturing, I remained in the hospital for several days while they negotiated the terms of my surgery with my father.

On a Saturday a nurse came to my room and told me that my father was in the lobby and wanted to see me. Up to that time in my life, my memories of him were not good, and I was very anxious, plus, I did not feel the greatest. The nurse went to escort my father to my room but soon returned alone. She said he had told her he would not sign off on my surgery unless I came to him in the waiting room. I told her I did not want to go.

After a short while the doctor came in and said the hospital was going to get a court order to do the surgery since it was becoming a life threatening situation. He then lifted me into a wheelchair and navigated me to the waiting area where he told us, *"You two talk and settle this by the time I return or I will be on the phone to the judge!"*

No one in the room was happy. I do not remember much about the conversation that took place, but I do remember I was happy when he left. A short time later the nurse came, shaved my belly, and took me to surgery; my appendix was removed that afternoon.

I went home a few days after the surgery and, being a young kid, I healed quickly and was back playing with my dog.

Late one afternoon, I was walking home from a walk, taking a shortcut through an empty field, when I was accosted by three older boys. They wanted to know if I had any money. *"Geez, did you guys pick the wrong target,"* went through my mind. When I told them no, they started shoving me around. They were older, larger and numbered three. After a few moments of this, Dugan did not like what was going on and started growling and chasing the boys. They could not get out of there fast enough, with Dugan literally chomping at their heels. I ran in the other direction and called for Dugan who was having a good time chasing the boys. He finally quit the chase and came running back to me. I hugged him and laughed at the three older kids, still running in the distance.

—— 8 —

ALL WAS OK in my world, even though our mother was home fewer days and even fewer nights. Basic necessities were in short supply, but we always seemed to get by.

There was one particular evening when the six of us kids sat down to the table to eat dinner. There was one can of pork-n-beans in the center of the table and that was it. OK, it may have been a large can. But when that was gone there was nothing more in the house to eat. Nancy apportioned out to each of our plates our share of the beans and we quietly ate our supper. I suppose I wondered, but I do not recall being concerned about our next meal. Every- day-life was day-to-day; our meals were, well, meal-to-meal.

I went to school the next day without breakfast but there was nothing unusual about that. To this day I do not eat the "most important meal of the day." I don't remember if I had lunch at school or not. I can't remember who took care of our younger brothers, Lee and Craig, but I came home that afternoon to a greeting from my dog and, for me, life was good.

There was a meeting of Don, Nancy and Carole with me in the kitchen. Nancy announced there was nothing in the house to eat.

I know this is going to sound like a bad TV drama but I swear this is what happened: Suddenly, there was a knock at the door. A group of ladies were there asking if this was the Nevels' house. Nancy, I believe, said that "Yes, it is."

They went back to their car and proceeded to bring in bag after bag after bag of food and placed it on the kitchen table. I had never seen so much food in my life. They said a quiet prayer for us before they left and they were gone as mysteriously as they arrived.

I had never seen those women before or since. They said a quiet, *"God Bless you,"* and left. I think we all assumed they were ladies from our church but it was a small church and none of us ever remember seeing them there. I have recently asked my siblings if they knew who those ladies were or where they were from and none of them have an answer.

Now, don't get me wrong, I'm sure there is a simple, logical explanation as to who these ladies were and how they found out about us. But even that does not take away from the miracle of their arrival at that most opportune time. Regardless of the logic, they were angels for us and, to me, still are.

This was not my first encounter with angels, nor would it be my last. Tommy Hamilton was the first. I remember that day he saved my life and when he got between our father and my sister. Then there was my teacher and Billie Burke who are to me magnificent angels who bestowed a miracle upon me. There would be many more that showed up in my life at the most opportune times. Call it coincidence, if you prefer, but to me they will always be angels.

I do not remember much about the next several months. But there came a day when our mother came home and told us our father was on his way to our home. I was in the middle of the seventh grade. I suppose Carole was in her ninth, Nancy her tenth and Don his eleventh grade.

Our mother came home with an authoritative pronouncement, *"I have taken care of you all this time. It is your fathers turn to take care of you for awhile."*

Lee and Craig were not there. It was just the older four of us and our mother. We were told to pack our things and that our father would be there shortly. There was no discussion. There never was with our mother.

Joseph William Nevels showed up a short time later. This was the first time I had seen him since the time I was in the hospital with appendicitis, not the best memory for me. Dutifully, we packed our few items. I had my clothes in a small box and my dog on a leash with his bowl and some food.

Our father looked at my dog and said, "We can't take the dog, we already have a dog."

I could not believe what I just heard. I looked at my mother but she just looked away. I began to cry and told them I would not go without my dog. There was a prolonged scene with my mother and father yelling at me but I would not part with my dog. Our mother was a very forceful person and I was not in the habit of challenging her, but on this day I refused to get in the car without my dog. The two of them counseled for a few moments while I calmed down and my father came back in a much more conciliatory mood.

"Larry," he said, "we already have a dog! My new wife has two kids and with you four that makes six. It is going to be a big adjustment for everyone, but, I will make you a deal. I have a friend who lives nearby where I can take your dog. I'll bet you will fall in love with our dog. But, after two weeks, if you still want your dog, we will come back here and get him."

I looked at my mother and she had a *"this is as good as it's going to get"* look on her face. I'm not a gambler but I know a sure thing when I see it. I knew exactly how I would feel in two weeks and I was still naïve enough to think a father would not lie to his son. I spent a few moments with my dog and told him I would see him in two weeks. Our father drove off with my dog as I stood there, quietly crying.

While he was gone our mother said her straight-faced goodbyes with a total lack of emotion. I asked about Lee and Craig but my mother did not answer. It wasn't long before our father returned, alone. We loaded our things into his car and the five of us quietly drove to Sacramento.

"Two weeks," I thought. "I hope I can make it for two weeks".

9

THIS WAS MY second trip to Sacramento, the last time being when my crayons turned to puddles in the glove box of our car. We arrived late in the evening, met our new step-mother and went to bed. I lay there that night thinking about my dog and imagining how Glinda, the Good Witch of the North might bring my friend to me. It would only be two weeks.

We had a new stepmother and a stepbrother and stepsister. I cannot today remember their faces or their names. They were neither memorable nor offensive, good people I am sure. I was enrolled into Starr King Junior High School as a seventh grader. There wasn't much left of the school year and everyone there had their friends so I just ambled from class to class and went home. I do remember the Perry Como song, *"Catch a Falling Star,"* was popular and I liked it. It reminded me of the Disney song, *"When You Wish Upon a Star."* I would go out at night and wish upon a star that my dog was OK and I would whisper that the two weeks had almost past.

When I was at our new home I had little to do with my new step-siblings and their dog. I was anxiously waiting for the two weeks to pass and imagined what it would be like when I was reunited with Dugan II.

It was a Saturday, two weeks to the day. I got up but our father was already gone. I waited all day for him to come home. When he did he avoided me as I tried to talk to him. Finally, I could not stand it any longer and I reminded him of the deal we had made two weeks earlier and asked when we could make the trip south to LA. He just looked at me and said, *"We have a dog,"* and walked away. As he was leaving the room, I reminded him, *"But you promised!"*

He looked at me with steely eyes and much more forcefully said again, *"We have a dog!"* and turned and walked away.

It was at that moment that I learned four things: 'naivety', 'betrayal', 'hatred' and what I thought was 'stupidity.' I was so naïve and naturally assumed my father would keep his word. How could someone betray a promise so easily to his son? As I considered what had happened, I realized he never intended to keep his promise. How could I have been so stupid? For the first time in my life I hated someone. I didn't like it, but there it was. It was then and there that I began to consider my escape.

It was a Sunday evening, probably weeks later, my brothers and sisters had found out about a church nearby, not too far from where we lived. Our father was away and my brother, I think, called them to ask if they could pick us up for Sunday night services. Our father referred to church as *"that hocus-pocus stuff"* and specifically forbade us to go. When my brothers and sisters told me about it I was anxious to strike back in any way a young kid could do, so I was game to go along.

In the middle of the evening service as we sat there our father came into the church, walked down the middle aisle and told us to get up and go with him. To my satisfaction my siblings hesitated until the minister said, *"Do as your father says,"* and we all walked out of the church as every eye in the place followed us out. There was a significant scene when we got home as he yelled and told us never to go back to that church. All four of us refused to promise we would not go back.

In a few weeks, maybe it was a month or so, we all finished the school year. My sisters maintained contact with a family that attended the same church we went to in Southern Cal. After much discussion, and with an intervention by our new stepmother, our father relented and let them go and live with that family. A week or so later they were gone and it was just Don and me with our father's family.

I was 12 years old and it was about 420 miles from Sacramento to the man's house in Long Beach, California where my father said he had taken my dog. Over the next few weeks I devised a plan to make my escape and make the trip to get my dog. I cannot recall how I got the man's address but I did. I was pretty resourceful.

It was summer in Sacramento; we have established earlier that it is hot in the summer there. My brother and I were in the habit of sleeping on outdoor lounge chairs in the back yard.

I called the Greyhound bus station and found that it would cost $12 dollars for one person to ride the bus from Sacramento to Los Angeles. It was about 10 miles from where we lived in East Sacramento, in the area of Carmichael, to the Greyhound Bus station on L Street in the downtown area. I then called a cab company and was told it would cost about $3.50 for a taxi from our neighborhood to the bus station. I added in fifty cents for a tip. I reasoned if there were a tip the taxi driver would ask fewer questions. From riding the bus system in and around the LA area I deduced I could get from the LA bus station to Long Beach for a couple bucks. All told and adding a little cushion I calculated I could make the trip for under $25. Remember, this was 1956.

While my brother was in the shower one evening I found that he had forty dollars in his wallet from a part-time job he had selling Christmas trees. I lifted $25 bucks the day before I was to make my great escape. Prior to commencing my plan I walked one block over and found a house with no lights on and noted the address and street. It was from there that I would put my plan into action.

The night I chose to leave, I covertly gathered up a couple extra pillows to make it look like I was asleep in the lawn chair. I hid a set of clothes in the garage and pretended to go to bed. I had purposely placed my lawn chair near the fence so the shadow would give me cover. When Don came out I gave him several moments until I was sure he was asleep, put the pillows under the covers and went into the garage to change clothes.

I had earlier located a pay phone at a gas station a few blocks away and called the cab company. I explained I was staying with my grandmother and needed to get to the bus station and gave the dispatcher the address I had noted the night before. I told him I would be waiting on the front porch. It was about 11:00 in the evening when the cab drove up and the cabbie asked where my parents were. I was 12 years old and I could see the cabbie was suspicious. I firmly explained I was staying with my grandmother who had gone to bed and I needed to get to the bus station to go home to my parents. He shrugged and off we went to the station.

I surmised that if my ruse were discovered that night they would eventually scour the bus station. So, I had found out when the last bus left for LA, and timed my escape so I would arrive at the station about 30 minutes before that time, just before midnight. I bought my ticket, boarded the bus and settled back for an all night trip.

We made several stops along the way, including Stockton, Modesto and Bakersfield but I stayed on the bus, just in case they were already looking for me.

I arrived at the Greyhound station in downtown Los Angeles the next morning. I inquired at the station as to which bus I should take to get to Long Beach. I had to switch a time or two but everyone was eager to point a young kid in the right direction. I had the address of the man my father had said would take care of my dog, so I asked which bus would come closest to his house. I got off the bus, asked a couple people how to get to the address a few blocks away and proceeded to knock on the door.

A man opened the door and I asked if he knew Joe Nevels. He said he did so I said I was there to get my dog. The man did not have a clue what I was talking about. I told the story about how my father, a few months earlier, had said he would bring my dog to this address. The man explained to me that Joe had in fact come over that day but did not have a dog.

"Do you know what he did with my dog?" I asked. He said my father visited for a few moments but he did not see a dog and it was never mentioned. .

The man asked if I needed a ride and I said. "No, my brother is waiting for me on the corner," and I left quickly, thinking he might call my father if he had time to think about it. I hurried away, intentionally in the wrong direction, went up a block and headed back to the bus stop.

I was dazed. I was absolutely convinced I would be reunited with my dog that morning. As I wandered away from the man's house I began to cry. I thought of what could possibly have happened to my dog. Perhaps he had taken him to someone else. I hoped he was in a good home. I was 12 years old and alone in Southern California, my plan had failed and I had nowhere to go.

My escape plan had come to an end. Beyond retrieving my dog, I had not made additional plans. After that, well, I just never thought beyond reuniting with my buddy. I thought I would contact my sisters but I did not know how. I found a phone at a gas station with a phonebook attached, not easy in Southern California, and fortunately found the name 'Howard Ervin' in Lakewood.

Brother Ervin was the pastor of our church in Lakewood, one of the many suburbs in the area. By now, it was past noon as I dialed his number and I was relieved when he answered. I told him where I was and he said he would be there shortly to pick me up.

We went over to his house where his wife and daughter, Mary Sue, were waiting for us with some lunch. He explained to me, "I received a phone call from the Sheriff's office asking if we had heard from you." He then told me he had promised to call them back if I showed up.

"You understand I have to call them as I promised, but I guess we can finish lunch." he said. He then told me he would see if they would let me stay with him. We had lunch and a coke while Brother Ervin called my sisters to let them know I was there. He then called the Long Beach Sheriff's office and was advised that I was listed as a runaway and they would either come to get me or he could bring me down to the station. He promised to bring me in that afternoon.

When we arrived at the police station, Brother Ervin tried to talk them into letting me stay with him but he was advised by the deputy that since I was listed as a run-away they had to keep me in the jail. After a short time of processing, they placed me in the juvenile section of the Long Beach County Sheriff's jail, and Howard Ervin had to leave. "What have I gotten myself into," I thought to myself, "a young kid in jail, with a possible history of emphysema and rheumatic fever who is quickly becoming a young man with a past."

10

IT WAS WEDNESDAY when I was put into the cell with two other juvee's, both 17, I think. They had been detained at the Mexican border with an older guy in a stolen car they were trying to sell to someone south of the border, probably for booze or something stronger. I did not have any pre-conceived notion about what type of person I might encounter in a lockup; of all the things I could think to worry about, that was not even on my radar. We had some books in the cell along with a monopoly game. My two cell mates quickly grabbed the cash and the dice from the monopoly game and began playing craps. They actually seemed to be OK guys; tried to sound tough when the jailers were around but they took the time to teach a 12 year old to play craps. We had Spanish rice for supper.

This policeman, one of the jailers I think, told me they had contacted my father and he said he would come down on Saturday to pick me up. According to the jailer, my father's comments went something like this, "I have never missed a day of work since I started and I'm not going to miss one for this. Let him sweat it out for a few days."

Brother Ervin brought my sisters to visit at least once, maybe twice. Other than reading the books, I played craps with my cell mates and wondered where my buddy might be. The next night we had Spanish rice again for the evening meal.

My two cell mates were transferred out on Thursday and I was alone. I actually missed those guys and their tough stories, but I was alone in the cell.

Saturday came and about mid-day Don and our father showed

up. My father asked me how I paid for the trip and I confessed I had "borrowed" it from Don's wallet. Don took out his wallet and for the first time noticed $25 was missing.

Our father frowned at me and said, "So, in addition to being a run-away you are a thief."

I looked him square in the eye and said something like, "Yes, it's a family tradition!"

There was fire in my father's eyes as he motioned to me and said, "Let's go."

"No!" I said as I formed my body into a ball on the back of my rack. I assumed he was going to grab me and pull me out of the cell but as he came forward the guard got between us and said to my father, "Let's go talk about this."

The two of them left and I told Don I was sorry about the $25, but I had no choice. He said, "Don't worry about it." We talked for a few moments until the guard came in and said the detective wanted to talk with me.

The detective escorted me into an office where there was a man in a suit behind a desk. "Please sit down, Larry," he said. "Tell me, why did you run away?"

I told him the story about my dog and how our father had dragged us out of church. He had this incredulous look on his face. "Does he beat you?" he asked.

"No, Sir," I answered.

"So, let me get this straight: You ran away because of your dog and because he won't let you go to church?"

"Yes, sir," was my reply.

He looked at me with a wry smile on his face and as he shook his head he said, "Well, this is a first." He looked up at the other jailer and commented, "I would give anything if the kids we get in here would go to church just once."

He then turned to me and after a short pause, he said, "Larry, I have to explain to you the law in California in this situation. We cannot make you go with your father. You must do that on your own free will. He can trick you to go with him, but we can't do that. However, if you don't go with him you will go back to your cell until we can get you before a judge. We cannot keep you here. On Monday, we will transfer you to juvenile hall in downtown Los Angeles. I have to tell you, there are some pretty rough kids in the LA Juvenile Hall. If you were to ask for my advice, I would suggest you go with your father and brother, but that has to be your decision."

He paused a moment to let the words sink in and said, "The guard will now take you back to your cell. I will tell your father the same thing I just told you. If he chooses, he will then come to your cell and ask you to go with him. At that time it becomes your decision. Do you understand what I just told you?"

"Yes, Sir," I said.

The detective motioned to the guard who took me back to my cell.

"*What should I do?*" I thought to myself. I did not want to spend another night in that jail. I could not eat another meal of Spanish rice.

Don was the first to come into my cell. "JW wants me to talk you into coming home with us. He said he did not drive all this way to go back empty handed," Don said to me.

"Do you think I should go back with you?" I asked.

"Well, that's up to you, Larry."

At that point, it could have gone either way. But I have to admit, I was leaning towards going with them.

Don left and, after a few moments, the detective came in with our father who gruffly said, "Let's go!"

I don't know where it came from, but before I could think, the word, "NO!" came out of my mouth, again.

His voice went from rough to angry. "*Come on Larry, enough of this foolishness.*"

"Where is my dog?" I shouted at him.

His anger overcame his self control and he blurted out, "I let him go on the LA freeway," he shouted. "Are you coming or not?"

I was stunned! I could not believe what I just heard. This was a possibility I never considered. He let my buddy go on the Los Angeles freeway. Tears welled up in my eyes along with more anger than I had ever felt. I hated this man before, but never like this. The detective had positioned himself between me and my father. I could see something in his look...while he said nothing, his eyes said, "*Don't go.*"

My father looked around and I suspect he thought he had come across badly in front of the detective. He tried to lower his tone and, in that wickedly sweet voice he sometimes used, he said, "Come on son, let's go home."

That friendly tone of his voice surprised me at first. I wanted to be with my brother and I really wanted out of that place. Then I remembered what the detective had said, *"He can trick you to go with him but we can't...He can trick you to go with him..."*

This man had fooled me more than once, never again. *"No!"* came out of my mouth. It was as if someone else had said it.

"Not another night in this place," I thought.

But before I could reconsider my father looked at me and said, *"You will never amount to anything!"* and he was gone from the cell.

The detective looked at me with a sincerely kind smile and said, "It's going to be OK," before he turned and left.

Don and I were alone in the cell. "Are you going to be OK?" Don asked.

"Sure!" I said. He told me he couldn't stay with our father much longer either, not with the three of us gone. We shook hands and he turned and walked out of the cell and down the hall.

After Don left I noted the cell door was open, there was no guard in sight. I briefly considered making a run for it but adding 'jail break' to my ever increasing rap sheet just didn't seem the right thing to do. I cried that night, alone in my cell. We had Spanish rice for supper.

On Sunday, Howard Ervin came by with Nancy and Carole. My sisters told me how proud they were of me for saying 'No' to our father. I didn't admit that I did not know where that refusal came from, and chose to bask in the small glory of being a 'tough guy.'

The next day was Monday and the detective came to my cell to tell me they were transporting me to Juvenile Hall in downtown Los Angeles. They escorted me out of my cell and told me they had to handcuff me for the trip. I was amazed and rather uncomfortable. "Its procedure," the detective said.

There was one other man being transferred that morning. The other man was older and was probably going to an adult jail downtown. The trip was uneventful, which means, I don't remember much about it, except being handcuffed in the back of a patrol car with another con beside me and driving down the freeway to who knows what in downtown LA. I looked up and down the freeway, looking for my dog.

When we arrived I was directed through a maze of security to a wing of a large building. Outside I could see other Juve's playing baseball. I was issued a set of cloths and introduced to the director of the wing. He showed me to my cell and then to a common room. By the time I was all checked-in to my new digs it was evening and I was directed to the chow hall. They served Spanish rice for dinner that night.

I appeared to be the youngest person there; certainly the smallest. That evening they locked me into my small private cell with a bed and a chair. Every thirty minutes, all night, someone would come to the window on my door, shine a light in my face and move on. I suppose you eventually got used to it and could sleep through the night, but that first night I woke up each time he came by. "What have I gotten myself into," I thought. "Perhaps I have made a big mistake."

The next day I met with, what I can only surmise was, a sort of counselor. He asked what I had done and I told him the same story I had told the detective in Long Beach. He said, "The detective in Long Beach called me about you. You don't belong here."

"*You are SO right*," I thought to myself. The next day I met with him again. He told me that within 72 hours I had to go before a judge. He said there was a home where they kept non-criminal juveniles and asked if I wanted to go there. "Sure," I replied." *In a flash*, I thought.

That evening in the common hall several older boys cornered me and told me they were planning an escape. They needed a small boy to make their plan work and if I knew what was good for me I would cooperate. It seems that once a week a laundry truck left juvenile hall. Their plan was to surround the truck, use everyone's belts to tie me to the drive shaft of the truck and when it stopped outside I was to free myself and proceed to a drainage pipe that could only be opened from the outside. They would be in the drainage pipe waiting for me. If I didn't cooperate they would kill me. If I didn't open the drainage gate they would track me down and kill me. I didn't say it was a *great* plan. I thought I could do better.

That evening the counselor and the guard with the flashlight came to my cell. The counselor told me that he had made the arrangements for me to go to the home but that I had to promise in writing not to run away. At that point, I would have signed a confession to the great brinks robbery to get out of there.

The next day the counselor escorted me through the maze of security doors to a large room. It looked like a court room from a Perry Mason TV show. Several of us boys sat in the pews and when your name was called you went to the table in front of the judge. When my name was called my counselor escorted me to the table.

A clerk read the basic reason I was in ju-ve: a runaway, no crime, no violence. The judge asked if a parent were present. The clerk said there was not.

"Of course not," I thought, "This is Wednesday, my father would not miss a day of work for this."

The judge made his comment, "Is there anyone here to speak on this young man's behalf?"

My wing counselor stood up and said, "Your Honor, I was going to recommend that Larry be placed in a temporary home until we could determine where he should go."

"Oh No," I thought, "*he must have found out about the escape plan. I will never get out of this place.*"

"There is a gentleman here your Honor," the counselor continued, "who would like to speak. His name is Leonard Tackles. He is a patrolman for the LA police force."

"Mr. Tackles, let's hear what you have," said the judge.

Leonard Tackles began, "Your Honor, I was contacted by the Rev. Howard Ervin, who is the pastor of the church this young man used to attend. After hearing what the Reverend had to say, I too believe Larry does not belong here. The good reverend told me his story and, if it is OK with Larry, I would like to invite him to come live with my family until this case can be resolved."

"Well," said the judge. "I do love a story with a happy ending; we get so few around here. What do you think young Mr. Nevels? Are you willing to stay with Mr. Tackles until this issue can be adjudicated?"

At that point I would have walked out with Jack the Ripper and while I had no idea what *a-jewd-a*…something meant I said, "*Yes Sir!*"

"*Besides,*' I thought, "*if he knows Brother Ervin…*"

I was convinced they were going to have Spanish rice and I was ready to get out of there. It was probably 40 years before I could eat Spanish rice again.

I was escorted back to my cell where I was given the cloths I was wearing when I ran away. I had to wait awhile, but eventually my counselor showed up and escorted me through a maze of doors that locked behind me until I was in a room with Leonard Tackles.

"*Let's go home, Larry,*" Mr. Tackles said as we walked out of Juvenile Hall.

11

(1959) I HAD only known Mr. Tackles for a little over an hour and already he seemed like an angel to me. During the long ride from the LA juvenile hall to his home in the suburbs, Mr. Tackles told me more about his family. He explained that he was married and had three boys. There was a fourth son but, a couple months earlier, he had wandered out an unlocked door, fell into their swimming pool and drowned. The entire family had fallen into an abyss of depression and guilt. When they heard about my situation they knew they just had to add another to bring the family back up to four sons.

During their time in the abyss they had turned to Rev. Howard Ervin for some understanding in their grief. His church had embraced the entire Tackles family and it was their love that carried them through their most terrible chapter.

A short time later I met the rest of the Tackles family and was surprised to find I would be the oldest of the children in the family. Being the youngest of the first litter of four in my family, the oldest was a position I had never experienced. I would share a room with Timmy Tackles who was about two years younger.

When they said they had a pool, my expectations were of a house similar to that of Billie Burkes. But this was a simple urban home with a pool that consumed about 90% of the backyard. I could not avoid noticing the lone glass door that opened to the pool-side and realized how quickly the accident must have occurred.

The house with the pool was put up for sale and in a few weeks we all moved into a new home in Buena Park, California, just two blocks from Knott's Berry Farm, and within viewing distance of the nightly fireworks at Disneyland. At the end of the summer, I started school as an eighth grader at Orange View Junior High School.

Don left our father's house that summer between his junior and senior year in high school. He moved in with another family from Howard Ervin's church, the Scotts, and enrolled in Dominguez High School for his senior year. Nancy and Carole had earlier moved in with another family from the same church.

~~~

During this time there was no fence around Knott's Berry Farm and no admission fee. I walked over there several times a week and just walked around and enjoyed some of the outdoor music venues. The Sons of the Pioneers were one group that regularly performed some of their most popular songs along with, Gene Autry, Roy Rogers and Dale Evans; to be a name dropper of some of those that were there. It was always around a campfire that these free concerts were performed and I was totally mesmerized by the fire and the music. There were many lesser known performers as well, but it all was calming for my soul.

I would always time my trips to watch the famous stagecoach-holdup where "bandits" on horses, with guns blazing, would stick up the stage as it made its trip around the park. I always wanted to ride that stage but it was a little expensive for me. In truth, anything above zero was expensive for me.

They also had a Christian book store in the middle of the park that played constant hymns in the background. I would browse the books and enjoy the music. They soon recognized me as a regular, who never bought anything, but they never seemed to mind as they cheerfully said hello each time I came in. I would roam through the saloon where someone was always playing on a tinny piano and you could smell the famous fried chicken as it wafted across that end of the park. No matter what troubles I may have felt, those trips through Knott's Berry Farm would calm me down.

~~~

While at Orange View JHS I signed up for The California Cadet Corp (CCC), whose mission was/is to develop leadership, citizenship, patriotism, academic excellence, basic military knowledge, and fitness. The CCC was established in California schools in 1911 and continued through the years until the Viet Nam conflict in the 1960's when it lost its funding. It was re-established in 1999 and as of 2007 there were 8,000 CCC cadets in the state.

Mr. Seidel was our instructor, a retired military man, from the Army, I suppose. I really liked him and he seemed to like me as well. Since we moved so much while I was growing up, our family never had much in the way of 'discretionary funds.' I was never able to join the Boy Scouts like many of my friends. There were no student costs associated with the CCC, so I was able to join and I thrived in that environment; pretence of things to come, I suppose. I can trace the beginnings of my zeal for leadership positions and fitness to that time in my life.

My new "parents", the Tackles, were not wealthy and the support of 4 boys was taxing. I had a crush on Mary Sue Ervin, the Rev. Howard Ervin's daughter, who was a couple years older. She played the piano like an angel and I desperately wanted to learn to play. The Tackles said I could take lessons if I found a job to pay for them.

From my days in Arkansas, I knew about delivering newspapers, so I got myself a paper route in the neighborhood. It meant rising at 4:00 a.m. every day, biking to the office to pick up the papers, folding them and delivering them before everyone left for work. I would usually finish by 6:00 a.m., ride home, and read and do my homework until everyone else awoke. During that time I decided to read the entire Bible and within that year that is exactly what I did.

In addition to the piano lessons, I used the money to buy a used bike at a neighborhood garage sale. Delivering the papers was the easy part; collecting the payments every month was not. I never knew there were so many excuses to avoid payment. Yet, if I missed a porch when I threw the papers, those who missed payments were the ones who complained the most to my managers. If I did not collect the money it was taken out of my monthly check so I had great incentive to bug those folks every day until they paid. I also learned some creative and forceful ways to convince people it was in their best interest to pay the first time I came around.

It wasn't until about half-way through that school year that I had enough money to pay for piano lessons. At the close of my first lesson, my teacher told me that she had given me the first 8-10 lessons that day and that I was going to be an easy study. My major problem was the

Tackles did not have a piano, so I drew a key board and practiced on that, which may be why I never learned to play by ear.

I only lived with the Tackles for about a year. It was a tough time for them, having just lost their son. But the fact that in the midst of their grief they chose to help someone else, taught me a valuable lesson. Now, over 50 years later, that has been my choice when I would find myself in the midst of grief or pain; go help someone. It really puts everything in perspective. Even today, when relatives or friends come to me with problems or issues, I tell them, "Go help someone in need!" They look at me funny, but those who follow my suggestion report back, "*It works!*"

I always wondered at the odd phrase, "*Let the dead bury the dead*" but living with the Tackles helped me to understand…grief may be necessary but the living must continue to live. I will confess I never lost a child, and I hope I leave this world before I do. But I wonder if I would have the strength to live the lesson I observed that year with Mr. and Mrs. Leonard Tackles.

After that year with the Tackles, I moved constantly and never had the chance to continue my piano career. Mary Sue eventually married and went to Mexico as a missionary and, as far as I know, is still there.

Leonard Tackles, another time, another angel that came into my life at the right time and in the right place. '*Coincidence,*' some would say. But, I don't believe in coincidences. There were many angels before Leonard Tackles, many more after, too many for me to consider them to be random occurrences. Mrs. Tackles got pregnant again and this time had a daughter, after four sons. I got along with the other three sons but tended to avoid becoming too close to anyone. I saw my brother and sisters at church on Sunday. It became a pattern to go to church with the Tackles on Sunday morning, stay all day until after Sunday evening church. Howard Ervin, usually with Mary Sue, would then take me back to Buena Park.

On Wednesday, I would ride my bicycle the 20 or so miles from Buena Park to the church and Brother Ervin would bring me and my bicycle back home after church.

By now, life had taught me to keep a certain distance from people. Before long, I was convinced, everything will change and I would have to say goodbye. Sure enough, at the end of the school year I was off again but the entire Tackle's family remains dear to my heart.

── 12 ─

UNKNOWN TO THE rest of us, Nancy knew where our mother went after we were all sent to live with our father. It was Nancy our mother trusted most with that secret and the dutiful daughter, with years of living with the controlling woman that was our mother, kept the secret until her junior year in high school. It was Don's senior year, Carole's sophomore year and my last year in middle school, the eighth grade.

As the story came out it seems that our mother fell in love with a man in Long Beach, California. It must have been rather intense until well into the relationship she broke the news she had six children. In an understandable flash, he was gone and she was heartbroken. It wasn't long, however, that the loss was relieved when she was at a bar in Long Beach and met Sherman, a Boson's Mate in the United States Navy. At first she told the sailor that she had only one child, our youngest brother Craig, who was the second son of Bud, the truck-driver from Clarksville, Arkansas.

When things heated up she devised the plan that her first husband, Joseph William Nevels, should now care for his four children. That left Lee as the odd-child-out. She went crying to Sherman and confessed that she had two children, Lee and Craig. She then contacted Joseph William Nevels and told him it was his turn to care for the older four of us.

Nancy was sworn to secrecy but in event of an emergency our mother told her that they had moved to Beeville, Texas. That was the home of Chase Field Naval Air Station where Sherman Clark had been transferred.

In a sense of guilt, or some other emotion, Nancy confessed her knowledge of this to the family where she and Carole were living in Southern California. They, in turn, let Howard Ervin know about this development. Howard Ervin, Leonard Tackles, Don's 'parents' and Nancy and Carole's 'parents' met and decided that the right place for all of us was with our mother in Texas. It was decided that Howard Ervin and Nancy's 'foster-father' would drive us four kids to Beeville, Texas in Leonard Tackles VW van, to scope out the situation.

It was the spring (Easter) break 1960 when we all left So. Cal on the trek east to the little town in South Texas called Beeville, the home to Chase Field Naval Air Station, an advanced training base for Navy pilots about to get their wings. We arrived in the early afternoon after a virtual non-stop drive. Nancy knew the address and had made some contact with our mother but our mother had no idea we were coming. When we arrived at the almost ramshackle house we noted Lee and Craig playing in front. Neither of them recognized any of us and as soon as they noted we were eying the place they retreated inside.

The Rev. Ervin and Nancy knocked on the door which was answered by our mother. She was a woman who did not like surprises and I fully expected her to be angry by our unannounced arrival but to our pleasant surprise she wasn't angry, or hid it well if she were. She always respected Howard Ervin and I suspect he was a calming influence.

We all exchanged hugs and there were some tears as we spent the next hour or more discussing options. Sherman Clark had no idea we even existed let alone were at his home. Our mother agreed that she would tell him about the four older children and retreated to a bedroom to call him at the base. I asked Lee and Craig to show me around outside. It had been nearly two years since last we saw each other. I don't think Craig remembered me but Lee did. We stayed outside for quite awhile until someone motioned for us to come inside.

Don was about to graduate from high school in a couple months, just as the other three of us were about to finish our school year. We met with Sherman, our mother and made the decision to return to California with Howard Ervin, finish the school year, and return to Beeville in the summer. That would give everyone time to adjust to the idea and make arrangements for a larger house to accommodate more kids.

While stationed in California in the Navy I went by the Tackles house in Buena Park but they had moved. I recently (2010) made contact with Tim who now lives in the Northwest. He informed me both his father and mother had died and one brother had committed suicide in 1981. His other brother also lives in Washington. The rough and tumble Tim is now a Christian family counselor.

— 13 —

As the summer of 1960 ended, Don went off to Bible College in Springfield, Missouri. The rest of us moved into capehart military housing on the east side of Beeville.

It is amazing how life for many is a vicious circle, and a small circle at that, repeating itself over and over. It was not long after our arrival that our mother and Sherman were off to some bar in town, got into a fight, and our Mom would not come home. Not long after, Sherman would come home; always drunk. At first, I tried to rationalize his actions by attributing them to the fact that all of a sudden he had five kids at home instead of two or that he remained angry at our mother for lying to him about how many children she had. He certainly never missed an opportunity to remind her that she had abandoned four of her children and what a horrible mother that made her.

The school year finally started. Nancy was a senior, Carole a junior and I was a freshman. Nancy got a job as a waitress at The American Cafe in downtown Beeville. I got a part-time job working at a truckstop on Highway 59 that rolled from Houston to Laredo. It was my task to clean bugs off the windshields of the big rigs as they filled up with gas or while the drivers went inside to order chicken fried steak from the small restaurant that was attached.

Before Don left for college that first summer, the four of us started the Bible Baptist Church of Beeville. Carole played the piano, I led the singing, Nancy sat in the pew and Don practiced his future profession as a preacher. Don was trying to follow in the footsteps of Howard Ervin which we all revered as a man of God. Eventually, a few others began coming to the church and by the end of the summer we were up to 12-15 people in attendance. When Don left for college there were a couple months without a preacher but the Baptist Bible Fellowship sent some subs and eventually a full time church leader?

The older three of us all rode the bus from Navy Housing to A.C. Jones High School. I was excited to be in High School, even though I was a freshman. We all made friends quickly and, with the exception of the drama at home, things were going well.

There was always *high* drama at home. Our mother and step-father saw to that. He would go to work in the day and drink until late at night. More often than not they would begin fighting in the wee hours of the morning. When I say 'fight' I do not mean small verbal exchanges. These were serious, both verbally and physically. Often they began out at a bar where someone would try to intervene to stop physical attacks. On rare occasions they came home together but as soon as they were both home the event would continue into the later rounds in the front yard or in the house.

Now don't get me wrong, there is *never* justification for a man to hit a women or the other way around. But, having heard many of these verbal exchanges first hand our mother knew exactly which buttons to push to illicit a physical attack. I observed there was always a path to avoid the high drama of a physical attack. I even tried to pull my mother away at times or ask her to withdraw. That completely infuriated my mother and she attacked me before she returned to my step-father. She was a master at bear-baiting the man and I suppose he was too drunk to see it coming. There were no innocents in these encounters. I do not write these observations with any sort of satisfaction and in no way do I justify the attacks she endured. I have seen film of dog fights and it sickened me to see people force the dogs into anger and eventually a fight. Those fights between my mother and step-father were no less sickening and after a point it would become impossible and fruitless to determine the instigator.

Eventually, I came to the sad and weird conclusion that they purposefully provoked each other. It was some sort of perverted dance they were engaged in. The next day she wore her bruises and cuts as a twisted badge of honor, designed to illicit sympathy from anyone who saw her. She seldom hid her marks or wounds and seemed to seek out public exposure. As I said, I hated Sherman for the sorry SOB that he was for hitting a woman. But, over time I began to develop a great sadness for my mother and perhaps resentment as I witnessed her provocations and her sad attempts at sympathy afterwards.

Things got so bad at home that my two sisters began staying with friends from high school. That arrangement gave them a semi-normal life and I was happy for them. While that left me and my two younger brothers at home to deal with Sherman when he came home drunk, I was happy Carole and Nancy were not there. There was nothing they could have done.

It was about half-way through the spring semester, 1960, that Sherman came home drunk without our mother. I pretended to be asleep and he collapsed on the couch in the living room with a beer in one hand, a cigarette in the other. Sometime later I woke to a smell of something strange in the house and walked down the hall to the living room. To my horror, the curtains and carpet were on fire and the room was filled with smoke. I ran back to the bedroom and woke my two brothers, Lee and Craig, and pushed them out the back window. I told Lee to go next door and have someone call the fire department.

I then went back down the hall to the living room and began yelling at Sherman trying to wake him up. Because the carpet was on fire I could not get to him. As I was just about overcome with the smoke I yelled one last time and he awoke, jumped up and ran across the burning carpet out the front door. I went to the back bedroom and climbed out the same back window and found my brothers about the time the fire trucks arrived.

They put the fire out but the house was a virtual total loss. They took Sherman to the base hospital. It seems the fire in the carpet had melted the foam cushion; when he ran across the burning carpet the melted foam rubber became imbedded into the bottom of his bare feet. At the hospital they had to scrape the rubber off his feet with a wire brush. As I considered how close we all came to dying that night I admit I was so angry with him I hoped it hurt bad enough that he would not drink and smoke again. Lessons are things some people learn and others do not. While that may have been the first house he burned down, it would not be his last.

Sometime after the event was over our mother heard about the fire and came home. I can't remember where we spent the rest of that night but soon after I moved in with a member of the Church we had started,

Mr. and Mrs. Garrett & his family. I lived with them for the remainder of the school year. The Navy rebuilt the burned house and by the end of the school year my mother, brothers and step father moved back in. I stayed with the Garret's through most of that summer.

Sherman received orders from the Navy to Subic Bay in the Philippines. I begged my mother to let me stay with the Garrett's but she and Sherman said no. When they came to get me I ran away into the woods for a few hours but was coaxed back by Mr. Garrett who explained my place was with my family. He told me if things didn't work out I could come back and stay with them.

—————————————————————————————————— 14 –

SHERMAN FLEW OUT early and the four of us, my mother, two brothers and I drove out to San Francisco and stayed for a couple weeks at The Presidio, a U.S. Army base in the downtown area not far from Fisherman's Wharf. There, we had all our shots and processing before we boarded a plane and flew to Clark Air Force Base in the Philippines, where we boarded a bus for Subic Bay.

It was late in the summer of 1961 when we moved into base housing and I prepared to start my sophomore year at George Dewey High School, a DOD facility that served military & civilian dependents on the base.

In many ways it was a good 10 months, in other ways not so much. It was exciting to be in an exotic foreign country and in many ways the Philippines was just that.

I was introduced to high school sports there and made the football and basketball teams as a reserve. I learned that, while small in stature, I was fast. I credit that discovery to our coach, Ed Orrick, a Kentucky Wildcat who became the coach for all the sports and introduced football to George Dewey High School. He saw me running during P.E. and invited me to join the team in sprints. I would always win, even against the upper classmen.

Coach Orrick convinced me I could run even faster and showed me a few techniques to better my times in the sprints. More importantly, he gave me confidence. He made me a defensive back on the football team but I grew up watching Johnny Unitas and I wanted to be quarterback. When I told him my dream he made me the back-up QB. He told me,

"Larry, you can be anything you want to be." He said it in such a way that I thought he meant it, and I believed him. He never knew how that one comment would affect my life.

There is a mental block in most people when they run. They have two speeds, slow and what they think is 'fast.' When most people run fast they assume that is as fast as they can go. But a serious runner learns the mind is as great a factor in running as the body, and you can convince your mind there are additional gears that lead to faster running.

While he was not a sprinter, this principle was demonstrated by Roger Bannister in 1954. Until that moment many claimed the four-minute mile would never be broken. Why? The 'official' world record in the mile, as recognized by the International Amateur Athletics Federation, prior to Bannister was 4:01.3 set in 1945. Many, including Bannister, toyed with the mark running several 4:02's prior to the record. Besides being a nice round number, what is 4:00 minutes? It is merely one 100th of a second faster than 3:09.99, that's all!

Over my lifetime I have heard many arbitrary limitations placed on mankind. As much as I loved and respected him, I heard the Rev. Howard Ervin proclaim from the pulpit in the 1950's that *"God put man on the earth and man would never walk on the moon."* He never could have known that about 13 years later I would be a member of the Apollo 17 recovery team that welcomed back the last person to have walked on the moon, Gene Cernan.

Today, I hear mankind will never break the two hour mark in the marathon that, as of this writing, stands at 2 hours, 3 minutes and 59 seconds (set in 2008).

"Limitations" are insidious and I am not just talking about world records. Society, family, friends, life-in-general attempts to place limitations on us all, and we don't even realize it. In many cases, those perceived limitations become as real as a brick wall in people's minds.

Many years ago my daughter's first grade teacher announced in class before a math lesson, "I do not like math." She went on to say, "Girls just aren't as good at math as boys." I did not hear about this until much later, which was probably a good thing, but I was no less furious and my heart rate and blood pressure rise even now as I write this. Though my daughter has never made less than an "A" in any math class she has ever taken in public schools and in college, to this day my daughter still thinks she is not good at math.

A few years ago while teaching at high school I had a young lady in class, a senior. She was very bright, did well on every exam and wrote some of the most thought provoking essays I have read from a high school student. While reviewing her progress with her I asked what she was going to do after graduation. She said she would probably get a job somewhere. I asked if she was considering going to college. She replied, "Oh, I'm not smart enough to go to college." Well, she was certainly bright enough and I tried to convince her she should consider it. A couple days later her father come to the classroom and angrily asked me why I was filling his daughter with *"that college shit."* "We are not college people," he said.

A few years later I ran into her at a local store with a baby on her hip. She told me the father of her child had left them and she was trying to hold down two jobs to care for herself and her baby. I wished her the best and told her if she ever needed a recommendation to let me know. As I watched her walk away, I thought how different her life might have been for her if someone had sold her on the dream of higher education. It then occurred to me that *my own mother had four children by that age* and believed everything that was wrong with the world was because of "those damn college kids."

Now, don't get me wrong, I do not have anything against babies and I know college is not for everyone. But to have a parent, teacher or friend place limitations on you that would chain you for your entire life is such a tragedy. How many generations of children will we rear believing these myths about what they cannot do? We need more people like Coach Orrick who tell children, *"You can be anything you want to be,"* and mean it.

Coach Orrick's encouragement convinced me that my sprint speed only had the limitations I put on it. We didn't have a track to run on so my times were irrelevant to me. I *believed* I could run faster.

Many people presume the ever faster speeds we see in track can be attributed to the evolution of the human body. While that is a factor, none of those accomplishments would have been possible without the evolution of the human mind. We presume that evolution occurs over the millenniums but the mind can change in a moment. I have seen it happen...it has happened to me.

Thirty five days after Roger Bannister's record time, it was broken again and since 1954 a new world record in the mile has been set 18 times. Today, if you want to be competitive, at almost any level in the mile, you have to run at least somewhere under four minutes.

"Every morning in Africa, a gazelle wakes up. It knows it must outrun the fastest lion or it will be killed. Every morning in Africa, a lion wakes up. It knows it must run faster than the slowest gazelle, or it will starve. It doesn't matter whether you're a lion or a gazelle--when the sun comes up, you'd better be running." Roger Bannister

— 15 —

I DISCOVERED THERE was an American missionary in Olongapo, the town outside the base in the Philippines. I met him and discovered he knew my oldest brother who, by this time, was a missionary in Argentina. Every now and then I would attend his church in Olongapo City.

Olongapo was a pretty wild place, especially at night. It was filled with sailors with too much money and Filipinos with not enough. The object of the sailor was to have a good time...the object of the Filipino was to separate the sailor from his money. For the most part, both objectives were achieved every night.

As a high school kid I never went to Olongapo after dark but Sunday mornings things were pretty quiet. The church was meant for Filipinos and I was received as a guest. I made friends with a couple locals in a Sunday School class who invited me to take a trip to Manila.

We met just outside the base early one Saturday morning and stepped into a jitney for a ride to the local bus station. At that time, you could take one of two bus lines that made the trip to Manila, *The Philippine Rabbit* or a *Victory Liner*. Filipinos had their favorite but, for no particular reason that I could see, we boarded a *Victory Liner* and headed out for Manila, a 120 kilometer trip that would take 4-6 hours. The bus was full, not only with people but chickens, pigs and other assorted creatures.

Subic Bay is northwest of the Bataan Peninsula and one must cross the Zambales Mountain Range before you enter the plains that

69

take you into Manila. The mountain range is thick tropical jungle with roads that often were washed out in the monsoon season. These mountains were also once home to The Hukbalahap, or 'Huk's,' as they were referred to by the locals. These Huk's were originally a group formed in 1942 to combat the Japanese occupation of the Philippines during World War II. Their name was a contraction of the Filipino term "Hukbong Bayan Laban sa mga Hapon", which, in the official language (tagalong) of the country means *"People's Army Against the Japanese".* After the war they were supposed to disband but some units evolved into the military arm of the Communist Party of the Philippines. They became similar to, but not as powerful as, the Viet Cong in South Viet Nam. While they were defeated several times, remnants of the movement remained in these mountains until the late 1960's.

As we made our way on the Victory Liner through the Zambalas Mountains I dozed off, only to be awakened as the bus came to a sudden stop. I assumed it was another road wash-out. One of my friends made his way towards the front of the bus to see what the problem was. He hurried back and quietly said to me, "It's a road-block, get down."

I started to stand to see what was going on when my two friends pulled me down and started pulling bags and a crate of chickens on top of me. *"Be quiet,"* they said. *"Do not get up! No matter what happens; No matter what!"*

I was totally buried under an avalanche of bags and what happened next was explained to me after the event. It seems the men at the roadblock were heavily armed and in uniform. They made a cursory search of the bus and then demanded payment before they would let the bus pass. The driver walked down the aisle explaining they needed to collect money, give it to the men at the roadblock, and all would be fine. He had some pesos and collected more from the passengers and gave it to the men at the roadblock. There was a loud argument going on in Tagalog but the armed men finally let us move on. We were quite-a-way down the road before my friends removed the bags and the chickens from on top of me and told me it was OK to get up.

They explained that the men said they were Huks. One of my friends said, "Maybe they were, or maybe they were just bandits." I thought it was all kind of exciting but I could see my friends were very disturbed. I asked what would have happened had the Huk's noticed that I was an American.

"That's something I'm glad we will never find out," said my friend.

We were soon out of the mountains and onto the plains. The roads were much better, straighter at least, and the bus began driving much faster…more like the suicidal Filipino drivers I was accustomed to. We pulled into the outskirts of Manila and through the city to the bus station. From there we climbed aboard another jitney for the ride to the university.

One of my friends was an on-again off-again student at the university. This, I was told, was fairly common in the Philippines. Students would attend for a semester but then could not afford to continue so they would take time off from school and worked and saved enough money to continue for another semester. It was rare for someone to go straight through and graduate in four years. This more common hop-scotch method meant it may take eight to ten years to graduate. Returning part-time students were treated the same as any other student, including dorm privileges.

So, there we were in the dorm. It was more of a commune where everyone contributed something for the meals and they rotated cooks among the students or occasionally they had someone come in to cook.

On this particular night a lady from the neighborhood cooked our meal for a very few pesos and her dinner. She served lumpia (similar to Chinese egg-rolls but with Filipino spices), pancit (noodles), chicken adobo (a type of cooking from the time the Spanish ruled the country that involved stewing the meat with vinegar) and of course, Rice.

We washed it all down with Pepsi, being careful not to drink the last half inch. One did not drink the water unless you had a way to purify it and soda pop or beer often had residue at the bottom; you could avoid drinking this unknown residue by either decanting the drink into a glass or very carefully and slowly drinking the soda so as not to disturb the residue at the bottom. I must say, the food was excellent and I was sure to thank my hosts as well as the cook. Normally, they spoke Filipino (Tagalog) but they thought this was a great opportunity to show off their English speaking skills. Everyone shared a story and I told them about being stopped by the Huks on the trip over. They all said they had made the trip from Manila to Olongapo many times and had never had such an encounter. I suggested my friends staged it for my benefit, which they vehemently denied and were quite offended at the suggestion. I just laughed and explained, "American teasing," and all was well.

After the meal we talked some more and I answered dozens of questions about America. They were particularly interested in Texas. As we got ready for bed I noticed they had only a couple mosquito nets and they insisted I use one of them. I tried to convince them I would be fine, but they would have none of my protests. I was a guest and it was incumbent on them to give their best to a guest.

On Sunday morning half of them wanted me to go to the Catholic church and my friends wanted me to go to the missionary church. I figured out if we went to early Mass we could do both. The Catholic service was in Tagalog and Latin, both which left me in the dark but I got the idea. The missionary church was in Tagalog and English. There seemed to be more English but, perhaps that was for my benefit.

We then toured around Manila and visited several parks including Rizal Park, named for an executed hero of one of the revolutions against the Spanish. We visited The Manila Cathedral and Makiti, which is probably the most affluent area with stores, hotels and restaurants. It is the financial hub of the country, much like Wall Street in the U.S. We stopped and bought some things to eat on the way home and went to the bus station in the early afternoon. The trip back to Olongapo was uneventful, much to the relief of my friends.

One other trip I made with my Filipino friends was at Easter. We traveled to an isolated rural area, which I could not find again if my life depended on it. There were men and women there conducting self-flagellation as they crawled on their bloody knees for miles many with whips imbedded with glass beating themselves as they crawled along. In this village, it was considered an honor to be literally nailed to a cross and nearly crucified on the side of a hill. No Hollywood props or sleight of hand, so to speak. They actually nailed the person to the cross. These bloody rituals have been outlawed in the Philippines but I am told they still occur in these outlying areas.

While I was only there for ten months, I learned to admire and respect the Filipino people. If your only exposure to the people of the Philippines was outside a military base you have a very narrow knowledge. They are proud and generous, sometime to a fault. Though, by comparison, they may have had little, that never diminished their pride and hospitable nature. I have observed this natural tendency throughout my travels around the world. While it may appear counter-intuitive, it seems the more people have, the less generous they become. This has been verified in my own hometown at Christmas. I have noticed the most elaborate Christmas light displays seem to spring up on homes of middle class and lower middle class homes. The poor cannot afford light displays and the rich folks just put a wreath on their doors. Want more evidence? I have rung the bells on behalf of the Salvation Army at Christmas. The less fortunate among us seem the most likely to make a donation; perhaps not much, to be sure, but a donation nonetheless. The wealthy, they just scurry by and refuse to make eye contact.

In order to keep my faith in mankind, I want to hope that isn't the case, but there is quite a bit of empirical evidence to back up my observations.

~~~

In 1843, Danish artist Johan Thomas Lundbye created a woodcut depicting a poor child selling matches. A copy was sent to Hans Christian Andersen who, in 1845, wrote, *"The Little Match Girl,"* a moving story about a dying child's dreams and hopes. In 2007 David Lang composed, *The Little Match Girl Passion*, for two sopranos, a tenor and bass-baritone. That passion is one of the most moving pieces I have ever heard.

The story goes something like this: On a cold New Year's Eve, a young girl tries to sell matches on the street. She is not having much success and is freezing badly, but is afraid to go home because her father will beat her if she has not sold all her matches. She takes shelter in a stoop of an empty house and lights the matches one at a time for some warmth. In the glow of the first match she sees a vision of a Christmas tree and a table set with food for the holiday feast. With the lighting of the second match the young girl sees a shooting star, and remembers her grandmother telling her that each time there is a falling star it means someone has died and is going to Heaven. Reluctantly, she lights her next match and sees a vision of her grandmother, the only person to have shown her any kindness. She strikes one match after another in an attempt to keep the vision of her grandmother for as long as she can and finally, the last match goes out. The child dies and her grandmother carries her soul to heaven. The next morning, passers-by find the dead child in the stoop, frozen to death during the night.

Just relaying the plot of that story brings tears to my eyes. But then, I'm just an old softy, I suppose.

I don't care if you have a majestic light display or just a wreath on your door, Christmas is a time to skip the mall for a moment and remember there are many people out there, probably in your own neighborhood, who are hungry and freezing in the cold; metaphorically or factually speaking.

The whole point of the story is that no one should be left out in the cold. Not just at Christmas but any time of the year. Little did I know that soon, I would have my own story, but set in the warm Asiatic land that was the Philippines.

16

THANKSGIVING, (1961) STARTED with all the potential for a happy occasion. My mother had worked the day before and that morning to prepare the all-American meal. It featured a turkey with all the trimmings and we boys helped her by setting the table with the finest settings we had. Things were going well. Sherman was home and it appeared that we would actually have a great family thanksgiving meal. But our hopeful expectations were again shattered in an instant.

There was this typical formula for every birthday, Christmas, every holiday, including Thanksgiving. Something innocuous would be spoken by someone and either Sherman or our mother would hit the roof. It would take a forensic scientist to ascertain the exact comment that triggered the conflict and we had long ago given up on trying to figure out who had lit the fuse to cause such a conflagration.

After a horrible argument our mother grabbed the keys and went out the door, got in the car and drove off. Sherman at first did not see her leave but once he realized she was leaving he ran down the street after her. He could not catch her but he must have continued down the road because he never came back until the early hours of the next morning, drunk as usual.

We three boys should have been stunned but we weren't. This was the same dance played out every holiday and most every weekend. We looked at each other and I made a joke that there was plenty there for all of us, *"Let's eat,"* I said, and we did. We tried to make the best of these bad situations, but sometimes that was very hard to do. Over time we got pretty good at amnesia about what had just happened.

I had many great experiences that year at George Dewey High School, on the base, as well as my interactions with Filipinos. I wasn't there long enough to make many lasting friendships and I remember my classmates probably a little better than they remember me but that was intentional.

That's not a put-down on them. It just reveals that in those days I was, by self-imposed necessity, more of an observer and less the participant. I was the new kid, a sophomore, quiet and unassuming, and of course there was always the drama at home. Because of that I didn't want too much attention drawn to me. If I was more open and flamboyant and there were an incident at home everyone would know I was one of the players in the high-drama- Shakespearian tragedy that played itself out almost every night. If I stayed in the shadows people would say, "I hear there were children involved but I don't know who they were."

I'm sure word did get out since the Navy shore patrol was often involved to calm things down. That meant that official reports must have been submitted. But then, perhaps this was not all that unusual and the Navy in those days had the habit of keeping domestic issues like this "off the books." Sherman continued to advance in rank despite all the drinking and fighting. Soon he made Chief Petty Officer, which frankly, astounded me then and still does today.

I did play passively at football, running, basketball, chess and a few other activities at school but I was really just quietly honing my interpersonal skills, learning my way around people but not letting anyone become too close. That was OK with me because there is a certain safety in anonymity.

The resilience of the human condition to absorb these types of senseless issues continues to amaze me, especially among children, and there was more to come, much more.

17

My world came crashing down around me one spring evening in 1962. That evening started out with me setting out dinner for my brothers. My mother and Sherman left for their almost nightly dramatic event at the Chiefs' Club.

For months, the dance had gone something like this: my stepfather and mother would leave together. Sometime during the evening my mother would come home, grab a change of clothes and be off to who knows where. Sometimes she said she was going to spend the night with a girl friend. Most nights I asked her not to tell me where she was going. The next part of the dance was when Sherman came home, always drunk. The first thing he wanted to know was if my mother had come home and where had she gone.

There was the occasional slapping and pushing that went with the shouting and the threats and occasionally he held up a threatening fist, but, for the most part, I took it as a big show from a very sick man. When I heard him downstairs slamming doors my stomach would do a flip. To this day I hate to hear the slamming of doors, and I react now as I did 50 years ago.

I hated what I knew was about to happen, but my options were extremely limited. I got in the habit of putting Lee and Craig to bed in a back bedroom before he came home, just to keep them out of the line of fire.

Sherman was a tall lanky man, not big, but extremely strong, or so it seemed to a fourteen year old. Still, his strength and the drinking made for a dangerous combination. He had no apparent fear of death when alcohol was involved. He had probably lost more fights than he won, but that just made him meaner. I would see him some mornings and know immediately he had been in a fight the night before. I couldn't imagine the other guy looking worse than he did and still be vertical. By his mean temperament, I could tell he had lost whatever encounter he had the night before. A more rational person might avoid a fight after a long and distinguished history of being on the losing end, but I guess alcohol is not rational.

On rare occasions Sherman could be fun and willing to play ball with us boys, but one was always aware that, like some wild animal, he could turn without warning.

He did not command respect but he did demand it. I suppose he didn't know or care that any respect I showed the man was superficial and more for personal survival than anything real. If it were not for Lee and Craig, I would have found a way to get out of there.

I have learned that things happen and people come into your life for a purpose. Sometimes people come into your life for the sole purpose of showing you what not to become. Sadly, too many people do not learn the lesson.

This particular night was about to become *the* night. The night I would never forget. It started like scores before; everyone played the script to a tee and never missed a line. They went off together; my mother came home, my mother left...

"Don't tell me where you are going," I told her, "I don't want to lie when I tell him, *I don't Know*."

I put my younger brothers to bed in a back room. Sherman arrived home slamming doors...my stomach did its normal somersault. He came in, demanding to know where my mother had gone. "I don't know," I said.

"You are a liar, tell me where she is," he said.

So far everyone had played their part, like a long running Broadway play with no missed lines.

I don't remember when the first fist struck my face and sent me stumbling across the room but I thought, *"Hey, that's not in the script,"* or something to that effect. In a flash Sherman was standing over me wailing away, with open slaps at the start. He caught me on the side of my head across my ear and suddenly there was a terrible ringing. *'Hey, someone answer the phone.'*

He yelled, but the ringing was so loud I couldn't make out what he was saying. I assumed he wanted me to tell him the location of my mother so I just kept saying, *"I don't know where she is."*

"You're a liar," he kept yelling and hit me few more times. The coward lorded over me and suddenly made a fist and knocked me down, but I do not remember any pain. His eyes were blank, with no emotion or concern. He stopped rather suddenly and stared at me. I thought it was over. He had never been this violent and I assumed he had come to his senses.

Then things became scary.

"Why aren't you crying?" he slurred. I was angry, mad, furious, ashamed, determined and considering my options. I thought of making a run for the door but even if I made it that would leave him alone with my brothers. I quickly surveyed the room for something with which to defend myself. Nothing caught my eye and he was inches from my face, so close I could smell the putrid liquor on his breath. It made me want to gag. I just stared into his eyes, determined to show no fear.

"Why aren't you crying?" he said again as he took another swing at me. I half expected what he would do and almost dodged the glancing blow. He was now over me with one foot on either side bending over, wailing faster and faster. *"Cry!"* he yelled. *"Cry and I will stop."*

But I didn't cry, I wouldn't cry! I remember thinking, *"You may kill me but you will never see me cry!"*

He had his belt off and made several loops around his fist. I stared directly into his eyes as he took another swing. Again I pulled back at the very last moment and it was another glancing blow, but enough to sting. I had figured out his timing and, though I couldn't avoid the blows entirely, I quickly learned how to avoid a crushing blow. He kept yelling at me to cry and I just glared at him.

I don't know how long the entire event lasted, moments, minutes, many minutes, I really don't know. It seemed an eternity in slow motion. He stood upright and I slid back still glaring directly at him. He turned and without another word slinked back into his bedroom like an animal that had grown weary of torturing his prey.

I went into the kitchen, the farthest place in the house from his room. I grabbed a towel and washed my face; there was some blood but not as much as I expected. I had a sense of satisfaction; I had survived the beating and won...he could not make me cry.

I know that may sound like a feebly innocuous victory, but in that situation, a victory was a victory, no matter how insignificant.

I quietly checked on my brothers and walked passed his room but did not hear anything from inside. For a moment I seriously considered getting a knife from the kitchen and taking my revenge, but that thought passed quickly. Still, no jury of my peers would have convicted me.

I was dressed in jeans, a shirt, tennis shoes and socks. I walked through the kitchen, out the back door, down the stairs to the street below. The road led down the hill for about a mile to the bay. At the bottom of the hill was a 'T'; to the right was Subic Bay Naval Station; to the left was a longer road to Cubi Point Naval Air Station. For no particular reason I took a left and just walked. It was early in the morning, no moon, pitch-dark with a few lights in the very far distance. I don't know how far I walked, probably a couple miles in all when I came to a road to the right that led to a fuel pier. There was no one in sight, so I climbed the fence and walked out to the end of the pier.

Off to my right I could see the lights of the ships at the Naval Base of Subic Bay, even farther I could see the lights of Olongapo City. To my left, in the distance, I could see the lights of Cubi Point with its tower beacon sweeping around every few moments.

For the first time, in the early morning hours on the end of a long fuel pier extending into Subic Bay, all alone, I began to cry. Soft sobs at first but then uncontrollable torrents of tears as my anguish came pouring out. I was embarrassed and ashamed that I could not, did not, fight back. I was totally humiliated that I did not charge him in a final bonsai-charge that well may have meant my death; but, it would have been a death with dignity. I should have gotten that knife.

Looking back, there was no logical basis for my shame. That coward of a man was much larger and stronger than me and could have broken me like a twig. But, I considered none of that in those moments at the end of the pier. The pain I felt deep inside was horrible and growing to unimaginably immense proportions. So much was my anguish that I seriously began to think, *"The pain of living far outweighs the pain of dying!"* I stood high on the end of that pier and through the misty distortion of my tears, I looked far down to the water; my knees were becoming weak, my entire body felt as if it were on the verge of exploding. The water below lapped at the piles that made up the pier, almost singing an invitation to me, *"Come, and all your pain will be gone."*

The anguish of my heart was beyond the limits of human endurance, or so it seemed to me. I stepped closer to the point where the pier changed from horizontal to vertical. My head was spinning; my entire body was shaking out of control. Soon it would be over.

At the very literal edge, where life crossed over to death, there shown a bright light through my tears. I looked up and, as I did, a giant ball of fire careened across the night sky. The light was so bright, for a moment at least, it was almost as if it were the middle of the day instead of the dark of night. I could see far across the bay into the mountains beyond; I could make out Grande Island which lies in the mouth of Subic Bay and was normally invisible at night. I quickly rubbed my shirt across my eyes to clear my vision just in time to see the giant ball of fire silently disappear behind the mountains on the other side of the bay.

Throughout this event, the night was silent but the fireball stunned me with its majesty and beauty. Perhaps I was delirious, but there was a voice, as clear as any conversation I have ever had, that softly filled the night, *"Not Yet, My Son,"* was what I heard.

I know…many will say there is a logical explanation for what I "thought" I heard but even if there is, it doesn't diminish the impact it had on me. Instantly, I could feel arms were around me, comforting me. My heartbeat was back to normal, the shame was gone, my eyes became clear, and I swear I heard the voice again as it said, *"All will be well."*

I stepped back from the edge of the pier and looked all around for someone who was talking to me but I was alone; alone, but not alone. There was a presence, a peace that comforted me, assuring and reassuring me. It was wonderful, magical, and certainly spiritual.

I suppose 100 people could have 100 explanations for what happened that night, and that's OK. I know what I saw, what I heard and I know what I felt. It is as vivid and real to me 50 years later as it was that night.

Some people are quick to discount anything that tastes of the spiritual. But the reality is, many of us have a real sense for things that are not of this world. I understand the doubters but years of experiences and encounters of inexplicable origin have convinced me these are not mathematical anomalies. I've seen it too many times, several of which are recounted on these pages…many more that are not.

18

THIS WAS NOT the only time I felt such a presence or heard such a voice. The next was about ten years later when, as a Navy pilot I returned to the same place. Only this time I was stationed at Cubi Point Naval Air Station.

I was on our squadron baseball team and we were pitted against a team from the Naval Hospital at Cubi Point. I was at bat, got a hit and rounded first base to stretch it into a double. As I slid into second base, the umpire motioned and said, "Safe!"

There was a doctor from the hospital playing second base and, after attempting to tag me, looked at me and said, *"Whoa, buddy, your eyes are really jaundiced. You may have hepatitis."*

The next day I told our flight surgeon of the event. After a casual examination he concurred with the first doctor and sent me up to the hospital to have some tests run. At the hospital, they drew some blood and did a cursory physical exam. When I went back the doctor said, "Your blood counts are all over the scale. What is supposed to be high is low and what is supposed to be low is high."

"So, Doc, what does it all mean," I asked.

The Doc explained, "I honestly don't know for sure, but we are going to find out. It's possible it is hepatitis. Or, it could be liver cancer. I just don't know."

Navy doctors were not constrained by the niceties of the civilian world and many would lay out the possibilities right there for all to see. Personally, I liked that approach but the words, *"liver cancer"* were not very appealing.

The big "C", even as only a possibility, is never welcome news but I wasn't too concerned since I had faced an entire litany of "maybes" from doctors. When they call it "practicing medicine" they aren't kidding.

"We need to do a liver biopsy," the doctor said.

I went in the next day for the biopsy and, if all went well, I would be back at the BOQ in time for dinner. Things did not go well.

I was prepped for the procedure and told I would be awake the entire time. The doctor explained the procedure would be mildly uncomfortable but nothing to worry about. He explained they would numb the area on my right side before the procedure, but that would only affect the surface area. At the time, a liver biopsy was taken by inserting a large hollow needle in between two ribs, through the pleural cavity and into the liver. Once the needle was in place a wire 'hook' was inserted into the needle to the liver and a piece of the organ was' hooked' and retrieved through the needle. If all went well, they would get a sample worthy of biopsy on the first try.

In a civilian world I would have to sign 20 different disclosure papers and initial all in 40 different places. Those niceties were ignored in the Navy which, I didn't really mind. I would either make it or I wouldn't.

The first thing I noted was the size of the needle. It appeared more suited for a horse than a human. I asked the doctor if he had ever done one of these procedures. He replied, *"Sure, I watched a couple at Harvard Med."* I was impressed with the Harvard Med part…the other, not so much.

He then said, *"You may feel a little pressure,"* as he quickly forced the needle through the ribs and into my organ cavity. "A little pressure" was a slight understatement. OK, maybe a great understatement. It was more what I imagine a .45 caliber bullet might feel like going into your side. Actually, I learned later they are not dissimilar. The force necessary to get this horse needle between two ribs was intense; it literally took my breath away and I began fading out. Being a Navy pilot, I knew about tunnel vision. That is when, what you see, becomes dark around the edges and then increasingly darker until there is just a pin hole of light in the middle of your vision and then, totally blank as you become unconscious.

Tunnel vision can occur to a pilot if you pull too many "G's" or have oxygen deprivation. I don't think I had either condition when this pin-hole closed shut and I was out.

When I say 'out' you may think I mean "knocked out, unconscious". While that may have been true, I was also *out*; literally, out of my body.

Now, I am aware how this sounds, but I'm telling the truth. I was above the operating table. I saw the back of the large round light they used to see everything in detail. I saw the table I was on; I saw myself lying on the table; the doctor and a nurse had their back to me, staring at the biopsy needle. *"Is it a good one?"* the nurse asked.

"I think so," replied the doctor. "Maybe we should get another".

From my perch above the scene, I noted a nurse standing beside me as she yelled, *"Doctor, I can't get a pulse. His BP is falling"*.

The doctor turned around and said, "Oh my God!" He was checking my heart with his stethoscope. He then began pounding on my chest. *"Get the crash cart, we're losing him,"* he yelled to the other nurse.

I watched as the doctor pounded on my chest and a nurse wheeled in the crash cart.

Then, in a flash I returned to my body. I know my eyes were open, but all was black. Slowly, or so it seemed, I saw reverse tunnel vision with a white dot in the middle getting bigger and bigger. I tried to speak, to tell them I was still alive, and not to give up on me, but I could not speak or move. I think I was barely breathing but I could not talk or move any muscle in my body. The doctor kept pounding on my chest, the nurse handed the crash cart paddles towards him. "I think he's back," said the doctor. "I have a pulse, BP?"

"Coming up," said the nurse.

A short time later the doctor said, "He's back with us."

Finally, I could speak again. "Is everything all right?" I asked.

"Yes," replied the doctor, "You went on a little trip but you're back with us now".

"If you only knew," I thought, thinking it better to keep the out-of-body stuff to myself.

A couple moments later I asked the doctor, "Did you get a good biopsy?"

"What we got will do," he replied with a tone that echoed relief and resignation.

I lay there in the operating room for quite awhile, until all my vitals were normal. I was never left alone. The nurse was always there, and the doctor came in and out of the room, but was never gone more than a few moments.

Finally, he spoke to me. "Larry, you gave us a little scare there. We need you to stay the night."

At least once an hour during the night a nurse came in and checked my blood pressure. About three in the morning a nurse came in again. I was drowsy, more than half asleep, and hoped it would be fast so I could go back to 100% sleep. Suddenly, she screamed, *"I can't get a BP"* as she pushed the Code Blue button on the wall. Alarms started to sound and lights started to flash. Holy Crap, I thought the whole place must be on fire. It wasn't long before every nurse in the hospital was in my room. I opened my eyes as one of the senior nurses checked my BP.

"It's a little low but he's fine." She then looked at me looking back at her and said, *"Quit doing that, Larry."*

I smiled and said, "Just trying to keep you on your toes."

The next morning I met with the doctor, who said I was looking good. "I feel fine, Doc. What happened?"

He explained, "Well, normally, prior to these biopsies, we give the patient a pre-biopsy injection of atropine. You, however, appeared in such good shape that I didn't think it was necessary. When I penetrated your pleural cavity it was evidently a great shock to your system; these things sometimes happen. In the future I will always give the patient the atropine."

By late morning I left the hospital and drove back down the hill to my BOQ room. I think they were almost as happy to see me go as I was to leave.

I did not mention to anyone about my *out-of-body-experience.* I didn't want to take a chance the doctors would keep me longer or that they would think I was nuts. "Out-of-body experiences" and "seeing UFO's", (I'm not saying I ever saw a UFO), are two things that can get a pilot grounded.

About four to six months later I was in Hong Kong. A fellow pilot told me about this "neat bar" in a posh hotel downtown. "Stews stay there," he said, referring to the stewardesses from the airlines. We dropped by and sat at a table near where there was a group of young ladies we assumed were 'stews.' After awhile we chatted them up and discovered they were nurses from the Navy Hospital at Cubi Point.

I said, "Really. I spent the night there a couple months back. My heart stopped during a liver biopsy."

One of the nurses looked at me and said, "I recognize you, you're the one who died!"

"Well, no one actually referred it to me in those terms," I said.

"No, really!" she replied. "You were dead for a couple moments. We thought we had lost you."

"Hey, thanks for bringing me back," I said.

"Now, every time before a biopsy we talk about your case," she told me.

"Well," I replied, "Everyone should have some sort of claim to fame and at least one contribution to medicine."

Oh, BTW, the biopsy came back normal. The doctor diagnosed me with something called Gilbert's Syndrome (G/S) (pronounced as the French, (gill-bear), an interesting little condition.

Gilbert's Syndrome is evidently a hereditary condition that manifests itself with increased bilirubin in the blood which causes jaundice and is found in less than 5% of the population. Its symptoms are jaundice and severe fatigue. The interesting thing is, medical studies have shown individuals with G/S have a significant decrease in incidence of coronary arterial disease and are thus at a lower risk for future heart conditions. Another study found that subjects with G/S had a much lower degree of atherosclerosis than those with normal levels of bilirubin. The study went so far as to discuss intentional, artificially raising bilirubin levels, as a means of prevention of cardiovascular disease and other oxidative and inflammatory diseases. Hey, I don't know if any of this is true; I'm just sayin'…whatever it is, look on the bright side.

19

I HAVE NO idea how I got back home after that early morning encounter on the fuel pier on Subic Bay. I suppose I walked the two miles or so.

Sometime within the next few days I had a rare serious talk with my mother. Rare because, when it came to her kids, my mother was a very controlling person who seldom listened to her off-spring. There was rarely any discussion…she talked, you listened. But I didn't care what she thought anymore.

"If I stay here, one of us is going to die," I told her with such firmness she knew I was serious, and serious I was. There was no doubt in my mind there would be another event as occurred a few nights earlier and when it happened I would do everything in my power to kill him, and, if I didn't succeed, he would most likely kill me.

I told her the Garrett's had invited me to stay with them if I came back to Beeville. That was kinda true but at that point truth became relative.

I was extremely conflicted about leaving my younger brothers in the middle of that mess that pretended to be a home. I rationalize that he had never hurt them and in the end I knew I had to get out of there.

My mother made some phone calls and visited some people on the base and a few weeks later she and I were on the flight line at Cubi Point Naval Air Station. A C-47 'Gooney Bird' was making a daily run to Clark Air Force Base on the other side of the Zambales Mountain range.

During that short flight I walked up to the cockpit and checked it out. The pilot in the left seat gave me a short tour of the instruments and controls and asked if I had ever thought about flying.

"I don't know," I said, "this is the second airplane I have ever been in."

It never occurred to me that there might be a possibility that, in nine years, I would be wearing the same Navy Wings of Gold as that pilot and 'I' would be sitting in the left seat flying my own naval aircraft from Cubi Point to Clark.

At Clark AFB I said goodbye to my mother and boarded a 707 charter flight to San Francisco.

During my 11 months in the Philippines we had no fresh milk. All they had was reconstituted milk, powdered or evaporated. There was milk in Olongapo, but it was known to carry TB so we were constantly warned to avoid it.

When I arrived at the San Francisco airport the first thing I did was go to a lounge at the airport and ordered the tallest glass of milk they had with the instruction to, "Keep'em coming."

From SF airport I transferred to a Braniff flight to San Antonio, Texas and caught a bus to Beeville.

~~~

One of the things I have observed in all of this is that there are basically one of two choices that children make. One is to follow the same path as their parents and the other is a radical rejection of everything from their parents thus creating an entirely new path. It seems the generation immediately after my grandparents, for the most part, followed the same destructive path they observed from their parents, while the very next generation, myself included, radically changed and rejected their parents example and chose a new direction for our lives. Perhaps the revolution of the 1960's had something to do with all that. It became the standard of those times to question everything, including our parents' choices.

Most of my siblings are highly educated and leading successful lives apparently without the bondage of alcohol or substance abuse. I'm not saying we are without issues, but considering the crucible we came through while growing up, I suppose we are comparatively well adjusted.

Life is a choice, actually, many choices. The more radically we severe ourselves from our parents, the more choices we are required to make. We are, after all, blazing a new trail each day and are forced to choose from many different paths. It can be, at the same time exhilarating and terrifying. But then, that's why it's so much fun.

— 20 —

THAT SUMMER, 1962, in Beeville, Texas, I moved into the modest Garrett family home on the west side of town. They didn't have much but there was so much love in that home it just didn't seem to matter.

I went up to the local high school and serendipitously met the head football coach, Dave Green. He asked if I played football and I explained I had played quarterback at the last school I attended. I may have left out the part about being a back-up who saw limited time on the field, or that it was actually flag football. He told me they needed a quarterback on the JV team and to show up in August for two-a-days. He explained that being a junior transfer I was not eligible for varsity, which I probably would not have made anyway.

The Garrett's had a daughter and two sons. There were bunk beds in the boys' bedroom, where they placed a single bed for me. It was a bit crowded but no one seemed to mind. The house had one bathroom which took some juggling, but we managed.

The Garrett family was another one of those serendipitous angels that just happened to be there at the right time and right place and willing to take a stranger into their home. Both parents worked outside the home but they still struggled to get by. I got a part time job but it didn't bring much in. I think I was making seventy five cents an hour.

Fifty years later that family continues to inspire me to help others even when I think I can't.

You just haven't lived until you've enjoyed two-a-day football practice in August in South Texas. Just to add to the excitement the

89

practice field really didn't have grass; it was 100 yards of stickers, rocks and dust. Coach Dave Green's motto was, "whatever didn't kill you made you stronger." Coach Green played his college ball at the University of Texas at Austin, as a defensive lineman, I believe. Supposedly, he broke his leg in the first half of the Cotton Bowl and still played the second half. That mentality meant that he had little patience for those who complained about our less than ideal practice conditions.

I made first team quarterback on the junior varsity. We survived pre-season and actually went undefeated that year...I think we tied one game and won all the rest. We ran an option offense with little passing which was good because my hands were small for the ball and passing was not my strength. Back in those days the quarterback on the field called the plays and it was very seldom that a coach sent a play in from the sidelines. Instead of sending in plays they had designed a series of consecutive plays where each one was a variation of the previous one. I caught on to the system quickly and got pretty good at being the field-general as quarterback. As any season goes, I made some mistakes but my speed was dangerous if I ever got outside. It's odd to me; I seem to remember every fumble but have to force myself to remember the touchdowns, even though the latter were far more numerous than the former. I guess that's just human nature.

At the end of football season I went out for basketball. I couldn't shoot that well but made up for it by being short. After a couple of weeks Coach Don Scott admitted I was great on defense and no one out-hustled me on the floor, as he dismissed me from the team. Sometime later I was made aware that Coach Green wanted me running track, which was probably the best move for me at the time.

Our track practice field was the same as that for football. They just brought a bulldozer in and cut a few lanes around the field. When we ran a 100 yard dash, 220 or 440 the time was just a guess. The faster you ran on an ill-prepared field, the more likely you were to have an injury. The only time we ran on a real track was at a meet out of town. That year I participated in the 100, 220, 440, sprint relay (440) and mile relay. I won a few individual races and probably finished "in the money" (first, second or third) most of the time. Our greatest success was in the relays where I think we set some school records, though they only stood for a few years.

My junior year I was introduced to theater and had leading roles in at least two plays. I received my first on-stage kiss from Patty Dillingham and got the nickname "Barrymore" from our football coach. Anytime I did anything wrong at practice it was, "Come-on, Barrymore, you can do better than that."

Towards the end of my junior year I began to realize I had missed something along the way, academic appreciation. My grades were OK-to-good; not great, but well enough, or so I thought. My early life was consumed with survival, which seemed to dominate my time, my thoughts, my being. I know, many people had it worse than me and some of them probably coped better academically, but life is priorities and eating and having a place to sleep ranks right up there. Eleven years of moving in and out of schools, more often than not in the middle of the school year kept me in constant academic survival mode. Each new school was at a different place along the academic calendar and each had its own unique style, so I had to spend most of my time just catching-on and catching-up, forget getting ahead. I made friends, but knowing I would likely be leaving soon would limit the depth of those friendships. More often than not my classmates had known each other since pre-school and busting into that friendship circle was seldom easy and at times impossible.

But A.C. Jones High School in Beeville seemed a little different somehow. For one thing, they had a Navy base nearby that infused new students each year into the system. I was not alone as a 'newbie' to the school and my classmates were used to welcoming the new kids on the block. Of course, it also meant that as new kids arrived others left, so my departure after my freshman year went virtually unnoticed. I did have a little edge-up when returning to start my junior year, since there were many familiar faces.

Of course, I had sports that automatically served to introduce me to new people. There is a 'fraternity of pain' that unites all who survive two-a-day practices in Texas summer heat. There is also a great equalizer in sports since the coaches didn't care about anything but putting the best person available in each position. If you did the job better than someone else it was yours. It didn't matter much who your daddy was. Oh, I suppose that wasn't entirely true but for the most part the best one at practice got to play in the games. The fact that I made starting quarterback on the football team my junior year, even if it was the JV, gave me a certain amount of credibility.

By the end of that junior year, and for the first time in my young life, I noticed my classmates talking about going to college. To be honest, that possibility had never entered my mind. If it did, I thought that perhaps I might go to Bible College as had my siblings, Don, Nancy & Carole. Until that time, even the faint dream of going to college to be trained in a profession was such a far-away, remote possibility that I could not even conjure up the image. I thought, even if college were free, I *still* couldn't afford it. One still needed to eat and sleep and no one had ever explained to me how that could be arranged. I had no idea how much college cost, but since I had nothing, it was pretty much a mute point. So, while I tried to make good grades, it wasn't to go to college. My pride made me continue to try hard and, quite frankly, I did not want to look bad among my peers. Perhaps less than pristine motivations, but it kept me in the running. When you are a mouse lost in an unknown maze all you try to do is find a little cheese.

But now a new possibility was beginning to open for me. Someone explained that I could work and go to school, someone else mentioned scholarships and loans. It was slim, but suddenly I began to see a glimmer of possibility. It was still such a wild stretch of the imagination but even a glimmer was more than I ever had before. Most of my friends had been preparing their entire lives, at least their high school lives, under the common assumption they would go to college somewhere. I had one more year of school remaining to redirect my ship out of the fog of uncertainty and onto a course towards something, quite frankly, foreign and unknown. But then, that was the story of my life.

Near the end of my junior year of high school the Garrett's announced they were moving to Cameron, Texas. I suppose I could have gone along but I had found a spot where I felt I belonged, with friends, sports, drama and other ties to the community. I began a search for another place to live. I was scheduled to be a contributor in football and track and, besides, I really wanted to finish high school where I had made some friends. I told Coach Green about my homeless situation and he began looking for a place for me as well. The search did not go well and the end of school was approaching which meant the departure of the Garrets and no place to lay my skinny bones.

The county judge was president of the Beeville Quarterback Club, and when Coach Green let him know I was looking for a home, they approached me with a proposition. Beeville is the county seat of Bee County and therefore the home of the county courthouse. They had a small apartment inside the courthouse which, in the past had been living quarters for bachelor janitors. The present janitor was married and the apartment was being used for storage. The deal was I could live in the apartment for my senior year at no cost if I could find a way to provide for my meals and transportation. I had a part time job at a local car dealership doing odd jobs and they offered me a full time position until fall football practice started.

Summer came and the Garrets left right away to get settled in their new town and new school for their kids. I moved my meager belongings into the small one room apartment in the Bee Country Courthouse.

The last day of school we were directed to turn in our books and I was assigned to go to Mr. Gallagher's room to process my stuff. I had Mr. Gallagher for a couple classes and he was aware of my search for a home. With him in the classroom that day was Mrs. Polly Fenner, a math teacher. While I had never had her as a teacher I knew who she was. She had a reputation at school as a strict task master in the classroom, but fair and an excellent teacher.

As I was turning in all my books, Mr. Gallagher asked me if I had found a place to live for my senior year. I explained the arrangement that the county judge and Coach Green had set up for me and he expressed great satisfaction the issue had been resolved. Mrs. Fenner listened to our conversation but did not say anything to me.

A few days later I was sent notice that Daddy Mac wanted to see me. The principal of A.C. Jones High School was Lester McCoy and the vice principal was Archie Hatcher. The seniors had tagged Lester McCoy with the title 'Daddy Mac,' while the vice principal was known to seniors as 'Uncle Archie.' The privilege to use these monikers was reserved only for seniors.

'Daddy Mac' explained that a math teacher, Mrs. Fenner, lived on a cattle ranch about 15 miles west of town and wanted to know if I would be available to work on their ranch for a couple weeks.

I wasn't real wild about my job at the car dealership. When I took the job I had hopes that it would be a chance to learn mechanics but it turned out I was doing everything but working on cars, all the little jobs no one else wanted to do, nothing to do with fixing vehicles.

So, a chance to work on a cattle ranch created a spark of interest and anticipation. "Perhaps I would be doing odd jobs there that no one else wanted to do but it was only for a few weeks," or so my rationale went. Since they were so far out of town and I had no transportation, working out there would mean temporarily giving up my digs in the courthouse.

21

PACKING MY THINGS was about a two minute process. I had two pairs of old jeans, a couple older long sleeve and short sleeve shirts, one pair of tennis shoes, a few unmentionables and I and my cardboard suitcase were out of there.

I have to admit, I was happy to be leaving that lonely room in the courthouse for awhile. They locked the building at night and it was kind of creepy being the only living person inside. There were stories, you see, stories of shootings and sounds that reverberated in the empty space. Of course I didn't believe any of that. Still, I couldn't deny the sounds were there.

The Fenners lived on a several hundred acre ranch west of Beeville in the little Hamlet of Cadiz.

Which begs a question…what is the difference between a community, a hamlet, a village and a town? These terms originate from Old English so I will use that as my reference. The first, a community, is a loosely gathered group of homes…when you get a church, it becomes a Hamlet…when you get a church and a pub, it becomes a village and when you get structure and a governing body it became a town. A city? Well, that's just a mess.

Cadiz, Texas had a few house in the area and a church so I call it a Hamlet, though it is referred to as 'community' among many of the locals.

Polly Fenner was a high school math teacher while John Fenner was a 'gentleman' rancher, with more emphasis on *gentleman* than rancher.

John was a high school all-state football player at Breckenridge High School in San Antonio, Texas and also played for a short time at Texas A&M until WW-II broke out. The Fenner family went way back in Beeville, with his grandfather and father even being mentioned in a Louis L'Amour western novel about the area. His father was an engineer and had a hand in designing and building the original River Walk in San Antonio, which was the reason John Fenner went to high school there. Upon graduation John went to Texas A&M on a football scholarship, but his academic credentials were suspect. I suppose, in a way, he was saved on December 7, 1941 and the breakout of WW-II. He and most of the Cadet Corps at A&M were commissioned as officers in the Army; even though most had not yet graduated. John was sent to help guard the Panama Canal, where he came down with malaria after about a year. He returned to the states and was hospitalized at Fort Sam Houston in San Antonio for the better part of two years, virtually missing the remainder of the war. Polly lived in San Antonio and worked at a switchboard monitoring international calls to report any state secrets that might be sent out.

After the war John returned to A&M but it was unclear if he ever graduated. He began working for the State of Texas as a highway engineer during which time he hooked up with Polly.

Pauline (Mauritz) Fenner was the total antithesis of John. She entered the University of Texas at Austin at age 14, at the time, the youngest person to do so. Four years later she graduated with a master's degree in Classical Languages. With help from her father no doubt, she got a job as an English teacher in Ganado, Texas, her home town.

Polly's parents were both from Sweden and immigrated to America in the late 1800's. Her father was one of the pioneers of rice farming in Texas and became a big fish in the small town of Ganado, Texas. They not only owned all the rice dryers, they owned the only store and eventually the bank in town. During the great depression he was able to acquire great tracts of land along the Texas Coastal Bend. His fortune increased greatly with the discovery of oil and natural gas on his land.

Polly Mauritz and John Fenner met while he was working as a

highway engineer for the State of Texas and she was teaching school. John was an accomplished golfer, and when Polly inherited a princely sum after her father's death, John left the highway department, played a lot of golf and eventually became the gentleman farmer he was when we met. They never could have children, so they adopted a son and later a daughter, Jack and Lindsey.

When I came to work for them I shared a bedroom with Jack, who was entering the ninth grade while I was going into my senior year. Lindsey had come down with a bad case of encephalitis when she was young, was in a coma for 18 months, and was handicapped as a result of her illness. Jack was a holy terror who turned out much more like John than Polly. He was a gifted athlete but did not like school and never graduated. He woke every morning, went to the bathroom, and smoked two to three cigarettes before breakfast.

My job at the Fenners was basically as a cowboy, doing all the odd jobs that go with that title. The first few days I was there they assigned me one of their horses, a saddle & tack and off we went through the mesquite and scrub brush of South Texas rounding up the herd for cutting, shots, branding and separating those to be sold at auction. For those who don't know, *cutting* is making steers out of bulls and yes, that involved *cutting*.

I took to horses very quickly and loved my job as *cowboy in training*. When I wasn't on a horse I was on a tractor pulling a *bush-hog* shredder cutting scrub brush. I was equally at home on my horse and on the tractor and, when I had nothing else to do, I would get on one or the other and just ride, sometimes for hours.

～～～

It is difficult to explain the peace and comfort I felt on my horse and on that tractor. I had a symbiotic relationship with my horse, we just connected right off. If ever I had some free time I would just saddle up and ride, and ride, and ride. The peace, the quiet, nature; I soaked it all in. It may have had something to do with being secure where I was and, for perhaps the first time in my young life, a feeling of being accepted. I knew they only invited me for "a couple weeks" and I wanted to squeeze in as much quality time as I could.

Up to now my entire life would never lend itself to looking much beyond the day. There was this constant uncertainty and it was inevitable

97

that planning ahead more often than not led to disappointment. I learned to resist looking beyond the moment for I had so little control over my future.

But riding the range 15 miles west of Beeville, Texas made me feel free for the first time in my life. Free from fear, uncertainty and demeaning condemnation.

The only thing comparable was flying solo in my airplane several years later. I think pilots and cowboys have much in common…riding the range and skipping through the clouds evoke a sense of freedom and connection to the universe that few other activities can duplicate.

Many times over the years I have considered, "should-a-been a cowboy."

That *couple of weeks* went by quickly and when I asked about my status they said, *Why don't you stay on for the summer,* and so I did.

The first week or so I was there Mr. Fenner took me to town to get some things so I would be able to do the jobs they wanted me to do on the ranch. He pointed out my one pair of tennis shoes just wouldn't do, so he took me to Turnipseed's Boot Shop in beautiful downtown Beeville and bought me a pair of boots. While we were there he told me I needed something to protect me from the South Texas sun and bought me a cowboy hat. Then it was more jeans, some chaps for riding through the Texas scrub brush, a pair of spurs and a couple shirts.

All the time, I was mentally adding up the cost of all this stuff and reminding myself I was being paid a buck an hour, which included room and board.

22

AFTER A FEW weeks I went into a serious funk. I mean, I kept track of how much the Fenners were spending on me and thought I would be indebted to these people for the rest of my life. I began to think, *I can't afford this job.* I started spending more time in my shared bedroom trying to figure out how I was going to pay all this back and wondering if I had made a terrible decision moving out there. The job was taxing but fun for me, but as much as I loved being a cowboy my tab was getting higher and higher with each passing day and my meager salary did not make a dent in my debt.

One weekend when I was particularly down, Polly came into my room and asked what the problem was. I explained my dilemma to her and she patiently listened to what I had to say. When I was finished, she contemplated my comments for a moment, stood up and said, *I'll be right back.* A few moments later she returned with two books in her hand.

She said, *"Larry, I always keep two books on my nightstand. One is my Bible and the other is a book called 'The Prophet' by Kahlil Gibran."* She explained to me about 'The Prophet', and how it was a series of vignettes about a wise man that roamed the Middle East and answered questions from the people who gathered there.

Polly told me, "I would like to read a couple parts of one of his vignettes to you. The first part was, "On Giving"..."*You give little when you give of your possessions. It is when you give of yourself that you truly give. It is well to give when asked but better to give unasked.*"

"This second part," she went on, "is for those who receive a gift: *"And you receivers…and you are all receivers. Assume no weight of gratitude, lest you lay a yoke upon yourself and upon he who gives, for to be mindful of your debt is to doubt the generosity of he who has given."*

She then expanded on her position, "John and I are in a position to give some things to you, and we do so with no strings attached or any expectations of any repayment from you." She concluded with, "Larry, someday, someone will come into your life that needs something and you will give to that person. And when you do, you will have repaid us everything we have given to you."

That was 50 years ago and I remember it like it was this morning. At that very moment I made a huge course correction in my life and those comments have served me well, many times, over the years.

I have indeed met people in need and I have tried to give generously of myself, and what meager fortune I may have. I have tried to live-up to the standard of Polly Fenner; a philosophy I set for myself with the Fenners as my inspiration.

THE SUMMER ENDED and no one told me to leave so I stayed with the Fenners for my senior year in high school.

Football season started and I began as back-up quarterback on the varsity team and starter at defensive back. I moved up to start at QB midway through the season. We won more than we lost, and even beat the previous year's state champion.

I could not believe my good fortune; I could come home at night to a non-violent home where there were people who legitimately cared about me. They came to my home games to watch me as the starting quarterback on the Mighty Fighting Beeville Trojans football team. I was earning a few bucks for spending money and gas, ginning up for the senior play, and a few others. There even was a glimmer of hope to do something after high school, life was good.

There are those of you out there who have no frame of reference for understanding the previous paragraph. Frankly, most of you probably came home without fear, had parents who attended your events, and you have had some amount of spending money all your lives. You have not experienced domestic fear, abject poverty, passed down shoes, and have never had a hopeless view of your future. It was not necessary for you to pretend at school that all was well and happy at home; that your Daddy was just too busy to come to the Father-Son Banquet. You never had to wonder if there would be anything to eat when you went home. You never had to find a place to hide during lunch because you didn't want anyone to know you had nothing to eat and you had no money to buy lunch at school. You never had to collect pop bottles along the road to turn in for their deposit so you could afford to buy a candy bar to quell the rumbling in your stomach.

Let me be clear, I do not want, nor am I expecting or seeking, your sympathy. Rather, I hope you will take another look at the advantages you have had and consider there are many out there who have had to face similar issues as mine, many still do. Perhaps you will consider there are those out there still with much less, who have no discernable future and a gentle helping hand would mean so much.

OK, enough of my *Hug-A-Bunny* philosophy. Give as you have been given to; if you are so moved.

Despite all the turmoil and uncertainty growing up, I never considered myself "poor," though looking back, I know I was.

It's true, my buddy, Sammy Davis down the street got the electric train I wanted for Christmas but I never resented him for it. He let me play with it now and then. Instead, I got a paper punch out train where you had to "put Tab A into Slot B", and hold the cars together with paper clips. In my imagination it was a great train.

My heart jumped when Tennessee Ernie Ford dedicated the song, *"Here Comes Peter Cotton Tail"* to me over the radio, the result of me sending him a postcard requesting that song.

Sometimes I consider my life an Aristotelian tragedy. Aristotle defined it this way, *"A tragedy is when the hero comes face to face with his true identity."*

Growing up, you become so accustomed to your place in life you never give it much attention. *It is what it is* and you smile and go on. You know most of the other kids don't have to live the way you do, but you also realize there are those out there much needier than you. So you accept your lot in life and keep moving forward.

But there eventually comes pivotal moments when you come *"face to face with your true identity."*

This was most apparent when I was 21. I had fallen for girl in college and I think she had fallen for me.

While I often referred to the Fenners as parents I had to be honest that they really weren't. For full disclosure, I had told the girl a few things about my life but it became a little sticky when trying to explain Mr. and Mrs. Fenner. They were not my parents, I was not adopted, they were not foster parents, yah-da, yah-da. Every simple explanation led to another question. I tried to minimize my past as best I could but

I was compelled to be honest. To my surprise, she was impressed with what I had done with my life.

But the tragedy began when she relayed some of that history to her parents. All of a sudden I was kryptonite; not from the girl, but from her parents. We remained an item for a couple years but her parents were relentless in painting me as a pariah. Eventually, it was too much and we parted.

It was over 20 years before I told another person even a sliver of my past. I was not necessarily ashamed of it, but found it emotionally necessary to keep it to myself. Personally, I found it high drama and a success story, but was suspicious of telling others for fear of another unexpected negative response.

~~~

Putting these several hundred pages on paper has been both difficult and exhilarating. My first iteration of this story was set in a fictional time and place. I wrote a few chapters, shared it with a few people, and they didn't seem too impressed. So I waited about two years and thought, "What the heck, I'm just going to tell my story, float it up the flagpole, and see who salutes it. If no one likes it, there is always the bottom of the birdcage."

Besides, I'm too far along in life to care much what other people might think and this is just me coming to terms with who I am...as Aristotle said, coming "face to face with my true identity." With all due respect to Aristotle, I view it more a triumph than a tragedy. As we all must do, I played the cards that were dealt me. But life is not entirely a game of chance; it is a test of wills, faith, determination and an unwillingness to become a victim of circumstance or failure. Is there a factor of serendipity? Perhaps, but still, life is not a spectator sport; it is the ultimate participatory challenge and the winners just keep getting up when they find themselves face down in the dirt.

We are gifted with amazing instincts and if we follow them, a good 50% of life's problems can be avoided. The remaining 50% we have to deal with the best way we can, again, by following our instincts. It is never too late to make a course correction. If you find yourself in the deep dark night, look for the North Star, get your bearings, and make a correction.

In the Bible it often says, "And it came to pass." It never says, "It came to stay." When you stand on the end of that pier, look up, and listen. You will not be disappointed.

24

NOT UNLIKE LIFE, running track had its good moments and bad. I pulled a hamstring early in the season my senior year at high school and was not able to run until the end of the season. By then, I ran the 220, 440 relay, and the mile relay. Coach wanted me to run the open 440, but I declined. I hated that distance; too long to sprint, too short to stride. It was several years later that the *Gilbert's Syndrome* was pointed out which mitigated my chances at ever being competitive at 400 or beyond. Still, Coach insisted I run the 440 relay. But I always found a reason to avoid the open 440! The 100, 440 relay or 220 were just right. 10 or 22 seconds, and I was done; no sweat, no agony.

I set as my goal to run the 440 under 50 seconds, the 220 under 22 and the 100 under 10 seconds. I reached and surpassed my goal in each race before my competitive running career ended.

I probably had more overall success in the drama department that year. I had lead parts in a couple plays and was voted *"Best Actor"* by our local Thespian troop which resulted in even more harassment from Coach Green. *"Come on, Barrymore,"* he would yell, *"you were voted the best lesbian in the school...you can do better than that!"* Political correctness was not one of Coach's strong points.

I made a great number of friends those two years at A.C. Jones High School, many of whom I keep in touch with on a rather irregular basis. My junior and senior years were the first time since first grade that I started and ended a year in the same school. That alone made for an exciting time for me. It was great to know friends for more than a short time. Though I had not known my classmates since first grade, as many of them did, it was a great new experience to start my senior year knowing most everyone.

Achieving a certain amount of success in sports and drama, and in the classroom, greatly increased my self-confidence and the possibility of higher education seemed more possible with each passing day. Prior to those last two years in public schools I had no vision of my future. My mother had a constant dim view of anyone who went to college and, growing up, there was no support system to create that vision within myself.

Everything changed by the middle of my senior year. I actually had the nerve to see myself just as capable as most of classmates.

When I first considered such the possibility of going to college, it overwhelmed me. But my mind always went back to Coach Orrick back at George Dewey High School in the Philippines, *"You can be anything you want to be."* I considered that, against all odds, I won medals at track meets, I made starting quarterback on the football team, I did well on stage, I was a senior class officer, I did OK in class and I had succeeded in everything I tried. Why not college?

Midway through my senior year I visited the University of Texas at Austin, Texas A&I, Kingsville, and Texas Lutheran College (TLC), Seguin.

I happened to visit TLC while they were in the middle of spring football practice. I went with Bobby, a receiver on the Mighty Beeville Trojan football team. Bobby was hoping to get a football scholarship to help with expenses at school.

Out on the practice field we met Fred Hightower, the head coach for the Mighty Fighting Bulldogs of TLC. (Every football team in Texas is always prefaced with 'Mighty Fighting' something or other).

Bobby visited with Coach Hightower awhile as I watched the team practice. I noticed the grass on their practice field was so much nicer than our high school stadium, without the stickers.

After Bobby and Coach finished their conversation, the coach asked me if I played ball. I said yes, that I played quarterback in Beeville. He mentioned they might be in need of a quarterback and invited both of us to fill out a *Prospective Athlete Card*. Not wanting to offend the coach, and quite frankly on a lark, I filled out one of his cards.

High school graduation came and I received my acceptance letters to Texas Lutheran and Texas A&I. The sheer size of the University of

Texas at Austin was a little overwhelming to me so I never applied there. My thoughts kept coming back to TLC and I surmised it would be a good fit. If only I could find a way to pay for it. Being a private school, TLC was among the most expensive of all schools in the state.

I was then faced with the prospect of finding a way to pay for this more expensive institute of higher learning. I applied for every scholarship I could find. In the end, I got 11 small scholarships from the community of Beeville and A.C. Jones High School. $500 here, $250 there, pretty soon they all added up. Remember, this was 1964, tuition was a lot less than now. I applied for, and received, a National Defense Loan, a federal program whereby one could borrow the money for school but did not have to repay until after graduation. Despite all that I was still a little short. I calculated I could get a job at night and that just might put me over the top.

Frankly, it was all a bit much for me. A couple months earlier I couldn't spell *university,* or have any idea how I could afford to go to college. Now, here I was accepted and almost paid for, at least the first year.

A few weeks after graduation I got a phone call from Fred Hightower. He was the football coach at TLC. He said he had visited with Coach Dave Green and watched some film of games from my senior year and would like to offer me a football/track scholarship to TLC. I was stunned and did not know what to say. I mean, I weighed in at 140 pounds, probably in full football regalia. I told the coach I would think about it and call him back.

I told Mr. Fenner about the phone call and he was actually more excited than me. "You are going to take it aren't you?" he asked.

"I don't know," I replied, "quarterback of a college football team?"

I really didn't know what to do. The very idea of playing college ball was both exciting and terrifying. I considered that an athletic scholarship would put me over the top financially, if only for the first year. As I lay on my bed considering my options, Mr. Fenner came into my room.

"What do you think, Larry, you gonna do it?" he asked.

"I just don't know,' I responded.

"Let me give you something to think about. You could pass up even trying and for the rest of your life you will wonder, "Could I have made

106

the team?" Or, you could give it a try, and maybe make the team, or maybe not. But at least you would know." After that he walked out.

I think it was Linus Van Pelt that said, *"There's no heavier burden than great potential."* Well, "great potential" was not my albatross, so I didn't have that as a burden. I was more of an "over-achiever," probably because I wasn't smart enough to realize my own limitations. The other part was that I was not afraid to try anything. I mean, if I failed, no one was going to say, *"Oh, and he had so much potential."* No, in my case, if I succeeded, it was more likely people would say, *"Are you shiting me?"* I got a lot of that over the years.

The next day I called Fred Hightower and told him I would like to give it a try and he would get my very best effort.

"That's what Coach Green told me Larry. I'll send you the paperwork. See you in August," he said.

I spent the rest of the summer working to save up for school and getting in shape. I had a pair of heavy boon-docker boots and I would run up and down the road in front of our house 15 miles west of Beeville for hours late in the evening and into the night doing sprints and longer distances. I drank at least one milkshake a day trying to gain weight but I evidently burned more calories running and my weight never changed. I didn't tell too many people I had a football/track scholarship to college since the few I did tell had that, *"Are you kidding me?"* look in their eye. I realized that would only pull me down, and I wasn't about to live down to other people's expectations.

⁓⁓⁓

No one in my life ever sold to me the vision of potential, the value of grades, or the wisdom of choosing my friends carefully. I had to learn it all on my own. When you live most of your life in survival mode you learn to throw what little water you have on the fire that is closest to your feet. But many angels came to me in the form of Coach Orrick, the Tackles, friends at Jones High School, the Garretts, the Fenners, Coach Hightower and many more. Each of those unknowingly gave me the gift of taking time to look within myself and search for the vision beyond what I was, to one that revealed to me what I just might become. It wasn't a perfect vision, rather a path through a dark unknown forest. But now, I was not afraid of the dark, the unknown, and I had the admittedly unfounded confidence I could slay any dragon that might attempt to block my path.

25

ONE OF THE greatest gifts of my life was to have had the honor and privilege to know Polly and John Fenner. I lived with them only a year, my senior year in high school, but from them I learned so much about life, the way I wanted to live, and who I wanted to become. I did not have a lot of positive role models growing up, and I shudder at what I may have become without the Fenners there for me at just the right moment. If ever I had any doubt about people coming into our lives at just the right time and place, they totally erased even the consideration of any such doubts. Those comments are no disrespect to the many people who came and went from my life, but there was something grounded about the Fenners. They were an unlikely couple since they were total polar opposites from each other, but somehow, they made it work, and it was there that I learned about 'vision'.

Polly was the intellectual who constantly read and was compelled to always be doing something productive. She had books on her bed stand, next to the couch and in the kitchen. She even had a book in the bathroom. If ever there was a spare moment she always had a book nearby to pick up and read. If she watched television she would read during the commercials. Her day was organized and efficient, designed to complete the most amount of tasks in the time allotted. I *never* saw her sitting idly. If there were a moment of sitting it included some sort of hand-work or reading. She was a born leader and that showed at school, in church and social clubs. She was involved in many activities, usually as president, president-elect or immediate past president.

Polly's college degree was in classical languages, but when there was an opening at the high school for a math teacher she jumped at the challenge and soon became head of the math department. She spent her summers going to college taking math classes in order to be the best possible teacher. She had a close friend who was also a math teacher who never seemed to change her curriculum. When the friend retired she commented to Polly that she had taught math for 30 years. Polly said, *"No, you taught one year…30 times."*

As I said, John was the polar opposite. He was an accomplished golfer, avid hunter and fisherman and loved his Johnny Walker red label. After breakfast he spent his morning watching Andy Griffith re-runs until the lunch crowd hit the domino parlor downtown. His afternoons were spent playing 42 or some other form of dominos until late in the day. Every afternoon, before coming home, he would stop by the local meat market and pick up something to grill. This was not an occasional event. He grilled probably 300 of the 365 days that year I lived with them. He had two acres of corn planted behind the house and each night in the season, I and my friends would jump the fence, pick some fresh sweet corn, and grill it along with the steak. While he was grilling we would listen to the Houston Astros as they found creative ways to lose ballgames.

John would take us down to Aransas Pass, where they kept a boat, to go out into the gulf fishing for ling or amber jack. Or, we might go down the inter-coastal canal, pass the land-cut to a small island, where we would spend several days in a makeshift fishing shack, seining for shrimp in the morning and fishing Baffin Bay for spotted trout or redfish in the afternoon. In the evening we boiled the shrimp and grilled the fish. When our ice chests were full of filets we would make our way home. *"Limits? We don't need no stinking limits."*

When hunting season came we would head off to a camp near Uvalde for a few days hunting white-tail deer; or down to the family place near Ganado, Texas doing the same in the forests or the empty rice fields. We would kill a doe the first day, marinate the hind quarter over night and John would slow cook the critter the entire next day outside in a pit. For breakfast John would make huevos-rancheros and serve them beside bacon or fried slices of back-strap and warm tortillas.

John had hunted most of his life and what he enjoyed most, at this stage, was taking Jack, me and some of our friends out to camp where he could place us in blinds and he would do all the cooking. At night we would play cards and dominos and tell lies about hunting, fishing or some other sport achievement. I suppose they were not actually lies, just creative memories of actual occurrences.

While by no means perfect people, Polly and John Fenner were about everything I could have ever wanted from a mother and father at that time in my life. Between the two of them, I learned two distinctly different ways to live and I found a sweet-spot somewhere in the middle. I learned hard work, education and 'dedication to a cause' from Polly and I learned how to have a good time from John. It was everything I missed in the previous 17 years.

26

MR. FENNER DROVE me to TLC the day before we were to report for two-a-day workouts. My scholarship did not pay enough for me to afford the dorm with the other athletes, so I checked into the cheapest dorm on campus long before the other students arrived. John left me with encouraging and supportive words. He basically said, do your best and don't worry about the falling chips. *"They are going to fall where they are going to fall,"* he said.

That first night, all alone in that 100-year-old dorm, I wondered what I had gotten myself into. *"What was I thinking? I'm going out there tomorrow, trying to make quarterback on a college football team."* It was a long, lonely night.

The next morning I showed up at the gym to check out my equipment for football. I got the smallest pair of shoulder pads they had and they were still a little loose. As we went onto the track surrounding the field the coach had everyone run a mile to see what shape we were in. At about 145 pounds I was this little kid among these giants. There was one other guy in the 190 range. The rest were over 200 pounds. But as the mile run started I began to pass people, the linemen first, then I caught up with the backs and ends. As it turned out, I came in first in the mile run; all that running over the summer had paid off. While winning the mile showed I was in shape, it meant little towards making the team. Except it did catch the attention of the coaches. We then ran some basic drills: tackling, blocking and all the basics. That afternoon for the second half of two-a-days the backs and ends ran sprints and I won every one. Hmm, maybe I do bring something to the table.

Being first in the mile run and sprints did not mean I won over friends or made the team. The linemen didn't seem to care, it was expected the smaller guys would beat them. But among the backs and ends it appeared I was *showing off* and some resented it. It didn't help that I couldn't afford to stay in the dorm with all the other athletes. That was where much of the bonding and closeness was born. It wasn't anything serious but I could sense I wasn't totally accepted.

As the workouts continued I didn't win all the sprints. I'm not necessarily proud of that, but we all have this need to fit in.

Things happen much faster in college sports than in high school. It stands to reason since these teams are filled with only the top one to five percent of all the high school teams. They hit harder, run faster, block better, and throw farther. If high school is 33 1/3 rpm, college is 45 and I suppose the pros are 78. As fall practice progressed, this distinction became clearer. The only skills I brought to the table were speed and leadership in the huddle. I wasn't sure it was enough to make the team.

They did plenty of drills I had never seen, but I did my best and went full speed every time. That did not go unnoticed by the coaches. In tackling drills I just let it all out. The coach threw the ball to a running back and I was supposed to tackle him. I had developed a kamikaze mentality as I planted my helmet into his chest while going as fast as was humanly possible, for me at least. The guy and I went down and as I got up I noticed a smile on the coach's face. Not sure what that meant but it was better than a frown. If I didn't make the team it wouldn't be because I was a slacker during practice.

At the end of two-a-days they posted a list of names of those who made the team and I was on it; but that was just the first cut. There were two more cuts before our first game and I made it on them both. No one was more surprised than me. I called John to let him know I actually made the team.

I didn't make the traveling team until mid-season, but I played off-and-on at quarterback, defensive back and special teams. To be honest, I could run the offense, but that *small hand thing* kept my passing statistics low. I did learn to change my throwing technique to compensate for that physical limitation, but there was only so much I could do. The size of my hand was not going to change no matter what I did and the ball was not going to get smaller.

We won more than we lost that season and I still had my scholarship for track. But still, I entered spring training as a long shot. I still won the sprints, I showed no apparent fear of death while tackling as a defensive back. The spring game was between the black and the gold, our school colors. I was quarterback for the black team, the second stringers. I didn't complete many passes, but I got outside on a couple sweeps and no one could catch me.

A couple of weeks after the spring game Coach Hightower called me in to tell me they were extending my scholarship for another year. Frankly, I was surprised, but very pleased. Being invited to play one year may have been a fluke since I was an unknown quantity. But being invited back for a second year was special, a validation that maybe, just maybe, I belonged there and I could compete.

Track season had started but we took a break from running for spring football training. After the spring game I dedicated my fulltime to the sprints and the relays. I felt my best chance was in the 100 yard dash or the 220. We had a couple seniors in the 100 so, like in high school, coach put me in the 220 and the relays, the 440 sprint relay and mile relay. I loved the sprint relay and we seemed to win quite a bit, just as we had in high school. I had run the mile relay in high school but hated it. 440 yards was still slightly beyond my endurance level, but, I gave it all I had and made it on the mile relay team.

It wasn't until years later that I discovered I had *Gilbert's Syndrome*, which made the longer distances even harder for me. Because of that syndrome, my body could not filter out the uric acid from my blood stream fast enough for anything over about 220 yards. As a result, hard as I might try, I would run out of gas after running full speed for about 400 yards. The shorter sprints were over too quickly to make a difference and it wasn't until the 440 or the mile relay that it would reveal itself. Still, I gutted it out and ran my lap in under 49 seconds. But, it about killed me.

I thought I just was not tough enough and could/should have done better. Hard as I might train I could not improve on my time. At the conference track meet in the spring of my freshman year I won second in the 220, first in the 440 and mile relays. My sophomore year I won first again in both relays and second again in the 220. I wasn't going to the Olympics but I did all right; I felt I earned my scholarship.

I spent one summer in beautiful Lubbock Texas, living with an

113

old high school teammate, Bobby. He had chosen Texas Tech because it was the farther from Beeville than any other school that was still in the state. I visited him early that summer as he was registering for classes. I needed a biology class so I wandered over to the science table. The numbering system at Texas Tech differed greatly from TLC. It was about two weeks into the class before I learned the one I had chosen was for biology majors. It was a tough class but I stayed with it and did OK. Bobby always had a knack for getting the cushy jobs, while mine were always a bit more taxing. During the summer after high school he had this summer job inside an air conditioned office while I was out in the summer heat loading 700-pound cotton bales or trucks with cotton-seed. I needed to get in shape for football so I didn't mind. After trying to tackle a 700-pound bail of cotton those 250-pound running backs didn't seem such a challenge.

27

I LOVED COLLEGE, well, almost everything about it. Making new friends, being a football star (OK, maybe just a player), being on my own, I even loved my classes, most of them, at least.

To be honest, I was not a great student, but I think I passed everything and was never on probation, as several in my dorm were, and they weren't involved in the challenge and energy draining aspect of sports.

Playing football and running track were physically demanding and it was hard to channel my focus and energy to academics after hours on the practice field. It seemed to me that everything in life was harder for me than most. Whether it was making the team or achieving better grades in the classroom, it was a constant struggle for me. There were those in the dorm that never cracked a book outside the classroom, went out drinking every night, and breezed through exams with 'A's. I hated them! Well, not really, but I did envy them and I constantly wondered what was wrong with me. It seems we always compare ourselves with the best in others. Not a wise thing to do, but it seems too often to be the case.

After many years, I have concluded it all comes down to the ability to focus and concentration. It took an amazing amount of energy for me to focus and concentrate on sports. By the time I went to class I had little left. During class, my brain seemed to have a mind of its own beyond my ability to control. I would constantly wander off the task at hand. It seemed that I focused so much on being the field-general on the football practice field that my mind would not, could not, concentrate on the lecture or assignment in class. I constantly found myself looking out the window, with my thoughts traveling to who knows where, and no memory of what took me there or how long I had been away. I would try to reorient my thoughts back to the task at hand but soon, there I was, looking out the window and off into some other unknown ethereal place.

Today, I would probably be diagnosed with AADD, Adult Attention Deficit Disorder, but in those days you were just either 'stupid' or 'lazy,' there was no other option. I didn't think I was either one of those, but I could not determine why everything was so difficult for me, and why I always had to work harder than everyone else just to get by.

Eventually, I did come to realize this was not a factor in everything I did. Where it involved motor skills such as are necessary in sports or flying an aircraft I could focus and concentrate with the best of them. I learned the offense and defense quickly and had a knack for calling the right plays at the right time.

In the air, I knew my operating and emergency procedures, my response time was above average, my decisions were decisive and correct. I was an instinctual pilot. To a certain degree, not unlike riding my horse on the ground, I was a natural in the air. Flying made sense to me from the very start. I knew my limits and the limits of my aircraft and I colored inside the lines. I did take chances but they were calculated and measured. I knew what I could handle and what was beyond my limits.

Flying for twenty years you will encounter some tight spots and I had my share. But I followed my instincts and the inner voice that kept the lines from blurring. I responded well in emergency situations, I was positive and resolute. I could handle all the extremes in weather conditions I encountered. I had the same number of landings as take-offs, a major goal of any pilot. I never damaged or loss an airplane and no one who was counting on my skills as a pilot was ever injured and certainly, no one was killed.

But, in my early academic days things were not always so pristine. It was literally painful for me to conjure up the energy needed to make anything beyond modest to 'kinda-good' grades. And, it seems it was temporal, not universal. About 10 years after my undergraduate college days I went back to school for a masters degree and got a 4.0 with a double major, the only one in my class to do so.

I suppose it is possible I am rationalizing a bit about those things I may have lacked. I do recall there were moments of clarity when I was in college when everything became so clear and in those marginal moments I would ace an exam. Those moments of clarity were rare through high school, a little more frequent in college and came even more towards the end of my university career. They were common by the time I joined the Navy and by the time I did my master's studies I kinda felt I had arrived. Perhaps I was growing up and learning how to study and how to focus and concentrate on exams.

Or, it's possible it was a matter of directed motivation. When your life depends on how well you understand and learn the skills necessary for a successful career in flying, perhaps an environment for clarity is created. I'm open to any explanation.

28

WHILE I WAS in college, Mr. Fenner was diagnosed with melanoma, a serious form of skin cancer. Today, if it is caught early enough, there is about a 90% survival rate. But in 1967 the mortality rate was closer to 90%. He went to M.D. Anderson hospital in Houston and had surgery, but they discovered it had already spread to his lymph nodes. He seemed well enough through my college years but when he attended my graduation I could see the effects of the illness and the treatments had begun to take their toll.

The only time I ever saw John Fenner cry was at my college graduation. Despite the tough mantel he projected, there was a gentleness and sensitivity to the man that most people missed. He was much more sentimental than Polly, the pragmatist. If there were an issue, Polly would immediately give you the logical solution, while John, surprisingly, would consider other more ethereal options.

When I first moved out to live with them I always called them Mr. or Mrs. Fenner. It wasn't long before they suggested I refer to them as Aunt Polly and Uncle John. Sometime during college I began to introduce John as *dad*. He was, in fact, the closest person to a dad I ever had. In my mind I always had a clear distinction between father and dad. Father was biological, dad was earned and reflected respect and honor. John deserved the title of *Dad*.

It took quite a bit longer to come to terms with calling Polly "mom", but I eventually did. If that offended her, she remained stoic and never let it show. It wasn't anything about her that kept me back, she was a great person. I may have had a sense that it was dishonoring or betraying my own mother. It seems she still had this emotional control over me. Eventually, Polly became mom, a lofty place she deserved long before I was able to say it.

Texas Lutheran College was a good experience for me. Though a small school, it was academically one of the most respected in the state. Like Beeville, I made friends easily there. One of the pluses of moving around as much as I did was the ability to make friends quickly. After my freshman year Gilbert Franke and I were roommates for the remainder of our college careers.

Gilbert was/is a rural intellectual. He hailed from Uvalde, Texas and was a student of the classics, but could fit in with the rest of us down-home folks just as easily. He and I were about on par as far as monetary resources, which put us on a natural equal plane.

Gil was light years ahead of me academically but you would never know it by how he acted. He seemed to envy me for whatever reason, which, I could never understand. He and I would have long philosophical talks about both simple and complex issues. Gil was Pre-Theo, which meant he was planning on going into the ministry after TLC. But, he remained down to earth, certainly not a preachy or holier-than-thou type of a guy. He liberally joined in our raucous times without compromising his core beliefs. I taught him how to use the pay phone down the hall without having to put money in, and he and I both confiscated a telephone for our personal use.

We lived on the West Side of Old Main, the original building on campus that was nearly 100 years old and had not held its age well. But, it had the least expensive dorm rates. On the bottom floor was the school business office and some other offices. The remaining three floors above were a men's dorm.

It seems there was a Ma Bell AT&T truck in the parking lot with its back door open exposing all the technicians' parts and telephones. I can't recall which one of us actually separated the truck from one of the phones but hey, I'll take the rap since Gil is now a man of the cloth. Suddenly we were in our room and there it was along with a roll of telephone wire. We located a junction box and tapped into a phone line that we thought was not in use. We hooked up our new phone through the central box and into our room. The result was, we had our own personal telephone we could use to make local calls after hours. I forgot myself once and picked up the phone during the day only to have someone else on the line. I asked who was there and he said, "The President of Texas Lutheran College." I quickly retreated by telling him it must have been a random bad connection and hung up before he had the chance to question my identity.

Each floor of Old Main had a couple toilets, three or four sinks, a couple showers and one bathtub. The tub was never used; well, almost never.

It seems I was at the San Antonio Zoo in front of the alligator exhibit when I looked down and there at my feet was a baby alligator. I picked it up and tried to get it to go back to the other 'gaters but it kept following me. I swear it did, at least, that's my story. It seemed like the only humanitarian thing to do was to pick it up and put it in my coat pocket. When I got back to the dorm it suddenly occurred to me that I didn't have a clue what to do with the critter. So, we filled the tub with a couple inches of water and that was the home for our alligator for the next several months. Alligators actually grow faster than what you might think, especially when they are well fed, using scraps from the commons by a bunch of guys in a men's dorm.

On another occasion someone threw a cup of water from an upper floor down the stairwell to someone else on a floor below. Cups of water went back and forth and these evidently turned into waste baskets, then buckets and finally fire hoses. By the time the melee was over the entire East Side of Old Main was soaked, with the greatest victim being the business office on the first floor. Something to do with gravity, I suppose. The next day when the staff showed up and discovered the results of the monsoon, someone came up to ask what had happened.

"Leaky pipes in the bathroom!" I said. "This place is almost a hundred years old, you know. Oh, you might want to stay away from the bathtub."

I could probably write an entirely separate book on our experiences at Texas Liquor Consumers, otherwise known at TLC. Suffice it to say, those four years were not dull.

As football season began my sophomore year with the normal two-a-days I was beginning to wonder about my future as a college football player. I had proven to myself I could make the team, not just once, but twice. I was maybe up to 150 pounds by now, and getting beat-up on a day-to-day basis by much bigger guys was beginning to lose its charm.

In the spring of my sophomore year at TLC I received some earth-shaking news. I got my draft notice from a nice lady in Sinton, Texas. I was directed to go to San Antonio for a physical, which I easily passed. As I recall, warm-and-vertical were the two major requirements. Soon after, I received another letter from the lady in Sinton explaining that I had two more years to get my degree. After May of 1968, she wrote, I would be eligible for the draft and in line for this all expense-paid trip to beautiful Southeast Asia. *Viet Nam!*

I began to seriously look at what I needed to do in order to graduate within that timeframe and it was clear I needed some fast and fancy footwork to get there by spring of 1968. It was then that I made the decision to hang up my jock strap and football cleats and concentrate on my studies. I admit I had struggled trying to do both academics and athletics. I saw many on the team that excelled at both, and I felt inferior that I could not. But, facts were facts, and I needed to conserve my time and energy for some extended educational workloads. Being an education major, which was a requirement for a couple of my scholarships, I still had to do student teaching, which would require limiting the number of courses I could take during that time. I went to summer school to try to close the gap. My girlfriend's parents thought I should be working instead of going to school over the summer. They didn't like me all that much which was an anomaly in my dealings with the ladies. More often than not, the parents seemed to like me more than the girls. There were two exceptions, the two I dated most in college. Maybe they saw something. I know I had a lot to learn.

During my time in college, I always had several extra jobs to meet the bills over and above my limited scholarships. Those jobs also provided some spending money for dates and things. At closing time, I cleaned "The Dog Pound", our rustic and ancient, student union center. The trio of Gil, Jimmy and I sold homecoming mums one year. I was the Assistant Sports Publicist for one year and took the top-job my senior year. I was the sports editor of our college newspaper for one year but that didn't pay anything.

I also had a job in Seguin working at Goetz Funeral Home. I worked the night shift where I would usher in mourners who wished to have a late night visitation. I tried to convince the owners that a catchy phrase like *"Goetz Get'em"* would improve business but they weren't buying it. They did have this old funeral hearse which we borrowed to drive to a party. Four of us drove up to the party, dressed in black suits and solemnly carried this casket inside to the party. Everyone there knew I worked at the funeral home and didn't know what to expect. When we opened the casket it was full of ice, beer and colas.

One night, while I was on duty, an ambulance showed up with a deceased Texas Highway Patrol officer. It seems he had stopped a car for speeding near Stockdale, Texas and when he motioned for the driver to roll down his window, he was shot in the face and probably died instantly. He was a mess and there was no one there to clean him up. The driver of the ambulance told me his widow was on the way to see him. He was an awful sight and I imagine how terrible it would be for his wife to see him like that. This was not in my job description but I cleaned him up the best I could and tried to put the things on his face back where they generally belonged. He still looked pretty bad but I concluded it was a lot better than when he came in.

His young wife arrive and I tried to convince her that it would be better to remember him as he went to work that day, not like he was now. But, she would have none of my suggestions and insisted on seeing him. Fortunately, she had her mother and her sister with her and when I removed the sheet to reveal his face the widow fainted. Her sister and I carried to a couch in another room where she quickly came around. After awhile her mother and sister left while she stayed and held his hand, which was still warm. I stayed with her through the night. It was so touching to watch that young widowed bride holding her husband's hand through the night as it slowly turned from warm to cold. I wondered if I would ever find someone who loved me that much.

29

THERE ARE TWO types of people in this world, those who put people in categories and those who don't. While you are considering that, keep in mind, we are taught lessons throughout our lives that fall into two major categories: to make us a better person and/or to prepare us for the next lesson we are to learn. You see, life is like algebra, if you miss the basic concepts, all the rest will only confuse you. Fortunately, the force within will continue to offer you the lessons you need to solve these riddles.

As I write these reflections, more and more people come to mind and, in their honor, I want to mention each one, though I am not sure that is wise or possible. I am compelled in that direction because I am so thankful and blessed for each and every person who has crossed my path over these many years...the good, the bad and the beautiful. All these people have inspired me to be a better person, most by their positive influence, and a few by teaching me what I did not want to become.

There is a force within each of us that attracts the person with the specific gift we need. That same force compels us into lives of others who need what we have to offer.

If you believe, as I do, there is a design for each specific person that crosses your path; you must accept that, when they leave, there is an equally compelling motive for their departure. They have been sent to teach us something, sometimes very small details, about becoming a better person; other times monumental seismic shifts in our thinking. But vital and necessary lessons all.

The women in my life were no exception to these rules and, in fact, they were among my greatest teachers. Yes, I've had my heart broken and, I suppose, I've left a few damaged hearts along the way. But, looking back, I had much to learn about relationships, and it was a blessing that I had those acquaintances that taught me most about who I am and what I want to become. I am thankful and blessed for each one, for they gave me the building blocks that would prepare me for "the ultimate one" that would eventually cross my path, and become my life partner. Evidently, I had a lot to learn because that didn't happen for over 50 years. Believe me, with few role models, I suppose I'm lucky it took only 50 years. Each person has given me something I needed to understand the complexities of being a lover, friend, husband and father. To each of them I acknowledge a profound and sincere gratitude.

My parental role models, from my parents, were not what I needed or wanted in my life. As bad as parental models can be, many still adopt their traits, and live them out all over again, creating a train wreck of emotionally challenged generations that began, who knows where, and will continue until someone breaks the chain.

Still, I readily admit, the answer we imagine can be suspect. That is the insidious nature of emotional scars. No matter how much superficial make-up we apply, the scars remain.

The goal is not to remove the scars. I've tried for years to do that. I discovered that to cover them up and ignore them is futile. Frankly, I'm not sure it is at all possible, and probably a waste of energy.

The only thing I know to do is to daily face the devil, look him in the eye as I shake my finger at him, and laugh...yes, laugh, as I announce, *"you are not going to win today!"*

Over a lifetime, we are exposed, many times, to all the skills we need to become happy productive beings. It becomes incumbent on each of us to accept or reject those life lessons. Accepting means self-fulfillment, rejecting leads to more opportunities to learn, and refusing to move forward with these building blocks of inner life leads to frustration at a minimum and inner turmoil and emotional illnesses in the extreme.

I have tried my best to be a positive force in my children's lives, to be the father they choose to emulate, not avoid. But I am no perfect vessel and I hope they ignore my flaws, take the best of what meager crumbs I have to offer, what their mother/step-mother has to offer, and use that as a basis, around which to build their own lives.

To my children I say, each person who comes into your life does so for a reason. No matter the outcome of that relationship, focus like a laser on what there is to learn. Sometimes it is to learn how to be, and sometimes it is to learn what to avoid.

Someday, the person who is meant for you will arrive and, the more you learn today, the better that relationship will be. It's a wonderful ride, so rejoice over whomever comes your way, for they are sent to prepare you for the ultimate prize. Even in a loss, grieve a little, then hold your head high as you discover and consider the gentle new information you have now acquired.

30

IT WAS JANUARY 1968, my senior year at TLC. I knew in May I would either be drafted or would have to join one of the military services. I was walking through the Commons with Jimmy, also a senior, and noted these guys in cool white uniforms who were recruiting for pilots. Jimmy suggested we take their tests.

The recruiters explained that in order to be accepted into the pipeline to become a Naval Aviator, you must pass the Aviation Selection Test Battery (ASTB). This is a test that, evidently, has not changed much since World War II. It consists of timed subsets in mathematics, verbal, mechanical-comprehension, aviation and nautical information, a spatial apperception test and a survey gauging interest in aviation. You then have to take a battery of physical, psychological and background tests followed by an in depth flight physical. Your vision can be no worse than 20/40, correctable to 20/20 and you cannot be color-blind or have problems with depth perception.

"About 1% out of the 10,000 who sit for these exams each year actually get accepted", the lieutenant told us. A little hyperbole perhaps, but he made his point.

To be honest, I was a bit uncertain. I mean, I had been in four airplanes in my life, all as a passenger. I barely knew which end of the plane was intended for the pilot. Only one percent out of 10,000 get selected? I guess I could be a one-per-center.

Two comments passed through my mind: the first was Coach Orrick in the P.I. telling me, *"You can be anything you want to be."* Then it was John Fenner saying, *"For the rest of your life you will wonder, could I have made the team?"*

What the heck, all they could say was '*no*,' they couldn't shoot us; at least, I was pretty sure they couldn't. Besides, it had to be better than digging foxholes in the mud of the jungles of Vietnam. Jimmy was game and I decided to go for it as well.

I had never taken such tests. They were long, but interesting, fascinating actually. Most tests I had taken in school, public and college, were so boring. But these tested my mettle and captivated my imagination.

Afterwards, the Lieutenant told me I had passed all the subsets and that I made a perfect score in the spatial perception test, a feat he had never seen, or so he said. That surprised me since my flying experience was zero.

The spatial perception test evaluated a person's ability to match external and internal views of an aircraft based on visual cues regarding its direction and orientation relative to the ground. Each item consisted of a view from inside the cockpit. You were expected to match that view to one of five external views. That test evaluated one's ability to visualize the orientation of objects in three-dimensional space. Sounds complex even still, but I guess it just made sense to me.

The recruiters gave me some forms to fill out and told me I would be contacted in a few weeks for my flight physical.

Sure enough, a couple weeks later I received a ticket to fly on Braniff Airlines from San Antonio to Dallas, where a driver would pick me up to take me to Naval Air Station Dallas for an all day physical exam. At the end of the physical I had to meet this Lieutenant Commander for an interview. When we completed the exam, I and another candidate were directed to his office, where I waited outside while he interviewed the first guy.

As I sat outside the office, I could hear everything they discussed during the interview. One of the questions was, "What kind of aircraft do you want to fly?"

'Whoa,' I thought. My mind started racing. I didn't want to sound like an idiot but I had no idea what planes the Navy even had. I knew about WW-II Corsairs and the A-1 Skyraider, but I was pretty sure those were obsolete. I did a quick inventory of the room and noted the walls had several pictures of different aircraft. I saw a picture of a Navy jet...underneath it said, 'F-4 Phantom.'

I was called into the Lieutenant Commander's office and was asked the same battery of questions as the previous guy. Then he came to the last part and asked, "So, what kind of aircraft do you want to fly?"

My immediate answer was, *"The F-4 Phantom, Sir!"*

He looked at me and said, *"I don't get it, everyone wants to fly the Phantom."*

I wanted to say, "Hey, change that picture out there to a blimp and we'll all say a blimp". But I bit my tongue, shook his hand, and later in the afternoon, they took me back to the airport for the flight back to San Antonio.

I waited for about a month without hearing anything from the Navy. Again, as I was walking through the Commons, I came across a set of recruiters in Air Force Blue. When I told them I had already passed the Navy flight physical they told me the Navy physical was more in-depth than the Air Force physical, and they would contact the Navy for my results.

Within a day or two I received a call from NAS Dallas telling me not to sign with the Air Force and they would send me another ticket to fly to Dallas. All they had to do was dilate my eyes and, if all went well, they would swear me into the Navy right on the spot.

The flight to Dallas left early so I got up at zero-dark-thirty, dressed in the dark so as not to disturb my room-mate, Gil. I arrived at the San Antonio airport and was waiting to get on my flight when I looked down and noticed I was wearing one brown shoe and one black shoe. "Oh, great", I thought, "Almost all my life I've only had one pair of shoes and now that I have two pair and I screw it up! I'm going to Dallas to sign up to fly multi-million dollar high performance naval aircraft and I can't even put my shoes on right."

I landed at Dallas and was met by the same driver as when I came for my flight physical. The first thing he noticed was my shoes. "So you're going to be an officer," he said, "It figures."

We arrived at NAS Dallas and I was directed to ophthalmology to have my eyes dilated, for the first time in my life. I completed the exam successfully, and they gave me a pair of temporary sunglasses to protect me from the bright spring Texas sun. They told me my eyes would be ok in about an hour, but that passed with no change; then another hour, still no change. In fact, my eyes hurt so badly in the sun they gave me a second pair of sunglasses to wear over the first. Finally, they took me back to the same Lieutenant Commander who interviewed me a few weeks earlier and who was going to swear me into the Navy. He looked down at my shoes and commented, "So, you can't decide if you are going to be a brown shoe or a black shoe."

You see, in the Navy, Surface Warfare officers wear black shoes while Naval Aviators wear brown shoes, or so it was in 1968.

I raised my hand and repeated the oath and someone said "Take your glasses off so we can take a picture". I did and the flash from the camera caused excruciating pain in my eyes.

I quickly replaced my glasses and the same driver took me back to Dallas Love Field for the flight back to San Antonio. The bright Texas sun plus the flash of the camera meant that I could barely see anything, so the sailor escorted me to the waiting area and handed me off to a stewardess (that's what they were called in 1968) who guided me to my seat on the plane. Just before take-off, the stewardess come back to where I was sitting and asked why that sailor was escorting me. With two pair of dark glasses and barely able to see anything I explained that I had just signed up to fly airplanes for the Navy.

"You're kidding, right?" she asked.

I replied, "No. There is a war going on, you know, and they'll take just about anyone! Besides, I'll bet I can see just as well as the guy that's flying this airplane".

She then asked me to sit down and added, "You're scaring the other passengers."

Back in San Antonio, my eyes had not even started to clear up. I knew I could not make the 30 mile drive back to Seguin, so I called my room-mate and he and another friend drove over to pick me up. Gil drove my car and me back to school. It was not until the next day that my eyes finally cleared back to normal.

I did my student teaching in San Antonio at Randolph AFB High School in English, history, speech & drama. The UIL One-Act play I helped direct won state championship that year.

My girlfriend had transferred to the University of Houston my junior year and we attempted a long-distance romance, but between the distance and the fact her parents never hid their disdain for me, should have been a clue the romance was over. She visited me once while I was in officer pre-flight training in Pensacola and we made plans for her to come back for Thanksgiving. I got busy in the Navy and a few weeks before Thanksgiving I called her about coming; she informed me she was engaged.

I asked her, "Does this mean our engagement is off?" I think she just said, "Yes". Actually, we were never really engaged but it sounded good at the time; I mean, what do you say at a time like that?

At that time in my life I had not fully developed my *people-coming-and-going-for-a- reason* theory and to be honest, it may have been little solace even if I had. When reality collides with theory, well, theory doesn't stand a chance. Still, the facts are, I learned so much in that and all previous/subsequent relationships. Despite the losses, I would not have missed that education for the world. Since that time, many people have come and gone and it never gets easy. It doesn't matter if you are the one leaving or they leave you, it's always difficult. But oh, the wisdom gained and lessons learned are so worth the loss. Each one of those wonderful young ladies gave me something so very special and I am forever grateful for their gifts. I hope I left them with something as well, but, that is their story to tell.

31

I WAS IN Aviation Officer Candidate School, Class 24-68, which meant the 24th class of 1968. I arrived in Pensacola to report for indoctrination in early August. My orders stated I had to report by midnight, but I had been warned not to report before 11:30 p.m. I drove through the main gate of Naval Air Station Pensacola where the civilian guard directed me to Pass & Tag, got my car tag, and decided to roam around a bit. I slowly drove by Building #699, known as 'INDOC,' for 'indoctrination,' where I was directed to report, 'no-later-than' midnight. It was rather ancient in appearance, probably having stood there since WW-II, and it had seen many different uses. Even driving slowly by I could hear the yelling and screaming from inside and probably some wailing and gnashing of teeth. Having been through many two-a-day football training days, I was anxious, but not intimidated.

As I drove around, I noted that almost everyone was saluting in my direction. Having been a military brat for a short time, I realized I had an 'officers' sticker on my car and they were threatened with something just short of death, if they did not salute the "officer" in the car.

"If they only knew," crossed my mind.

I finished my cursory tour of the base, and headed down to Pensacola Beach to pass the time and to get a bite to eat before all hell broke loose.

Even though my orders said to report by midnight, I didn't want to go in as a complete target so I decided not to be a total last-minute type of guy. Still, I didn't see any point in getting there any earlier than necessary, so I showed up at 11:15pm, and immediately there began a systematic attempt to exorcise my body of anything civilian.

From my year in the California Cadet Corps, I knew the basics of marching, saluting and all the little stuff but that did not reduce the screams from the upper classmen or the number of pushups I had to do every time I didn't respond quickly enough, or not to their liking. I just kept telling myself that it was just like two-a-days and they were playing a similar game trying to get into my head, and I just went along with the whole thing. I had been a freshman on the football team and understood harassment, I actually found it amusing. My greatest fear was that I would burst out laughing, but, I controlled that temptation.

I was issued my 'poopy-suit', an all green oversized cotton jump suit which made the hot August Florida sun even hotter, boon-docker boots, both which seemed oversized for me, along with underwear and socks. There were no DI's, (Drill Instructors) that night, only what I found later to be students like myself, who were about to graduate. I was never a fraternity guy but I did go through initiation into the "T" Association, the club for athletes at Texas Lutheran and throughout other universities in Texas. My first night at AOCS was about the same as that experience. I just smiled (internally) and said (internally), *"Hit me with your best shot."*

The next morning at 4:30 am we were awakened by a record playing reveille. It was interesting, there was about a seven second delay from the time the needle hit the record and the music started. That must have been one over-used disc because we would hear the scratching of the record over the intercom well before the music actually started. It wasn't long that, just like Pavlov's dogs, we would hit the deck and were almost dressed during that period between when the scratching began and the music started.

Sometime early that second day we met our Indoc DI, Drill Instructor. These guys were combat Marines very recently returned from fighting the Viet Cong in the jungles of Vietnam, who had 11 weeks to teach us the basics of military life and prepare us to become Ensigns in the U.S. Navy. We had one DI for our first week through Indoc, and then were assigned another to take us through to commissioning.

Marine DI's, with their Smokey-the-Bear hats, were among the best in the Corps. That being said, they had little patience with 120 recently graduated college students who, immediately after commissioning, would make twice their salaries. Still, they did their job and did it well. I soon surmised the basic concept was to break us down as completely as they could and rebuild us in the Navy/Marine way, as quickly as possible. The second purpose was to identify those who did not buy into the program and get them to DOR, *Drop on Request*, also as quickly as possible.

The first week of "Indoc" we started with close to 120 in my class, lost ten or so in the first 24 hours and by the end of the week we were down to about 90. DI's and student officers constantly reminded, and somewhat encouraged, us to DOR. It seems they could not drop us from the class, but they could make life so miserable you wanted to DOR. Once you caught onto the game, which many never did, it really wasn't so bad.

Our particular DI referred to everyone as "Dollies." We spent hours on 'the grinder' learning to march and conducting close-order drills. Our Indoc DI became so frustrated one day he yelled to us, *"If you Dollies don't learn to march you are never going to get liberty."* Some wise-guy, who shall remain anonymous, in the back of the 90+ formation yelled, *"Give me liberty or give me death."*

"Who said that?" screamed the DI.

The voice came back with, *"Patrick Henry!"*

At that, the DI *almost* had the crack of a smile but then proceeded to run us around the base for several miles; it was worth it.

The next ten weeks after Indoc were filled with the basics of training: military, physical, leadership, rifle and academics, with a smattering of aviation thrown in, just to remind us why we were there. We had 20 minutes to eat our meals but that time started when the first person entered the chow line and that meant those towards the end of the 90 of us had very little time to eat. I was an "N," almost in the middle, so I had time to gobble down some morsels before we were directed back to formation. To be honest, it was August/September and all we really wanted were tall glasses of the green and blue "bug juice" over ice, as much as we could consume in the short time allotted.

You may have seen the movie, *"An Officer and a Gentleman"* (1982). That cinema offering begins in Subic Bay in the Philippines. The lead character (Richard Gere) is the son of a Navy Chief Boatswain's Mate who drinks too much and abuses his son on a regular basis. Sound familiar? It may become even more familiar. The son grows up, manages to go to college, and joins the Navy with the hopes of becoming a Navy pilot. But first, he must make it through the rigors of AOCS, Aviation Officer Candidate School.

The movie is set in the state of Washington because, due to content, the U.S. Navy would not allow them to use Naval Air Station Pensacola, Florida where the actual AOCS is located. The lead character, Zach Mayo, is confronted by a Marine Drill Instructor (DI,) played by Louis Gossett, Jr. While there is enough within the movie to give a certain feel about AOCS, most of it is pure Hollywood. I am told it is loosely based on my class. In the movie a guy hangs himself over a girl, the same as occurred in my class; more about that later. There are a few other similarities, but it is probably a composite of many classes.

The most common heard term in AOCS is "Attention to detail." When these DI's are finished, those students who survive will go into Navy flight training and, if successful there, will be charged with operating multi-million dollar high performance aircraft in a combat situation flying off aircraft carriers. In order to survive in naval aviation you have to have a keen sense of *attention to detail*. In aviation, especially flying off aircraft carriers in combat, it is usually the pressure and the little things that kill you.

The DI's were focused on applying constant pressure in every aspect of the 11 weeks of training. But the Navy had another card up its sleeve to filter out the marginal future pilots before they spent millions on us.

In the August heat in Pensacola, one tends to prioritize things on a daily basis. What was most important to me at that moment was that the NAMI building was one of the few on the base that had air conditioning in 1968. You cannot imagine the respite it was to spend a few hours out of the hot and humid Pensacola August afternoon and inside the igloo that NAMI seemed to be.

We knew it as NAMI, the Naval Aerospace Medical Institute. While NAMI's objectives are many fold, at the early part of the Naval aviation food-chain they prodded, poked, hooked up sensors to our hearts, heads and just about every other of our extremities to discover if there were any anomalies that might be a disqualifying element. They were especially interested in our eyes for anything our initial exams may have missed. They also gave us additional extensive psychological exams and explored our social history in great detail.

One of the questions I remember on a psych test was, "Would you rather (a) hit your thumb with a hammer or (b) throw up on a bus?"

Now, I suppose it's entirely possible the future of the free world could swing either way, depending on which of those choices you made, but its purpose still escapes me over 50 years later. I don't know if I chose 'A' or 'B' but, evidently, I got it right.

Now, don't get me wrong, I agree with the Navy's efforts to weed out anyone who might possibly be physically or mentally suspect. When it comes to fingers on the nuclear buttons I want the very best and the most stable personalities we have in that position. When I am sitting in an aircraft being shot off the end of a carrier in the darkness of night, with the rain storming down, I want only the very top notch pilots at those controls.

After my last test the corpsman informed me, "The doctor will see you shortly." As I waited, I noted my health record sitting on the doctor's table. Soon, my curiosity got the best of me, and I peeked to see what comments were written there.

At the end of my entire personal history analysis, they assigned two grades; the first was a percentile estimate for the chances of the candidate finishing flight training, and another for the chances of that person completing a career in the Navy. The staff had no intentions of us seeing these projections, but, while stranded in that room, I glanced at my results on the doctor's desk. I noted that, based on my social history, my chances of completing flight training and having a career in the Navy were very low.

~~~~~

Now that really pissed me off. Many times in the past, I had been labeled, based on circumstances over which I had no control. I didn't pick my parents or direct them to do the things they did. I never told them to marry, divorce, marry again, and again, so many times I've lost track. I didn't pour their liquor or force them to drink it. I didn't go to sleep drinking and smoking and burn the house down, twice, while we barely escaped with our lives. In the midst of all of this, we survived the best way we could.

I have spent my life, from childhood through to present day, coming to terms with where I've come from and who I am, to who I want to be. The stories you are reading are true, I have lived them, been cursed by them, and have overcome them. I have never told this story in the details contained within these pages. There has always been the risk that people will view me differently...it is a risk not without merit. Some people, aware of some of these things, have labeled me with a scarlet letter, not based on what I have overcome, but based on vague perceptions and preconceived notions of what I am or might become.

Even at this point, after I've passed all the exams, proven myself physically fit, more than able to deal with the pressure and attention to detail needed to survive in this risky aviation environment, I am labeled, yet again, by some guy who surmises that "due to social history the odds of this man finishing flight training or a career in the Navy are very low."

Statistically, maybe they were right. But how do you calculate the human spirit, one's personal drive and determination. There is a factor within the human condition that cannot, and never will be, calculated by science or statistics.

I admit, there were times when flight training was difficult and challenged me to exceed beyond what I thought I could do. That occurs to everyone going through naval aviation training. It is both physically and academically demanding, and many are tossed along the way. But I met all the challenges face to face, and was often inspired by what my father had said and what that doctor had written.

"You sons-a-bitches are NOT going to beat me." And they didn't.

After about an hour it became apparent they had forgotten about me, but I just lay on that table, saying not a word, until finally the corpsman came back and said, *"My God, are you still here?"*

Shortly thereafter the Doc came in and, after a short discussion; I was quickly dismissed to find my way back to Building 699. The Doc quickly praised my results on the physical and psychological exams, but did not address the "social history" comments or the percentile numbers.

I did not hurry during the walk back to Bldg. 699, and arrived just in time to march to the chow hall.

Ah, one of life's small, but significant, victories.

I did wonder that evening about the 'social history' comments, and

136

if, after going through all this crap, I was going to be dropped from the program based on statistics. I decided to treat it like cuts in a football program. I would do my best and if I didn't make the cut for whatever reason, well, so be it. I slept well that night.

── 32 ──

SOMETIME IN THE first few weeks of AOCS, a call went out for college experienced football players to join the 'Pensacola Goshawks', a service football team that played against other military service teams, mostly in the South. Since I had some football experience, I went to tryouts. I wrote down I had college experience at quarterback and defensive back.

The coach looked me over and said, "Lots-a-luck, Kid. Roger Staubach is on the team."

It seems that Roger had recently returned from Vietnam and had a year or two of service obligation left before going to the Dallas Cowboys. So, they sent him to play for the Navy Goshawks in Pensacola. Needless to say, I went out for 'D' Back.

If the Dallas Cowboys had known the terrible condition of the field we had to play on they might have reconsidered their draft pick. During that first week of practice, as I was running DB drills, I stepped in a hole and severely sprained my foot & ankle. I was on crutches for about a week and my short football career with *Roger the Dodger* was over.

There is much written about AOCS, how the DI's would bust our chops for even the most minor of infractions. How we had to fold our underwear 6x6, and it was measured with a ruler during every inspection. If it were even a tenth of an inch off, it went out the window, along with dusty rifles, poorly shined shoes, etc, etc. It was that, "attention to detail thing." If they really got pissed, our entire room, beds, lockers, everything was out the window, and we were on the second floor. We scrubbed the hall floors and bathrooms with tooth brushes, just to make a point. The six in our room were 'squared away' and never had that happen to us, but everyone joined the fun if even one room was below par. Right after attention to detail there was 'teamwork', if one went down, we all went down.

Of the eight in my room only two received their Navy wings. Of course, I was one and the other became a POW in North Viet Nam. One was killed in a car accident, three DOR'd (Drop-on-Request) and two were kicked out after failing one of the many phases of flight training.

We had to qualify on the obstacle course the last week of AOCS. If we failed to qualify, we would have to start the 11 weeks all over. I was determined that my ankle was not going to push me back a class, so the first time I ever ran the obstacle course was a couple days before the end of AOCS. I was so frightened I would be rolled back that I finished with the best time in our class. Who said 'fear' is not a motivator?

Each cadet was evaluated in the five areas of training and got anywhere from one to five bars to wear on their collars based on those areas. We had two five-bars in my class. I was a four bar cadet, earning a bar in military, leadership, academics and rifle; I missed athletics due to my ankle. Those with five bars wore white nametags and were known to the rest of us as "Snowflakes." As it turned out, within weeks after our commissioning, both of our two five-bar 'snowflakes' became conscientious objectors and never entered flight training. I'm sure the psychiatrists at NAMI had a field day with that one.

Our class officer was USMC *Major Stephen W. Pless*, a somewhat eccentric Helo pilot who had been selected for, but not yet presented, the Medal of Honor for action in Viet Nam; the only Marine aviator awarded the Medal of Honor in that war. The Major, who survived 780 combat helicopter missions in Vietnam, was tragically killed in a motorcycle accident in Pensacola, Florida, on July 20, 1969, just six months after being presented his Medal of Honor by President Lyndon Johnson at a White House ceremony.

There was a drawbridge over the inter-coastal canal that separated Pensacola on one side and the beaches, bars and businesses on the other side. The official report of the accident apparently was stated in the newspapers as this: *"As Pless approached the bridge's center span, he did not notice until too late that the span was open. Pless was unable to stop in time and his motorcycle went off the bridge and into Pensacola Bay. After a seven-hour search, divers pulled Pless's body from the water."*

But many of us, who had first-hand knowledge of the man, speculated there was more to the story and more likely he had died as he had lived, always on the edge. We crossed that bridge many times and, it would have been virtually impossible to *"not notice until too late that the span was open."* It was night, the barriers were down, the red lights were flashing. The *Navy Scuttlebutt* had always been that, in a Steve McQueen moment, he attempted to jump the drawbridge as it was going up and he didn't make it.

He bragged to us that during happy hour at the Officers Club he told a Marine widow that he had shot her husband with his pistol as the trapped pilot was unable to get out of a downed burning Helo in Vietnam. Pless insisted the trapped Helo pilot begged the major to shoot him, and not to leave him to burn to death in the Helo. A noble gesture but hardly a conversation a widow needed to hear at happy hour.

This is not an attempt to disparage a Marine MOH recipient. A list of just some of his medals, in addition to the MOH, are the Silver Star, the Distinguished Flying Cross, the Bronze Star, 38 Air Medals, the Navy Commendation Medal with V for Valor, the Purple Heart, all speak for themselves. He was a true war hero. Still, my personal contact and observation of the man demonstrated an eccentricity I have rarely observed before or since in an American armed forces officer.

～～

We had a formal "Dining Out" with the Admiral the last weekend before graduation and commissioning. Those who were married brought their spouses while, for the rest of us, they brought in a bus load of young ladies from a girls school in Mobile. We single guys got in a line and our date was the next one off the bus. My date, Sarah, was a very nice young lady; not that I made the girls weak at the knees. Still, we had a great time. We were directed to only share our first names.

Being a 'four bar', Sarah and I sat at the Admirals table along with Jim, a rough and tumble half-Polish, half-Indian from Oklahoma. We were about to end 11 weeks of 20 minute meals three times a day eating as fast as we could. It was hard to switch gears for the Dining-Out.

Sometime during the meal, Jim was eating like crazy and yelled across the table, "Pass the fuckin' salt."

The entire room went silent and all eyes turned to the Admiral and his wife. It was probably only a few seconds but it seemed as if the whole world had stopped. Then the Admiral broke the moment when he said, "Well, you heard him, pass him the fuckin' salt."

The moment was over and we all went back to our meal. The rest of the evening went well. Sarah and I walked on the beach before I took her back to the bus that took them to a local hotel. I kissed her gently on the cheek and told her I had a good time, which was very true. She smiled and said she had a great time as well.

A week later a letter found its way to me from Sarah addressed only to 'Larry, Class 24-68'. She wrote:

Dear Larry, I just wanted you to know how much I enjoyed the evening with you last week. You were a perfect gentleman. I know I wasn't the prettiest girl at the party but still you made me feel like I was. You made me feel like a princess the entire evening. It was the best time I have ever had and I have you to thank for that. I wish you the very best in your Naval career and I hope you never forget the great time you showed me."

She signed the letter "Sarah" but it did not have a return address. Sarah will never know the impact that evening, and her letter, had on me. People come into your life for a reason and the lesson was not lost on me. Kindness prevails in *almost all* circumstances.

33

OUR CLASS GRADUATED and we were commissioned Ensigns in the U.S. Navy. As we left the stage after being commissioned, there was our DI saluting each of us for the first time as Officers in the United States Navy. It is a Navy tradition that you give a silver dollar to the first enlisted person who salutes you. Those sly and cunning DI's knew this well and positioned themselves so they were the first to salute us. He made about ninety bucks that day and considering the price of silver, he did all right.

After a week at Indoc, you have your class DI for 10 weeks. During the first five weeks they become increasingly more demanding and they slowly ease off the final few weeks. We had come to respect and admire our DI and relished the opportunity to receive his salute and bestow a coin on the man who now made about half our salary. In addition, we all contributed toward buying him a silver plated .45 pistol. He was genuinely moved by the gift, which, evidently, was totally unexpected.

We were now commissioned Ensigns in the U.S. Navy, the very bottom of the officer food chain but it was a position each of us felt we had earned. Besides, we were glad to see AOCS in our rear view mirror.

We moved over to Naval Air Station Saufley Field on the other side of Pensacola. At the time, it was good to get away from NAS Pensacola, even if just a few miles. Most of us moved into the BOQ (Bachelor Officer Quarters) at Saufley Field and waited to begin primary flight training. But first, there were many more hours of classroom training before we ever saw the inside of an airplane.

When you received your commission coming out of AOCS, there seemed to be two options: a new GTO or you got *'The Ensign Mobile'*, a new 1968 Corvette Stingray. My favorite car of all time was, and is, the 1960 Corvette with its coves on the side, four headlights, which was unique at the time, and that tiger-tooth grill on the front. I thought the Stingray was a disgrace to the Corvette's short but proud history. I resisted buying one of the favorite two, mostly because I have always resisted going along with the crowd. But, in a weak moment after my college girlfriend broke up with me for a guy with a much nicer car, I bought the GTO. It may have more to do with the 1964 song by Danny and the Daytona's than anything else.

Frankly, I hated that car. I had buyer's remorse the next day and every day thereafter until I finally let it go. It did have redeeming aspects, it was fast.

This was 1968. Vietnam was probably at its peak and the AOCS classes were putting out about 80 or so students a week. All those flight students eventually clogged the aviation pipeline, so they put many of us on temporary hold. We had to report in at 8:00 a.m. every morning, but then we were on our own for the rest of the day. The pipeline was so clogged the wait went on for three months or more. At first, we all went to the beach, played volleyball, and went sailing in the bay.

I bought a small two-person sailboat. When I would meet an interesting young-thing I would tell her, *"I named my sailboat after you."*

"Really!" she would usually say in disbelief.

I would say, *"I promise, I named my boat after you. Come sailing with me tomorrow and I will prove it."*

Occasionally, this actually worked and when she showed-up I showed her what was written on the back of my sailboat, *"AFTER-U."* No one ever walked away and we usually had a nice day sailing around the bay.

Many of my recently commissioned shipmates could have spent the next several years playing and drinking on the beach all day, but after a short time, I grew tired of the routine. I had met a young lady on the beach, sailing in *"After-U,"* whose family owned a radio station in Milton, Florida, just a few miles from Pensacola. She told me they might be looking for a part-time DJ, so off I went to give it a try.

As part of my minor in speech I had taken some courses in radio and television and had worked on some Conoco commercials for KTSA in San Antonio. I also did some DJ work for KWED in Seguin, Texas.

The manager at WSRA, in beautiful downtown Milton, said they were looking for a lunch time DJ as well as a late night person. I told him I would do both.

At that time, it was forbidden for Naval Officers to work outside the Navy so, for my noon show, I became *"Jeffry Crunch, and the Crunch-for-Lunch-Bunch."* For the late night-early morning work I was just *"Jeffery, Ensign of the Air"*.

The daytime show was Pop Top-40 music, while at night my show was called, *"Other Kinds of Songs."* On that late show I would find songs on popular albums that I thought were very good even though they did not make the pop charts. I had a decent following into the late evenings but it tailed off in the wee hours of the morning. One morning about 3:00 a.m., I played a song off Bob Dylan's "Nashville Skyline" album and announced, if anyone could name the singer, they could have the album. I then said, *"Name the singer or the song"*...still nothing. I upped the ante to 5 albums; zippo. Finally, I said I would let them have my GTO and all they had to do was call in; still nothing. So, I turned everything off, locked up the station and went home. I almost got fired since their FCC license stated it was an all-night station and you had to stay on the air even if no one was out there in radio-land.

Those were the wild months. Several of us took up training to get qualified to sky-dive, and it seemed that everyone had a motorcycle. I began the parachute training but, a week before my jump two prospective pilots were injured in a jump. One landed on a Volkswagen on the road around the landing site and severely injured his leg. The Admiral decided the Navy had invested too much on us and the next jumper would be court-martialed.

While on that hold status I called John Fenner at least once a week. He was always so excited when I called. He told me he wanted to do something for me for being commissioned. I told him that as an officer, I needed to buy a sword, so he sent me $300 to buy one. I kept the money for a few months waiting for the time I actually needed a sword. That just never occurred, but the opportunity to get a motorcycle did, and that was just too tempting. I bought a Honda 350. It did well on the few beaches that allowed motorcycles.

Motorcycles and flying had a lot in common, I found. You were usually alone out there and you could do some crazy things. I spent several nights just riding on the sands between Pensacola and Ft Walton Beach. Just riding as far as I could, and then sleeping there on the beach next to my bike. As long as I got back by 0800 muster, all was well.

One Friday evening, I rode my 350 to Happy Hour at the Officers club, and was invited to join some friends out on Pensacola Beach. Driving out there, I came to a stoplight and my friends pulled up beside me. *"Do a wheelie, Larry,"* they yelled at me.

Now, I had never done a wheelie in my life so, I thought I would give it a try with a very small one. When the light turned green I hit the throttle, pulled the front of the bike back, to about 10 degrees, but started to slide back on the bike, which made me inadvertently add more power which brought the nose of the bike up to about the 45 degree position all the way through the intersection. It was the most beautiful wheelie I could have imagined but it scared the be-hey-zus out of me. As I got across the intersection I lowered the front of the bike and continued on. My friends pulled up beside me and yelled, "Wow!" I just smiled and waved, like I did that every day. That was the last wheelie I ever attempted.

My number finally came up and I had Marine Captain Lentz as my first flight instructor in the T-34B. But, before we actually flew we had to pass a flight procedure test. We had these cardboard mock-ups of the inside of a T-34 to practice and to take our test, about as low-tech as you can get. We had one flight student who got airsick every time he stepped inside one of those cardboard mockups. I think he eventually went out on one actual flight but filled his helmet bag and flight glove with vomit. He was dropped from the program.

I made my solo flight in the T-34 on the fourth of February, 1969 and moved on to the Naval Air Station Whiting Field for intermediate training in the T-28 Trojan.

The T-28 was actually first flown in 1949 and was used as a counter-insurgency aircraft, primarily during the Vietnam War. Nearly 2,000 were built and at least 20 different countries used the T-28 in their air forces and navies over the years.

I was at happy-hour one Friday night at the officers club at Whiting

Field. We were scheduled to go out on a solo flight the next day. One of my AOCS classmates was at Happy Hour and he seemed a little strange, but not that unusual, for him. He stated that, the next day, Saturday, it was his intention to fly his T-28 into the control tower at the base. We all assumed he had too much to drink and was just mouthing off.

The next day, Saturday, we went to fly our solos, but the weather was terrible. We sat around playing cards and referred to the overcast as "stratus secure-us" clouds until finally, a little after noon, they cancelled the day's flights and sent us home.

That afternoon, the pilot who threatened to fly his plane into the tower went back to his apartment, drew a picture of a face on a paper bag, put the bag over his head, and jumped through a skylight with a rope around his neck and hung himself. We all knew he was a troubled soul but it never occurred to any of us he was that desperate. The Naval Investigative Service (NIS) did a comprehensive investigation and questioned those of us who were in his AOCS class, or at happy hour that Friday.

I had been in the Navy less than seven months and that was the first shipmate I knew to die; but it would not be my last. Of the 120 we started that first day at Indoc, sixty nine actually made it to be commissioned. Of those, maybe thirty received their Navy Wings. Of that 30 maybe 15 are still alive. One became a POW in Vietnam, several died in plane crashes, some in car accidents, two by suicide, and a few others by natural causes. Only about five of us made it to retirement. NAMI, eat my dust!

Naval Aviation: it's a dangerous business, and not for the faint of heart.

While at Whiting Field I called home to see how John Fenner was doing. Polly said he was not feeling well and could not come to the phone. I knew something was serious. John had never turned down an opportunity to speak with me. I arranged to get emergency leave, jumped into my GTO and headed East on I-10. Before I reached the Florida-Alabama state line I was stopped by the police for speeding. I was stopped again in Mississippi, Louisiana and Texas before I made it to Beeville.

On arrival I went directly to the hospital to see John. It was a Monday evening. We watched the NCAA men's basketball national championship game together; UCLA beat Purdue. I had driven about 11 hours straight through, and both of us were tired. I told John I would be back in the morning. I went home, lay down on the couch, and went to sleep. About 2:00 a.m. Polly came home, woke me, and told me John was gone.

I stayed on for the funeral and then drove somberly back to Florida, quite a bit slower. I cried quite a bit during the trip back. I loved that man and I am pretty sure he loved me.

34

AFTER COMPLETING OUR intermediate training we all began training to make our first landings on an aircraft carrier. These would be conducted in the T-28C which had a tail hook and a shortened propeller blade for carrier landings. One of the unique qualities of a Navy pilot, as compared to all other pilots, is the ability to land on an aircraft carrier. At the time, one could not be given his Navy wings unless he had mastered this skill.

With the proper training, putting down on a moving target in the middle of the ocean went from "You've got to be kidding" to "Piece of cake." This was the best time in the whole training program. In order to go out to the carrier you had to complete a series of FCLP landings.

FCLP was a Navy acronym for Field Carrier Landing Practice, or learning all the procedures and mastering all the skills necessary on a normal airfield before you could go out to the ship. The best conditions for doing this were early in the morning and late in the afternoon. In between there was too much heat-effect off the ground to properly get the feel for what it was actually like at sea. So, we would take off early in the morning, fly for a couple hours, play cards, eat and nap during the heat of the day and continue in the late afternoon.

At the entrance to the outlying field where we trained for this was a sign, *"The Best Pilots in the World Are Trained Here."* One night someone, whose identity shall remain anonymous, went out there and changed that sign to read, *"The Best Card Players in the World Are Trained Here."* To our surprise, our instructors never noticed the revision and it stayed that way until long after we completed that phase of our training.

It wasn't long before we took off for Jacksonville, Florida in our T-28C's and from there, out to the USS Wasp (CV-18).

In those days, when you went out to the carrier for the first time it was solo; there was no instructor to make sure you did it right or to save your butt if you did it wrong. The night before we went to the boat they showed us a movie of all the mistakes pilots before us had made, most of which ended in fatal crashes. If you weren't nervous before, you were by the end of that movie. But then, it also made you take your procedures even more seriously as you checked and double checked that hook, flaps and gear were all down, airspeed was exact at each point of the approach and the glide path was perfect.

During the FCLP's and at the boat there is a Landing Signal Officer (LSO) who advised you if you were high, low, too fast or too slow or your lineup was off. Every FCLP and landing on a carrier is graded by the LSO. It didn't matter if this is your first landing or the hundredth, you always get a grade. If you were well off the intended flight path you would get a "Wave Off" from the LSO. If you messed up in close or missed a wire the LSO would shout, *"Bolter, Bolter, power and go"* which meant you should add take-off power and go around for another attempt.

There are four wires on a carrier deck and the perfect landing from the LSO is "OK pass, three-wire" which was unusual to get the first time out.

I flew my T-28 into the break at 1000 feet over the ship and turned downwind to the 180 position. That is, abeam the ship but flying exactly 180 degrees from the direction of the ship. There, you begin a slow descent, lower the gear, flaps and hook, and began your turn to line up directly behind the ship. At the 90 position, which is just as it sounds, 90 degrees to the path to the ship, you re-check that all is in order. You are constantly scanning your airspeed and working on your line up. As you roll out inbound to the ship, the LSO comes up and says, *"Call the Ball."* The Ball is part of the Fresnel lens, the optical landing system.

That system is calibrated to the exact glide path needed to safely land on the carrier. Although the lights are always on, the angle of the lens from the pilot's point of view determines the color and position of the visible light. If the amber "meatball" appears above the green horizontal bar, the pilot is too slightly high. If it is below, the pilot is a little low, and if the lights are red, the pilot is very low, not a good place to be for very long.

When the pilot sees the amber light he calls back to the LSO, "*Roger Ball.*" The object of this high-priced game boy is to fly the aircraft down to the carrier with the amber ball exactly in the middle of the lens. Theoretically, that should give you a 'three wire'. Sounds simple enough, but, in the real world, there is a seemingly infinite number of things that can go wrong and you have to be prepared to deal with all of them or go around and try again.

I approached the USS Wasp along with five of my fellow aviators on the clear day off Jacksonville. One at a time we broke to the left to get situated heading downwind just as we had practiced on the endless FCLP's the weeks previous to this moment. I turned off the 180, through the 90 and on final I called the ball. I rechecked everything and flew down the flight path to the ship. The LSO said little which surprised me. We made two Touch & Go landings before we made our first trap. That was to get the feel of the boat and to rid ourselves of some of the anxiety.

My third approach was to catch the wire and full stop on the boat. I touched down onto the USS Wasp and was surprised at the jolt from catching the wire.

I made a couple more touch-and-go landings followed by five arrested landings. I can tell you, that first full trap was the greatest feeling I had since that blind date I had in college, and a great relief. That night I ate Chinese, went to the dog races and slept well. I was *NAVY Carrier Qualified!*

With intermediate behind me and being boat qualified in a single engine aircraft I was off to Corpus Christi Naval Air Station in Texas for advanced multi-engine training.

My first view of the inside of a T-34 put me in awe, tackling the T-28 and the boat was a huge step, then there was the inside of the S-2 with its twin R-1820 engines and more than twice as many instruments to learn.

As awed as I was when I first stepped inside, by now I had confidence that I could learn whatever the Navy put before me. It all started with hours in the classroom again but soon we were in the air with another student and the instructor.

My flight partner would fly; then, we would switch seats and I would fly my instructional hop. One of the first flights was an area Fam-flight. The instructor would point out cities, islands and other landmarks and ask us questions about them. I aced that part, but didn't disclose that I had graduated from high school just 50 miles up the road in Beeville and these were old stomping grounds for me. Hey, a strategic advantage is best kept to yourself.

By now I had learned the system and breezed through advanced flight training. I took one long cross country with my instructor to Jackson, Mississippi where his father was a professor and where he had graduated. We left on a Friday and landed that afternoon. The next day we went to watch Ole Miss, with Archie Manning at quarterback, play Tennessee…the Rebels of Ole Miss beat the Volunteers 38-0.

A short while back, while visiting Memphis, we drove down to Jackson and noted that Manning continues to be honored on the campus of Ole Miss, where the speed limit is eighteen MPH. 18 being Manning's jersey number. You may recall Archie's two sons, Peyton and Eli.

In December 1969, I flew back to Jacksonville and got my multi-engine carrier qualifications on the USS Lexington. With the completion of advanced training I had jumped through all the hoops to finally earn my Navy Wings of Gold. I invited Polly Fenner to come down and pin on my wings in a ceremony at NAS Corpus Christi. It was the least I could do for a family that had done so much for me.

I considered telling my father and the doctor at NAMI in Pensacola about the event but thought better and just enjoyed the day.

35

A COUPLE OF months before we received our wings my fellow pilots and I had completed our d*ream sheets,* our preference for which aircraft we wanted to fly. Nearly all in my class put in to fly P-3's, but there just weren't that many openings, so most of us went off to secondary squadrons. I was sent to Fleet Composite Squadron 5 (VC-5), Detached to NAS Cubi Point in the Philippines. A little too ironic, I thought.

I still hated my Pontiac GTO and sold the thing to a friend from college. He got a good deal and I just wanted to get rid of that albatross. I bought it for all the wrong reasons and felt relieved it was gone. I also sold my motorcycle. In their place I bought a stock 1939 Chevrolet. Everything was original on the car and I packed it up with my things and headed west in Interstate 10. I broke down in El Paso, Phoenix and San Diego.

In San Diego I went to a couple survival schools. Everyone went to DWEST, Deep Water Survival Training for the Pacific, and after that, we spent a week going through SERE School: *Survival, Escape, Resistance and Evasion.* The school was all that and more.

There were about a hundred in our class and they were not all aviators, or even officers. Several were Intel officers, others were aircrewman. We started by spending the first night surviving on the beach eating whatever we could forage. Then we got on a bus that took us up into the mountains to a place called Warner Springs…sounds a lot nicer than it was.

We roamed around the mountains on foot for a couple of days, eating only what we could find or catch. Trust me, there is not much out there in January. We then spent a day trying to evade capture by our instructors. If you made it to a place called *Freedom Village* without being caught, you were given a sandwich. After several hours, I made it undetected to within 100 yards of *Freedom Village* when the siren went off, signaling the exercise was over. I didn't get the sandwich.

Most everyone else had already been caught and trucked to this simulated POW camp. The next two days we were POW's. Our guards and interrogators were all dressed as North Vietnamese and dramatically acted as such. They were very much into the whole thing, and a little too convincing, if you ask me.

I got water-boarded a couple times, shoved into a 3 ft by 3ft box for about 12 hours, brought out occasionally to be interrogated, which included some serious physical contact. The water boarding was scary but I just kept telling myself they can't actually kill us. Can they? I pretended to be more terrified than I was just to make them think it was effective.

They wanted us to confess to war crimes and, if we didn't, things became progressively worse. I was surprised by the number of people who cracked. I mean, we all knew it would all be over on Saturday. Still, several didn't make it. I am pretty sure all the pilots in our class made it through. I mean, we had been through hell in AOCS, and flight training was probably more stressful at times so, while this wasn't easy, we had the confidence we could make it. Each morning in the POW camp the guards had us in formation and we had to bow as they played the North Vietnamese national song and raised the flag with the red star.

By Saturday we weren't so sure it was going to end. Nothing they promised up until now had actually happened. They had us out in formation, bowing as they raised the red flag and when their song was over, they had us come up and there was' Old Glory' flying on the flagpole. Then they played *our* National Anthem. There was not a dry eye in the prison compound.

We each had to go through a quick physical and the doctor noted I was extremely jaundiced. "Holy Smokes", he said, "You have hepatitis." They called San Diego who sent up a helo and med-evaced me to Balboa Naval Hospital in San Diego.

At Balboa, they took all my clothes and put me in isolation for two days. No one could come into the room without a mask and overalls which they had to take off immediately upon leaving the room. The first day they told me I had tested positive for Hepatitis, the second day my tests were normal, the third day I was positive again. By the fourth all was normal again.

By the fifth day, they were comfortable that I did not have hepatitis when my color returned to normal, so they moved me out of isolation. But, since they weren't sure what was going on, I had a private room that happened to be next to the elevator.

Balboa was/is a Navy teaching hospital and every other day a new class of nurses came off that elevator. Being bored, I made a homemade sign and put it just outside my door a few minutes before the elevator opened bringing up a new class of nurses. The sign read, *"All Student Nurses Check-In Here."* I had a clipboard and directed them to line up alphabetically and give me their names and phone numbers.

My ruse was working pretty well, and I was about at the "M's, when their instructor, a crusty old Lieutenant Commander female nurse walk in and asked very sternly, *"What the hell is going on here?"*

I started to explain that I was just trying to help and that's as far as I got when she said, "I think you are well enough to leave lieutenant."

"Yes, Mam," I replied.

A short time later my doctor was making his rounds and told me, "The head nurse seems to think you are well enough to go."

"I think I am, Sir," I replied.

"Well, you can go for the weekend, but I want you back on Monday to run one more series of tests."

"Thank, you sir. Where can I get my clothes?"

"Well, when you arrived we thought you had hepatitis so all your clothes were burned," he explained. I told him I had my uniforms back in the BOQ at North Island Naval Air Station.

A short time later, dressed in hospital garb, I was in a navy car with a driver who took me back to NAS North Island BOQ. I made a call to a college friend who lived in Lubbock, Texas and asked if I could come for the weekend. He said "Sure!"

I drove to the airport in uniform and bought a military discount ticket from San Diego to Lubbock. In those days you could fly military-standby for next to nothing, if you were in uniform.

I got on the plane still wearing my hospital wrist band. I hadn't officially check-out of the hospital, so I still had to wear it. My seat was next to a First Class Petty Officer with about a hundred ribbons on his uniform. I had my wings, still probably warm, and one award, the National Defense Ribbon, which we referred to as the 'Battle of Indoc' ribbon. About halfway through the flight, one of the stews came up and asked why I was wearing a hospital wristband.

OK, let me say right off, how this started and how it ended was not planned, nor my intention, and I am not particularly proud about the events that occurred.

"Well," I said, "I was in this kinda POW camp and…"

No sooner were those words were out of my mouth than she stopped a fellow stew and said, "Amanda, this Navy Lieutenant was a POW."

"Really," Amanda said as she smiled at me. In my limited feeble defense, I did try to stop the rumor, "It wasn't really all that much, it was a sorta-kinda POW camp." But they would have none of my back-tracking. The fact that Amanda was really cute may have had something to do with my unenthusiastic denial. Before I knew it, the sailor next to me and I each had free drinks in front of us, and then another, and another.

Each time a stew walked by, she would pick up our half empty drinks and drop off another fresh one. The salty old sailor next to me never said a word. He just shook his head and enjoyed his drinks. By the time we landed in Lubbock, both the sailor and I were feeling pretty good. As I struggled down the aisle to get off the plane Amanda was at the exit.

"Oh, you're not going on to Dallas, what a pity," she said with an undeniable twinkle in her eye. I gave some serious thought to turning around and returning to my seat but I knew my friends were waiting.

I just shrugged and said, *"Sorry,"* as I left the aircraft. People come into your life for a reason and Amanda certainly cheered me up and made me smile.

I was back in San Diego on Monday and met with my doctor, who did one final series of tests. "If all is well with these tests you are out of here tomorrow," he told me. The next day he gave me a clean bill of health and sent me on my way. *"Etiology unknown,"* was what he wrote in my health record.

I got into my '39 Chevy and began the trek north, first to see my sister in L.A., and then on to San Francisco to drop my car off for shipment to the P.I. I then boarded a MAC flight for my transport across the Pacific.

～～

During the flight I couldn't help but consider the irony that I was on my way back to the Philippines, to the same base I had left just eight years earlier under dire circumstances. I reflected on those eight years…high school, college, flight training. It seemed an unlikely scenario, but here I was, on the amazing circle that is life.

36

A COUPLE DAYS later I landed at Clark Air force Base in the Philippines and, as I stepped off the airplane, there at the bottom of the ladder, was a Lieutenant in a flight suit asking for Ltjg Nevels. I motioned to him and he told me to get my bags and meet him at the US-2B on the flight line. My new squadron had sent him to pick me up and fly me back to Cubi Point, a 30 minute flight, but a bumpy six hour bus ride across the Zambalas Mountains. On arrival, he gave me a ride up the hill where I checked into the BOQ, my home for the next 18 months.

VC-5 Det Cubi was as close as you could get to McHale's Navy. Our Commanding Officer was in Okinawa, we had an OinC (Officer-in-Charge, Lieutenant Commander 'Holly.' At this early stage in my career I was too young to have much of an opinion about the conduct of a senior officer so I accepted him, with all his eccentricities, as our 'Skipper'.

It was1970, the Vietnam experiment was at its zenith, a plateau actually, which it maintained for several more years. Among the missions of VC-5 Det Cubi were towing targets for ships and aircraft, launch and recovery missile targets, airborne photography, and in those early days, support to VRC-50 with crews and aircraft to provide COD (Carrier Onboard Delivery) service to the carriers in and around Subic Bay and Vietnam.

COD is a military term used to describe aircraft which are able to ferry personnel, mail, and high-priority cargo on and off a ship, usually an aircraft carrier, though Helo's are used as COD's for other ships. But, like everything in the Navy, our job description always had the clause, *"and other tasks as determined by the needs of the Navy."*

I had flown the S-2 in advanced training and flying the US-2 was an easy transition. In a month or so after arrival, I was off flying missions as the aircraft commander. During my first several months we flew constantly from/to Cubi Pt-Danang-Camh Ranh Bay, South Vietnam carrying passengers and supplies.

Most of my squadron mates were married with families in base housing. I was a bachelor who loved to fly. I was constantly being asked to take the weekend and holiday flights for them so they could do things with their families. For me, Saturday & Sunday, July 4th or even Christmas was just another day. I could go to one of the beaches, the pool, or get drunk with buddies at the club; neither option had any more appeal to me there, than they did when I was in Pensacola. So, I usually accepted all the flights offered to me, which meant I ended most every month as the 'Top-Dog' in flight hours. That fact created a little ill-feeling from some of the other pilots but they still called on me to fly in their place when their wives had other plans.

Don't get me wrong, I managed to hit the beaches, the club, or off into Olongapo now and then, but never to excess. It didn't take long for me to grow tired of 'sin-city', a common description for Olonogapo. In addition to the sin, you could get hand-made boots, cloths, uniforms and furniture for, what seemed to us, ridiculously low prices.

It was the morning of July 4th ...I was heading out to meet HMAS Melbourne, a Royal Australian Aircraft Carrier. They greeted me on the radio with, *"Happy Birthday Mate, how are things in the colonies?"*

My reply was, *"Really great since all those redcoats left, how can the American Navy rescue the Aussies today?"* It was a little game we always played.

Did I mention I loved flying? I regret a little that I didn't go single engine more often because, being alone in the sky, through the clouds, over the mountains and down in the valleys were some of the freest moments I have ever experienced...along with being on my horse or motorcycle. But, even with a co-pilot, I loved it in the air. And to think, they were paying me to fly the mostly friendly skies.

Being a composite squadron meant we had multiple types of aircraft. In addition to the US-2's, there were A-4 Skyhawks, and one RC-45J. We also had Fire-Fish target boats and target missiles. But, being the Vietnam event was going great-guns, (pun intended) we were diverted from all that crap-flying to helping out with ferrying people, mail and essential parts into the war zone. We would also take parts and mail out to the aircraft carriers. You had to have 75 traps before you could take passengers to the boat, so I spent most of my time hauling mail and parts.

VRC-50 was the primary passenger airline from the coast to the ships but the pace of flying was so intense we were tasked with supplementing their efforts and I loved it.

Every *real* Navy pilot lives for the excitement of traps (landings) at the boat (aircraft carrier). It is the major factor that separates us from all other pilots. You can't imagine the rush of rolling out on final to see that gold meatball square in the middle of the Fresnel Lens Optical Landing System, catching a "3 wire", and getting an "OK Pass" from the LSO. Ok, so it's not the high performance jets, but the technique is the same and no one was more popular than I was when I approached the carrier and announced, ***"You have mail."*** The landing pattern was more often than not cleared and I was directed as, *'Number One for landing.'*

On deck, I had just enough time to deliver the mail, fix any problems with the aircraft, grab a quick soda, and then enjoy the excitement of the cat-shot (catapult) back into the air, and the flight back to Danang.

It's hard to say which gives the biggest rush, a trap (coming aboard) where you go from 120 mph to zero in about 2 seconds or a cat shot (leaving) where you go from zero to 120 in about 3 seconds. Either way, it's safe to say there is nothing more exciting you can do, with your clothes on at least.

Most any Navy pilot will confirm the greatest rush and the greatest relief is trapping at night, in the rain with a pitching deck. During the approach you are so anxious you are promising God just about anything and everything, if he will just get you on the deck *this one time*. I can tell you without fear of contradiction, there are no atheists on short final at the boat, in those extreme conditions.

Soon, we were shot off the front of the boat and on our way to Vietnam. Maybe it was just me, but it seemed that Danang was always in a perpetual monsoon from 2:00-5:00 pm every day, and that was my normal arrival time coming back from the boat. They had so many aircraft in and out that you were almost always assured of being put into a holding pattern. On this particular day, I was told I was #18 for landing. When I got low on fuel, I declared an emergency, only to be told, "You are #11 in the emergency pattern."

Finally, the red low-fuel warning lights came on and that tended to get my attention and increased the "pucker factor" just a mite. In terms of flight-time, one was not certain how much fuel remained when those lights came on, since it differed with every aircraft. But there you were, in the air with two red lights that seemed like the flaming red eyes of the devil laughing at you as you were stuck in the air, about to run out of fuel, and with no place to land.

Not wanting to dead stick the plane onto China Beach I went out over the coast, lowered beneath the clouds to about 800 feet and announced I was downwind requesting an emergency visual approach. Now the fun starts.

There are two small mountain peaks just to the west of the Danang airfield; so, I had to keep those off my right wing as I flew inside the normal pattern to keep the field in sight through the rain on my left wing. That meant I had to yank the yoke into about a 45 degree turn with lots of left rudder and roll out pretty much on final over the numbers on the end of the runway at about 20 ft. If an engine quit during that maneuver we were toast, but a calculated risk, considering my alternatives.

As luck would have it, there was this heavy shower over the runway as I flared to land and I lost sight of the runway centerline completely. I glanced out the side window with my peripheral vision to stay on the runway as we began to slow down. As we were rolling out the #2 engine quit, no fuel.

We made it to the parking area on #1, which also died just short of our final parking spot. I noted that, from the time those red lights came on until the engine died, was about 8-10 minutes. That was something good to know, if I'm ever in a similar situation, but only in that airplane.

37

When I arrived to the squadron, VC-5 Det Cubi, the only pilots qualified to fly the RC-45J were Holly, and Lt. Rick. Rick's tour was about up, so I asked Holly if I could get checked out in the 'Bug-smasher', as it was affectionately called. I flew with Rick most of the time and Holly gave me my check ride.

Our bug-smasher had many designators over the years. It was the Beech 18, a C-45, the Navigator, which as the name implies, had as its primary mission to train aerial navigators, but it also served as a general purpose transport.

The first Navy version was the SNB. I have no idea what the three letters stood for, but we always affectionately referred to our SNB as, "Secret Navy Bomber." It was built in 1945, a few months before I was born so, like me, it was about 25 years old at the time. It was in production from 1937 until 1969, as such, was one of Beech Aircraft's most successful and longest running production designs.

The plane was a "tail-dragger", which added to the skill required to land and take-off this gentle beast. Holly used to tell me there were two types of SNB pilots, "those who have ground-looped the plane, and those who will." I took that as a personal challenge. My first flight was on April 28th 1970, the last was June 28th 1971, and I never ground-looped.

The C-45 had five fuel tanks, two in each wing and one in the nose. The pilot had to manually select any one of the five tanks. But, it had only one fuel gauge which showed the amount of fuel in the selected tank only. Normally, we used the fuel from the 25-gallon nose tank first, which allowed the CG of the aircraft to move aft. Both engines ran from whichever tank was selected at the time. If the pilot was not vigilant in monitoring the fuel usage, the aircraft could instantly turn into a glider when both engines failed due to being on an empty fuel tank. Of course, at altitude the engines were easy enough to restart after selecting another fuel tank. However, if this happened during landing or take-off, it could be disastrous. Every instructor purposefully lets the engines quit at altitude to make the student pilot keenly aware to monitor fuel at all times. It was a lesson not easily forgotten.

The C-45 was fun to fly and the Navy did not require a copilot. We had a squadron policy to have at least an observer in the right seat, to keep watch for other aircraft. I would offer right-seat rides to anyone in the squadron, but there were surprisingly few takers. I didn't take it personally as they would tell me, "I fix'em, I don't fly'em."

We had a young engine mechanic in the squadron by the name of Nick Nevels, no relation, who jumped at the chance to go flying. He became my go-to-guy when I needed an observer.

As I have said, VC-5 was, in many ways, like McHale's Navy. Often, if I had the duty on weekends, I would fly the Bug-Smasher solo. As much as I enjoyed flying others in the Bug-Smasher, my favorite times were flying alone.

I would sometimes head over to Corregidor Island at the mouth of Manila Bay or down to some of the volcanoes south of Manila. The most famous was Taal Volcano – This small island is famous for being an island, within a lake, within an island, within a lake, within an island, within the ocean! Trust me, that's the correct description. It started out as a volcano within one of the islands that makes up the Philippines. The caldera of that volcano eventually filled with water and another smaller volcano appeared in the middle of that lake, which eventually filled with water as well and still another island appeared in the middle.

The most recent period of volcanic activity was from 1965 to 1977, and produced violent explosions that occur when rising magma makes contact with the surface water of the lake. Depending on the day you flew over, you might witness massive explosions, or it may just see steam climbing high into the sky. It was almost always a great show. I had to constantly remind myself they were paying me for all this fun.

I also got into the habit of taking the DOD school teachers up to Baguio in the mountains to the north, usually taking them up on Friday, and returning for them on Sunday. At 5,100 feet above sea level, Baguio is not quite a mile high and, as such, has a mild climate, especially a treat in the summertime in the PI. During my time there, it was home to a silver mine and a silver shop run by Nuns from a local convent. The runway was built by chopping off the top of a mountain and the runway, at the time, was about 3500 feet, which meant only our Bug-Smasher could land and take-off there. At the end of the runway was a drop of about a thousand feet, and at that altitude, even the Bug-Smasher had to take-off and dive down into the valley to get enough airspeed to continue back up and over the other mountains. Several times some of the teachers were a little skeptical about getting into our Secret Navy Bomber. When I asked what they were worried about, one asked, *"Is it safe? I mean, it's so old."*

My normal response was, *"Of course it's safe, how do you think it got so old!"*

Once, after I started the engines, one of the teachers commented, *"Those engines sure are loud!"*

I reminded her, *"The worst engines are the really quiet ones."* OK, maybe I was a bit of a wise-ass, but it sure was fun!

Baguio had no tower; every pilot was on his own. Most rural runways in the PI were without towers. If we wanted to land, we would make a low pass to chase off any water buffalo, and then come around and land. Being in the mountains, this was not necessary at Baguio, since there were few water buffalo up there, but we still always made a low pass just to be sure there were no vehicles on the runway.

On Sundays at this airport, they would have drag races with several hundred people there to observe. I almost always had a shopping list from the wives for silver items, so I would go up a couple hours before the teachers expected me to pick them up, and head off to the silver shop.

When I returned from shopping I had to get all the kids away from the airplane, load up, and taxi out for takeoff. I would taxi to the very beginning of the runway to get as much distance as possible to take-off. The two most useless things to a pilot are runway behind you and altitude above you.

On this particular day, two of the dragsters, a corvette and a souped-up jitney, pulled up just off each wing tip as I was about to take off. I held the brakes until I had full power and started down the runway. At the beginning, the 'vette and the jitney easily pulled out in front swerving left & right down the runway. About mid-field I caught up with them and, I was worried they would swerve in front of me. They settled down and I passed them and pulled the nose up as I approached the end of the runway. As I normally did, I lowered the nose down into the valley to pick up speed and then climbed up as I was turning around to make a pass back over the runway.

As I came back over the airfield I could see many of the spectators at the end of the runway, I suppose to see if I had crashed in the valley, not that uncommon an occurrence. I rocked my wings and they all waved, and off we flew back to Cubi Point.

Often, we would be tasked with photographing ships; they seemed to all want a picture entering Subic Bay. When we were finished I would often head out over the South China Sea in search of giant manta rays and hammerhead sharks. These critters would sun themselves on, or close, to the surface and they were so huge they were easy to spot from the air. If you were lucky you would see a ray jumping almost all the way out of the water. I've been told they can't actually get out of the water, but these beauties sure gave it a try. Some of these rays were huge and almost spanned the distance from one wingtip to the other, or so it appeared from our vantage point.

My last flight in the Bug-smasher was the last for the aircraft as well. The Navy decided it was too expensive to keep them going and they grounded them all. I was told that was the last C-45 still flying in the Navy. I can neither confirm nor refute that, but it was a great aircraft to fly.

38

OUR OFFICER-IN CHARGE, "Holly", was a strange bird. He would be your buddy one moment, and the next would be an explosion of anger, for no discernable reason. He was a geographical bachelor, which meant he was unaccompanied in the Philippines. He had a Filipino girlfriend who had moved into his BOQ room. For the most part, he and I got along. I stayed out of his line of fire as best I could, but he would confide in me his disdain about some of my fellow officers, which put me in an uncomfortable position. I did my ground job, flew at every opportunity, and volunteered for the away missions the married guys did not want to take. I suppose he thought I was gung-ho since I flew so much but, the truth be told, I was planning to get out of the navy at the first opportunity, *I just loved flying.*

Holly conducted AOM's (All Officers Meetings) first-thing every day. He had this flip-over calendar, and each day at the AOM he would flip the calendar over to the new day and read all our assignments for that day.

One Sunday, I was the duty officer and needed to go into Holly's office for something. I noted his flip-over calendar, and this idea struck me. I proceeded to take all the *Tuesdays* out of his calendar.

Monday came, and at the AOM he flipped the calendar from Sunday to Monday. The next day's AOM he flipped the calendar again and it said Wednesday. He went through the entire day with the assumption it was Wednesday. We just conducted business as usual assuming he would figure it out at any moment.

Friday eventually came and he didn't show up for work. Someone went up to the BOQ and saw him beside the pool, where many of us congregated on the weekend. Well, Sunday came along and there he was at work, thinking it was Monday. The duty officer tried to convince him it was Sunday, but he was having none of it.

To be fair, it was Vietnam, everyday seemed the same with planes flying 24/7. Perhaps the tempo slowed a bit on weekends, but not enough to notice. Nothing was ever mentioned about the calendar with no Tuesdays, but we did notice the next week that Holly had a new calendar.

During the summer, the college age kids who had parents stationed at Subic Bay or Cubi Point would come to visit, some for a couple months. Somehow, a couple of us got hooked up with the senior officer's daughters for the summer. There were a couple Admirals there, and it seemed they had a propensity for daughters.

I noted during my Naval Aviation career that Navy pilots, in general, had a tendency to have female off-spring. My unscientific survey noted that daughters were more frequent by somewhere between three and four to one. Someone suggested it was an oxygen and/or altitude thing. No proof there, but it just seemed that way. Oh, I had a daughter.

One of us started dating one of the daughters and pretty soon, three of us single guys were hooked up with three girls who were there for the summer. The companionship was nice, and I think everyone had a good time.

I got hooked up with Rachel. At the end of a particular evening with Rachel, she told me she and the other two were going out to Grande Island on the Admirals gig, a really nice motorized yacht. They told me their daddies were not going with them.

The Navy began using Grande Island as an R&R spot since it had pristine beaches and perfect coral reefs for diving.

We could not join them since we didn't have the summer off as they did, but I decided to give them an aerial escort. The next day I buzzed up the old bug-smasher and caught them heading out to the island. I gave their gig a couple lower-than-normal passes; actually, much lower than normal, rocked my wings, and went back to base.

The next day Holly got a call from the Admirals office inquiring if one of our aircraft had buzzed the admiral's gig. Apparently, the Admirals had changed their minds and had joined their daughters for the day. Fortunately for me, Holly was out flying and the duty officer just said he would look into it and get back to them. You see, I was the duty officer that day, and I did look into it.

I saw Rachel that night and told her about the phone call. She said, "Don't worry about it, I'll talk to Daddy." I never heard another word about the incident.

I had my 1939 Chevrolet in the shop for some maintenance and a paint job but it was finished by the beginning of that summer. I had it painted dark purple, with new running boards and a new interior and installed a new *ah-u-gah* horn. The Warren Beatty/Fay Dunaway movie, "Bonnie & Clyde," came out in the states in 1967 but had just reached the Philippines. Rachel and I dressed up like Bonnie and Clyde and drove my old Chevy into town. There we were, driving down Magsaysay Boulevard, the main street in downtown Olongapo, 'Ah-U-Ga' horn blaring at the jitneys, as we pulled up in front of our favorite club. I paid a couple kids a few pesos to watch my car as we went inside. Rachel had on a skirt, blouse and hat, not unlike Faye Dunaway, while I sported a black shirt, white tie and was wearing a fedora hat. She was a brunette Dunaway while I was a blond Warren Beatty. I even carried an old violin case. Gunfights were not uncommon on the streets of Olongapo, so we only did this once. Besides, I didn't have anything in the violin case.

The summer ended and Rachel went back to school. I got one letter from her expressing delight over a happy summer and I never heard from her after that, but, I think we both had a good time. Sometimes people come into your life for a very short time just to make passing the time a little more enjoyable, and that's OK too!

39

I BEGAN HANGING around the AFRS (Armed Forces Radio Station) on weekends and on my off days. I volunteered to substitute DJ on weekends, which they cheerfully accepted. One Sunday morning I drove over in my '39 Chevrolet and passed a British Frigate that was docked at the Subic Naval Base. I noticed they had three large speakers blaring AFRS music, one forward, one aft, and one amid-ship.

I began my stint at the station and started cruising through old records to find one to dedicate to the Brits. Then I saw it, the perfect song for the occasion. I introduced the record and dedicated it to the crew of the HMS Sirius (Not 100% sure of the name) visiting Subic Bay: "Here's Johnny Horton's #1 song, "The Battle of New Orleans.""

The next day, Monday, I took off for Bangkok in my trusty twin engine S-2 for an exercise with the Thai Navy. We parked at Don Muang Airport for the time we were on the ground. Things were tight on the field and they asked us to fold our wings to take up less space. A week later, as we were ready to leave, we began to unfold our wings when an outside observer noticed a massive hydraulic leak under the left wing. We determined we were not going anywhere until we got a new hydraulic valve. Home-base notified us the earliest they could get us a new valve was about five to seven days. We had spent most of our money on cloths, gemstones, food, and entertainment and we were broke.

As I was talking to our home squadron, the duty officer happened to mention someone from the Admiral's staff was asking if anyone at the squadron was working at the AFRS station on Sunday. Hmm, I thought, perhaps a good time to stay in Thailand.

When the proprietor of the gemstone store, where we had spent most of our money, heard we were stuck, he invited to take us on a van tour of Thailand. We all loaded up and headed off into the back country of Thailand. We visited Buddhist Temples and several national monuments until we came to a river five clicks (kilometers) or so from the Thai town of Kanchanaburi…

A 'click' is a kilometer…one kilometer equals 0.621371192 miles… so, five clicks is about 3.1 miles. I know, it would have been easier to just say 3.1 miles but not nearly as educational.

Our driver explained this was the site of the bridge depicted in the movie, 'The Bridge on the River Kwai.' The movie was inaccurate on many levels; perhaps the most egregious being it was not the River Kwai at all, but the Mae Klong River. I guess 'The Bridge on the River Mae Klong' just didn't have the Hollywood ring to it.

But, there it was, the remnants of a bridge, with an old rusted Japanese railway engine on display in between the modern new bridge and the remnants of the old bridge, a few hundred yards away. There was a large brass sign in Thai and English that explained the significance of the site and honoring the British, American, Indian and Thai dead, along with those from several other countries.

After having lunch on the site, and touring the bridge we boarded some Thai boats and went down the river a few miles to a WW-II military cemetery. It was there that many of the fatalities from the building of the railroad were eventually buried. The path to the cemetery was not well-traveled and our guide had to cut through some jungle brush along the way. There was an elderly Japanese caretaker who tried to keep things in order, but he had to be at least 70 years old.

The irony was not lost on us that a 70-year-old Japanese man would be tending the grounds, over hundreds of graves of Allied soldiers who died at the hands of the Japanese during the war. To be sure, there were also a few Japanese buried at the site, but he did not appear to favor those over any of the others. He smiled when our guide told him we were American military, and directed us to where the majority of the Americans were buried. He appeared genuinely respectful as he brushed a few leaves off some of the markers. Our guide explained that the man was abandoned for unknown reasons when the Japanese were defeated and it was his choice to stay behind and care for the cemetery for the past 25 years The caretaker only accepted donations of food as compensation for his work, refusing tips of any sort. He explained to our Thai guide, *"that would dishonor those who are buried here."* Our guide gave him some white rice wrapped in newspaper as we left and the man seemed grateful for that meager meal.

We stayed on and pulled a few weeds from the plots, knowing well the jungle would claim them back very quickly, and probably faster than the Japanese man could keep them clear. There were just too many and he was too old and fragile.

The elderly caretaker walked us down the path to the river and smiled as we got back into our boats for the trip up the river to the bridge. I can still see the toothless smile on the man who waved goodbye to us until we were out of sight around a bend in the river. I can only imagine the stories he could tell, or perhaps the demons he dealt with still.

From the Burmese western border on the first day, we headed east the next day to the Cambodian border. I am not sure where we were except our guide, the gemstone dealer, explained we were in the vicinity of the complex of Angkor Wat, an ancient Hindu temple built in the early 12th century.

He knew how to get us safely across the Cambodian border to some ruins but told us it was too dangerous to try to get into that ancient city. He did, however, take us into the jungles of Cambodia to some other ruins where an ancient king of the Khmer Empire had once had another smaller Hindu temple.

It appeared this area was one of the sources of gemstones for our guide, since he went to do some business while we roamed around the ancient grounds. The jungle floor was literally littered with hundreds, maybe thousands, of what appeared to be artifacts of some ancient civilization. In all, we had spent about two hours on the Cambodian side of the border when our guide returned with several packages. We had traveled a very isolated back road from Thailand into Cambodia, with no guards on either side of the border. The people on both sides were very friendly but few spoke English. Safely back to the Thai side, we headed back to Bangkok where our host treated us to a large Thai dinner that evening.

Within a few days we had our airplane repaired and we were off to Cam Ranh Bay, South Viet Nam, for a refueling stop before heading out over the South China Sea to do some DR flying back to Cubi Point.

We landed at Cam Ranh Bay in mid afternoon, pulled off the runway and onto the taxiway and headed to the refueling area. Suddenly, we got an order from ground control to hold our position. It was, as always, hot and we had our overhead hatches open for some fresh air.

As soon as we stopped there was an explosion in the distance and suddenly we saw about 10 black clad men running in the distance with backpacks. A voice came up on guard channel and said, "Sapper attack, Cam Ranh Bay," several times over. The Air Force taxi ways were as wide and long as a typical Navy runway so I asked ground control for permission to take off. We couldn't have made it to Cubi but we had enough fuel to stay airborne for an hour or so until the situation on the ground could be stabilized. Ground control said, "Negative, hold your position!"

We could see a couple Viet Cong (VC) sappers in the far distance tossing explosive satchels into the revetments. I took my .38 military issue Smith & Wesson survival pistol out of my vest, and we discussed a plan if they came our way. It wasn't long before the airfield was filled with soldiers and MP's. The whole thing was over in about 15 minutes. The attack had done minimal damage and most, if not all the VC, were killed or captured.

After about 45 minutes we were cleared to the Naval Air Facility refueling area where we took on enough fuel to get to Cubi Point and told the tower we would file our flight plan when airborne. It was time to get out of Dodge.

～～～

By the time we arrived back to Cubi Point, the whole issue with the Brit Frigate was forgotten, but the guys at AFRTS told me it was probably best for me to stay away for awhile.

We began workups to go out to the carrier by doing FCLP's (Field Carrier Landing Practices) at Cubi. Our home squadron was going to send a group of newly arrived pilots to go out to the boat with us.

Holly assigned me the roll of LSO (landing signal officer) in training. I would talk the aircraft in during the FCLP's with a certified LSO from VRC-50 giving me instructions.

After training late one afternoon, I drove up the hill to the BOQ, showered and hiked over to the Club for a couple of drinks. As I sat there, the Duty Officer walked in and said he had been looking all over for me. Holly had directed him to find me and tell me to go to Naval Air Station Sangley Point to pick up this pilot and bring him back to Cubi. It was getting close to sunset and the Bug-Smasher was interesting enough to fly in the daytime; the Navy had restricted us from flying the thing at night.

I looked at the sun outside the club and decided if I put my skates on I could probably make it to Sangley and back before it got too dark. I was in civvies, jeans and a T-shirt, so I told the duty officer to direct one of the maintenance people to fire up the bug-smasher and I would be right down. He asked me if I needed an observer in the right seat and I said I would have one on the trip back.

The SNB was turning and burning as I arrived, so I parked my car next to the plane, jumped out, climbed aboard the aircraft and taxied out for takeoff. In the air I filed for Sangley Point and back.

I landed and told ground-control to have my passenger meet me in front of the tower. He was standing there as I rolled up and he climbed into the plane. As we taxied out I directed him to stow his bags and climb into the right seat. As he strapped in, I noted he was a Commander in his whites and there I was with jeans and T-shirt; too late to worry about formalities now. Besides, he was getting a free ride to Cubi Point instead of a 10-hour bus ride.

I gave him the take-off check list and he started reading it to me. I knew it by heart but thought he might feel better if he actually read it. We were rolling down the runway as he was finishing the check-list and we were airborne to Cubi.

I pointed out Corregidor and the Bataan Peninsula from WW-II days, and he seemed to enjoy the tour.

As we arrived at our destination, I noted the sun had set but there was just enough dusk to call it a daytime landing. I rolled into the parking ramp and pulled in next to my car, the 1939 Chevrolet. I helped the commander with his bags and gave him a ride up the hill to the BOQ. His only comment was, *"Is everything here over 30 years old?"*

"No Sir," I replied, *"I'm only 25."* He never said much after that and I never saw him again. I drove back to the club and met up with my friends. "Hey," I said, "Who finished my drink?"

40

HOLLY WAS A hard drinker and womanizer. He had been passed over for Commander a couple times, and he was determined to show the bosses he deserved the promotion. Even we junior officers knew that if you got passed over your chances for being picked up the second time was small. Passed over a second time and your chances were infinitesimal. But, hope springs eternal among some.

Each squadron was allocated so much fuel each quarter. He got it in his head that if he didn't use all the fuel we were allocated the powers-that-be would be impressed and he would get promoted. We did only minimal flying that quarter and sure enough, there he was, turning fuel back in. All it meant was that we received less fuel the next quarter, and, when we had a higher pace of operations during that time, he had to ask for more fuel the last month of the quarter. The whole thing ended up as a strike against him for poor planning.

Holly was the most experienced S-2 driver in the Pacific. As such, he was the 'Model Manager' for the aircraft. Normally our twin engine S-2's had a generator on each engine. There came a shortage of generators in the Pacific so he petitioned CINPACFLT (Commander of the Pacific Fleet) to allow S-2's to fly with only one generator. That was approved providing it was daytime -VFR flying only.

It was August, 1970. The USS Oriskany was about to leave Subic Bay for Yankee Station off North Vietnam. We were in the process of finishing up our FCLP's and were going to meet the "O-boat" about 120 miles out of Cubi to renew our qualifications for carrier landings. We had four new pilots from our parent squadron, who had been doing their FCLP's with us prior to going out to the boat for the first time since advanced training in Corpus Christi. I had been doing carrier landings on an intermittent basis flying out of Cubi and Danang. Including the training command, I had about 75 traps, not a huge amount but I was pretty comfortable at the boat.

The plan was for a flight of four S-2's to fly out to the USS Oriskany and trap aboard. I would then go to the LSO platform to get the experience of actually bringing some aircraft aboard the ship as our LSO in Training. When the carrier was ready for us, the other 10 pilots would take turns getting six traps apiece. I would then leave the LSO platform, get my six traps, full stop, and we would launch all four aircraft for the trip back to Cubi.

Lt.jg's Glenn Grimes & Ken Hubona were flying one aircraft. Lt. jg Jim Finley was flying another. Holly was flying the third aircraft and had Lt.jg's Jack Dripps, Quint Gunn and Glen Spar in the aircraft. I flew the fourth plane.

Things did not start off that well. I had electrical problems with my aircraft, which they worked on before I could/would take off. When it looked like I was about ready to go, Holly directed the first three to take off and I would try to catch up. My aircraft finally checked-out and I took off for the "O-Boat," as the Oriskany was called.

I had only one generator, so I delayed taking off to be sure my electrical issue was resolved before heading out. Unfortunately, about halfway to the boat my only generator failed. I did have a battery but that lasted about two minutes after the generator went out. I was in and out of the clouds so I descended to get into the clear. I had no radios, no instruments and several other limiting factors. All I had was a wet compass to DR my way to the boat.

Eventually, off in the distance, I could see the boat. The area around an aircraft carrier can be really busy and they did not like strangers coming in without an announcement. Unfortunately, with no generator and a dead battery, I had no way to let them know I was there. I used my survival radio to announce my position on the guard channel but I have no idea if they heard me. We considered our survival radios as *US military devices for storing dead batteries.*

I hung out amid-ship, a mile or so out, and waited until I could see an opening. When things looked as good as they were going to get, I flew down over the carrier rocking my wings, a signal to them that I had no radios. I broke to the left, and at the 180 position I saw a green light signaling that I could land. There was an LSO but I had no way of hearing him. I just flew the best approach I could, knowing if I saw a red flare I would have to go around. The meatball was in the middle all the way down and I got a three-wire. The airplane director, in a yellow shirt, directed me to the parking area to fold my wings. I shut her down, went into maintenance, wrote up the gripe, told the maintenance chief my problem, and proceeded to the LSO platform.

Soon, the other three aircraft were airborne doing their landings. When I finished at the LSO platform, I got into one of the S-2's and did my 6 landings. It was nice to have a plane with radios. After my sixth landing I made a full-stop and got out while they re-fueled the plane. The plan, at departure from Cubi, had been that we would return in the same plane as we flew out there. I went to the maintenance shack to sign for my aircraft and noticed the gripe about the generators had not been fixed. I asked the chief about it, and he said our CO had said we would take it back *as is*. I just looked at him dumbfounded. *"That can't be right!"* The sun was about to set, we had 150 miles to get back to Cubi Point, which would take over an hour, and it was the monsoon season, which almost guaranteed rain on arrival.

As I was trying to explain to the maintenance chief that he must have misunderstood, Holly walked in. I said, *"Skipper, they haven't fixed the generator!"*

He said, "I told them we would take it as is. There is a shortage of generators and I don't want them on Yankee Station with one less generator."

I just looked at him, wondering what I should say. I was a Lt (JG), he was a Lieutenant Commander. He was the OinC of the squadron and he was the model-manager for the Pacific. This all occurred in a matter of seconds. Finally, I said, *"Sir, I can't fly that airplane without a generator!"*

He looked at me and said, *"Well, Nevels, if you can't hack it, I will take it!"*

If the world is going 331/3 rpm, life on the boat is at least 78. It took longer to read that last paragraph than the entire discussion lasted on the boat. I signed for my plane and proceeded to the flight deck. The engines were running, there was a pilot in the co-pilot seat, and one in the back. I did a quick check of the electrical system, called for the take-off check-list and notified the boat I was ready for take-off. The yellow shirt directed me out and I launched as the sun was setting. I circled abeam the carrier until all our aircraft were airborne. I learned later that Holly had briefed another pilot that he would fly on his wing back to Cubi Point. I watched as the next-to-last aircraft was launched and then I saw Holly's plane get airborne. I specifically wanted to see the landing gear go up. In the S-2, the landing gear was electrically activated and hydraulically operated. But there was a manual override for the electrical activation to bring the gear up with no electrical power.

"Knowing Holly he just might pull this off," I thought. I had no intention of making the Navy a career, but I didn't look forward to facing Holly every day after this. *"Crap, I don't care, I made the right decision and I would do it again!"*

The first several miles we were in the clear, VFR (Visual Flight Rules). But that changed about halfway home as we got into the soup. It got progressively worse the closer we got to the Philippines.

This was the monsoon season, and you could set your watch to the rain that always came in the afternoon and into the evenings this time of year. I could talk to the lead aircraft, with Holly on his wing, but I knew he had his hands full, so I only spoke when he asked something or wanted me to verify his position and altitude. I didn't want a mid-air to top off this day so I kept my distance. I wanted to help, but there was only so much I could do.

I could tell by the lead pilot's voice he did not like the position he was in. The responsibility was enormous and his voice reflected the tension he was under.

I let him know that, when we arrived in the vicinity of the airfield at Cubi Point, I would enter a holding pattern and let him fly a Ground Controlled Approach (GCA). After he and Holly had landed, I would make my approach.

"You can do it," I said in an attempt to calm his nerves.

"We are totally in the soup and I have no idea if Holly is still on my wing, we can't see a thing," he commented in an apparent attempt to calm his own nerves.

"Approach knows the situation, just follow their instructions," I answered.

The lead aircraft was Checkertail 26, Holly was in Checkertail 27,

I was Checkertail 24, someone else had Chekertail 25. It was night; I was in the soup the entire time and speculated how it must be, flying in Holly's plane, in the clouds, in the rain, at night, no wipers, no instruments, trying to maintain a visual on Checkertail 26.

Imagine you are driving 150 miles an hour down the interstate in a severe rainstorm with no lights, no windshield wipers, just trying to follow the red tail-lights of the car in front of you.

I listened as they began their GCA approach. The GCA controller acknowledged "radar contact," but did not acknowledge both aircraft. I hoped the two aircraft were so close they appeared as one blip on the radar.

As the controller directed, Checkertail 26 began his descent; then I heard the ground controller give the standard GCA approach directions. He never acknowledged seeing two aircraft. While that did not sound good, I continued to believe that Holly was close on his wing. Checkertail 26 completed his GCA and landed at Cubi Point. I kept expecting him to say, "Holly has landed right behind me" but there was nothing.

The controller asked me my intentions. I said I was going to continue in my holding pattern for awhile. The last thing I wanted was a mid-air with Holly if he was still in the air. Perhaps Holly had broken out below the clouds and was going to make a low altitude visual approach. In that case I didn't want to be in the way.

I asked Checkertail 26 what altitude he had broken out of the clouds on the approach. He said about 200-300 ft. Not good, I thought, but we've had worse. I stayed up there for about an hour more while all the remaining Checkertail aircraft made their approaches and landings.

I called control, who said the only other aircraft they had on radar was me, so I advised him I was ready for a GCA, hoping I didn't run into Holly. I came down, broke out at about 200 feet and landed at Cubi Point. As I taxied in to our parking area I contacted our squadron and asked if they had heard anything from Holly. "Nothing," was the answer.

We all stayed at the squadron staring out toward the runway fully expecting to see a plane land any second, but we were beginning to have serious doubts. No one wanted to be the first to say they were gone. We counted heads from the aircraft that had returned and we were four people short. That meant there were three other pilots in that plane with Holly, and all three of those pilots were from Okinawa. I started calculating when he would run out of fuel. It did not look good.

About mid-night, base-ops called to say some Filipino fisherman claimed to have seen an aircraft crash out near Grande Island at the mouth of Subic Bay. The Navy had sent out a rescue boat and would let us know. About 2:00 a.m. we got another call from Base Ops… the rescue boat had found a massive debris field and oil slick. No survivors!

"That son-of-a-bitch," I thought. *"All this, so you could make Commander! I hope those three pilots are kicking your ass all the way to Hell!"* I was pissed. I mean, really pissed. I was shaking with anger. I could only remember once, a few years earlier and a few miles down the road, being that angry.

Survival on an aircraft carrier, especially the flight deck, requires top-notch training and good instincts. Good instincts are mostly the result of top-notch training. The three victimized pilots were all Lt (jg's), probably in the squadron no more than a few months. I imagine they were not informed about the condition of the plane. They were just told to get into that aircraft for the flight back to Cubi.

It could easily have been me or any of us. Or, I could have been the hot-shot pilot trying to impress the old man and say, *"Sure, Skipper, I brought her out, I'll take her back!"*

The conversation that occurred in the maintenance shack lasted only a couple of seconds; there was no time to think it out rationally. What made me stand up to the Old Man? I don't know for sure. Part of that may be that I knew him, and my respect level was already low. Any rational thought I may apply to that question begs another question, *"Why me, why not one of the others?"* Was it by design or just a random act? The major difference that haunted my mind was, I had a choice. I knew the conditions and the other three pilots probably didn't. In the heat of the moment and against all odds a young junior officer had to make a decision in a matter of a few seconds to try to impress, or say *"No,"* to a senior officer. I chose to follow my instincts, knowing full well that any thoughts of a career in the Navy were now extinguished. But then, thankfully, at that time I had no thoughts of a Navy career.

The three Lt. jg's that got into that ill-fated aircraft were Jack Dripps, Quinten Gunn and Glen Spar. Ironically, and sadly, I do not remember much about them since they were from our parent squadron in Okinawa and had been there for only a short time. The one I remember the most was the culprit, "Holly."

While I may not remember much about them I do remember their faces, mostly in dreams; but occasionally, and randomly, in the middle of the day.

Like Private Ryan, I had a few more that were counting on me to *"live a good life"* in their stead.

There was the expected accident investigation, which almost always tried to find people to blame. Of course, the primary cause of the accident was pilot error, big-time, my words not theirs. But there were also several lesser reprimands that were assigned by the final reviewing officer, Admiral John McCain, CINCPAC, (Commander in Chief, Pacific). He was the father of Navy pilot and, at that time, a POW, and later Senator John McCain.

The Admiral assigned letters of reprimand to various officers in the chain of command, and gave a verbal reprimand to us junior officers, myself included. Those verbal reprimands were never expressed verbally to me, and never showed up in any of my permanent records. The basis for the reprimands was never articulated to any of us, which seemed to dilute any effectiveness they may have had. No one ever explained to any of us, verbally or otherwise, what we should have done differently.

Personally, the event had a huge impact on me and created entirely new criteria for making both personal and professional decisions. There was no pride to be found in anything that day, but I was pleased my instincts had directed me to make the right decision under extreme conditions. If anything, it gave me confidence to follow those instincts and to disregard the political, career or personal consequences. That lesson would serve me well over the next many years during my 20+ year career in the Navy, and later in civilian life. It was another significant and very personal *"Course Correction."*

⁓⁓⁓

Graveyard humor was rampant within our tiny band of merry pilots. Before each flight someone would always say, *"If you don't make it back can I have your stuff?"* Followed by someone else saying, *"I get your stereo."*

A few days after Holly's death a couple of us bachelors were assigned to go to his room and pack his things to send home. This small 'group' mushroomed into all those in the BOQ who knew the man. Holly had a well-stocked bar in his room and since that could not be sent back we proceeded to have a "*Going Away*" party with Holly's liquor. As morbid as that may sound, I think each of us there would have wanted the others to do the same for us, if we were to meet a similar fate.

41

KRAIGHER KRISTOFFERSON WAS our AOinC (Assistant Officer-in-Charge) at the time of the accident and assumed the duties as OinC until a replacement could be found. Kraigher was one of the good guys. He and his wife Gray would have us single junior officers over for dinner now and then and, before the evening was over, Kraigher would always pull out these demo records his brother had cut trying to get country stars to record his songs. Kraigher had this old beat up guitar and would try to play along with the songs. As the evening wore on it would become more raucous, load and probably obnoxious.

Of course, his brother was Kris Kristofferson, a virtual unknown at the time but that was about to change. Within a few months Johnny Cash recorded, *"Sunday Morning Coming Down"*, Janis Joplin recorded *"Me and Bobby McGee"* and Kris was on his way.

I was able to meet Kraigher and Kris's father and mother when we had a table next to them at dinner in the Cubi Point Officer's Club. That entire family would become one of the most interesting I would ever encounter. Their father was an Air Force Major General, Pan Am Pilot and oil company executive. The unusual name 'Kraigher' actually was the last name of the general's best friend and oil company partner. The general died not long after that visit to the Philippines to see their son.

Kraigher Kristofferson's command of our squadron was a needed calming period for us, during which the tragedy of Holly's crash could be digested and overcome. All our assignments went forward as tasked. Each officer and senior enlisted in the squadron came together. It was a proud and shining time for VC-5 Det Cubi Point. We all were disappointed when Kraigher's tour was up and he had to leave. He got out of the Navy and went to California where, I understand, he became a land developer. Not too many years later I was stationed in Hawaii and Kris came to do a concert in downtown Honolulu. I went down to the concert and actually met Kris but I doubt he would remember; we'll just leave it at that.

It wasn't long before we had another Lieutenant Commander as OinC and things returned to just about the level they were under Holly.

Our new OinC, Lieutenant Commander Art, started out hopeful but quickly went sideways and then straight down. He was also passed-over for promotion to Commander and viewed his tenure in VC-5 as a chance to prove to the selection boards they were wrong in their decision. Sound familiar? The world is just a circle and goes round-and-round.

As he met each one of us, on his first day in the squadron, he would look us over in a very obvious motion beginning at the top of our head to our feet. He then would stare at our nametag and do it again, it was a bit disconcerting. When he was finished with the last officer in the room he explained that he had an infallible method for remembering names and he went through this routine to find something unique about each one of us to associate it with our name. Harmless enough, we thought. He claimed he never forgot a name.

The next day he was late coming down the hill for our daily AOM (All Officers Meeting). We were all milling about smartly and started talking about his method of remembering names.

Someone came up with the idea that we all exchange nametags.

Our new OinC showed up a short time later and proudly began greeting us. His method was apparently good because he did remember each name. He looked at each of us in turn and when he got to me he greeted me with a cheery, *"Good Morning, Lieutenant Nevels."*

I pointed to my new nametag and said, *"No Sir I'm Lieutenant Harms, that's Lieutenant Nevels."*

He made the rounds of all the officers getting each one wrong. "I can't understand it," he commented, "I have never made this many mistakes."

"Probably the proximity to the equator," someone said, "Or the

Philippine sun, Sir," came from another. A third chimed in, "Both factors can really play tricks on you."

The next day we all had our proper nametags on and he missed all the names again. When he came to me he said, *"Good morning Lt. Harms."*

I replied, *"Sir, I am Lt. Nevels. That is Lt. Harms."*

He was getting suspicious and asked us for our ID cards. Since we now had the correct nametags our ID cards matched.

"Must be that equator thing," he said shaking his head.

Humor was a huge part of what helped us keep our sanity in the very insane world that was Vietnam, both in country as well as in the periphery that was Cubi Point. It was a day-to-day challenge to see how much humor we could conjure up without being disrespectful or disloyal. For certain, in those times, some things were so serious that if you didn't laugh at them, you would go crazy. After our recent squadron tragedy this fact came home to us in a very dramatic way.

I suppose the same applies, even today.

42

WITH RICK NELSON's departure and Holly's death, I was the only pilot in the squadron qualified to fly the RC-45J, the Bug-Smasher. No one else was interested in getting checked-out, so it became *my* personal airplane. What a great situation, I had my own private airplane and the government paid for all the maintenance and fuel. All I had to do was take a few pictures of some ships now and then and haul around a few dignitaries and senior officers. This was great!

Before Holly died I had 15 hours in the bird. After the crash, I accumulated 156 hours for a total of 171, which spanned 116 total flights before the aircraft was grounded for good by the Navy.

After the crash they took us out of the COD (Carrier Onboard Delivery) business but we still hauled passengers, mail, and vital parts to and from Vietnam. My LSO career ended before it really got started and those landings on the Oriskany were my last traps aboard a carrier. That was a big disappointment since I felt I was getting really good flying to and from the boat.

I flew the Bug-Smasher and the Stoofs (S-2's) which were both fun, but slow. I was always trying to get into something faster.

I ginned up a friendship with the OinC of an A-3 Skywarrior squadron that shared our hanger. I let him know anytime he needed a co-pilot I would love to fly with him. They were short of pilots and the few they had were getting worn out with too many flight hours. It wasn't long before I was flying with him to Vietnam on tactical missions. These were EKA-3B's: the 'E' stood for electronic counter- measures warfare, the 'K' meant it was also a tanker used for refueling other aircraft, the 'A' meant its original mission was as an attack aircraft, the 'B' was its designation as the second version of that model of aircraft. Because of their large size they were referred to as "Whales". When they discontinued the attack mission and took over electronic counter-measures as their primary job they were known as "Electric Whales". They normally had a crew of three, two pilots and one crewman who handled the electronic gear on the aircraft.

Despite being a high performance jet aircraft they had no ejection seats. There was a slide that could be opened behind the pilot's seats and one could slide out the bottom of the aircraft. If you had an emergency at low altitude you were toast. There was a variation of the plane called the Douglas A-3D Skywarrior. The pilots and crew contended the 'A-3D' stood for "*All 3 Dead*". My Skywarrior experience was short lived and I made only a half dozen or so flights with them but we got into the War-Zone and qualified for combat pay.

I had this urge to break the sound barrier, which none of the aircraft I had flown could come close. While at the Cubi Officers Club I struck up a conversation with an F-4 Phantom pilot. He approached me because his wife was there for a visit and he wanted to take her up to Baguio, a semi resort town in the mountains of Northern Luzon. He asked around and heard that the Bug-Smasher was the only plane on the base that could land and take-off up there. I agreed to take them if he would give me a ride in the Phantom and break the sound barrier.

The speed of sound is about 768 mph (Mach One), or one mile about every five seconds at that speed. The pilot gave me a quick review of ejection procedures and off we went. He let me fly the beast a short while, doing some simple maneuvers.

We were in the air for about an hour when he put us into a dive over the South China Sea and, bang, Mach One. Of course, pulling out he put us into a series of rolls. It seemed that was mandatory. There were a few "G's" as we pulled out, but nothing spectacular. The Phantom could go up to 'Mach Two' but I didn't press my luck.

A few days later I took them up to Baguio and picked them up after a few days, at a much more leisurely pace than in the Phantom. All three of us were happy. So, what I told that Lieutenant Commander in Dallas a few years earlier finally came true, I got to fly the F-4 Phantom.

Every pilot in the Navy has a particular call sign. Sometimes it's your choice, other times one is assigned. If your last name is Campbell you can be sure your call sign will be 'Soupy'. If you have the last name 'Rhodes', it will be "Dusty". With a name like Nevels, nothing really fit until I kept finagling flights in faster and faster aircraft. Soon, my call-sign was 'Speed' which seemed a bit ludicrous bouncing around in the Bug-Smasher at about 150 MPH. Hey, it beat the bus.

A buddy of mine, Ken, had been dating a local DOD school teacher, Marcia, and they decided to get married. I was leaving for a week to work with the Nationalist Chinese Navy in Taipei, on the north end of Taiwan and Tainan on the south end. Ken asked me if I would get a Lhasa Apso pup for him to give to his bride, Marcia, as a wedding gift. While in Taipei, I met this Taiwanese girl who was trying to learn English so she could get a government job. (That's my story and I'm sticking to it.)

It seems that Chinese have this problem with R's. No matter how hard they try, the letter comes out sounding like a 'W'. Being a bit sinister I told her my name was *Ralph*. When she tried to pronounce my name it came out "Walph". No matter how hard she tried it was "Walph". She finally said, "Walph, Walph, sound like dog!" Well, she took me to a dog-shop where I found this Lhasa Apso for Ken and Marcia.

The Lhasa Apso was introduced to China when emissaries from Tibet gave them to the Chinese royalty as gifts. Of course, Lhasa is the capital of Tibet while Apso means 'bearded' in Tibetan. They are referred to as, *the Lion dog of Tibet* in one of the Chinese dialects. The Lhasa Apso was bred as an interior sentinel in the Buddhist monasteries, who alerted the monks to any intruders who entered, by waking up the larger, less sensitive guard dogs.

This particular Lhasa cried all night in the hotel room where I was staying in Taipei. I figured he just wanted some company. So, the next day I bought a second dog from the same shop to keep him company. That resulted in both dogs crying all night.

The third night I flew down to Tainan, on the southern end of the island of Taiwan. In order to get some sleep I found a hotel with a kennel and someone to care for the two dogs while I went flying with the Chinese Navy.

My assignment was pulling targets for these Chinese Navy warships. We pulled the target about a mile behind us which may seem like quite a distance' unless someone is shooting at it. These five Nationalist Chinese ships lined-up, bow to stern, and I was to fly abeam the five ships. I would start my stop-watch when I passed the first ship and so-many seconds later I would give that ship the command to "commence fire" and so-many seconds later I would call out, "Cease fire!" Then I would do the same for the second ship and the rest on down the line. This technique kept the cone of fire away from my aircraft. At the briefing I explained all this and asked if they understood.

They all said *"Roger, Roger."* Of course it came out as *"Wah-ger, Wah-ger."* I asked my English translator if they understood and he said, *"Wah-ger, Wah-ger."* I asked one of the Chinese Naval officers if I could hit him in the nose. He smiled and replied, *"Wah-ger, Wah-ger."* I knew I was in trouble.

The next day as I passed the first ship I started the watch and, at the precise time, I gave the direction, *"Ship Number one, commence fire."* Well, all five ships opened fire at the same time. There was more flak up there than any B-17 had seen over Germany during World War II. I yelled out *"Cease Fire, Cease Fire"* for a full minute. There must have been a lag from the time I called for a cease fire and they got the message down to the gunners.

I hit the emergency release of the target, made a hard right turn away from the ships and descended to just above the water as fast as that sucker would go. We had an emergency shotgun shell that sent a knife to cut the cable to the target, which I activated. They kept shooting at the target all the way down until it hit the ocean and then they headed over and picked up the target. I had a crewman in the back of the airplane who was launching the target and rolling out the wire. He came up on the aircraft's intercom to tell me we had been hit.

I continued away from the ships until I was out of range and turned towards Tainan. I climbed up and checked all the controls and everything seemed to be working. I turned it over to my co-pilot and went back to check the damage. There was about a four-inch hole in the vertical stabilizer but it appeared to miss any of the controls, wires and hydraulic lines back there.

We landed at Tainan and checked the damage from the outside. The Chinese maintenance team was eager to fix the hole as quickly as possible. Our man supervised the repair and the next day we went to discuss what had occurred. They wanted to continue the exercise but I told them I would not go out again without a Chinese Naval Officer, who spoke English, in the aircraft with me. I went over the instructions again with the ships gunnery officers; showed them what went wrong and explained again the procedure. I asked my English speaking translator if they understood everything I had just said. He looked at me and said, "Woger, Woger". The next day we went out again and to my relief, everything went like clockwork.

Don't get me wrong, the Chinese Nationalist Navy is excellent at what they do. Once they figured out the procedure they were dead-on to the target.

One day of flying happened to fall on a Thursday and it was Thanksgiving Day, which meant nothing to the Chinese. That evening I went to about a dozen restaurants until I found one that served turkey. So we spent the evening eating turkey fried rice, at least they said it was turkey. We had a good time in Taiwan and after a week I safely returned to Cubi Point with two Lhasa Apsos. I named mine 'Ralph' while Ken and Marcia named theirs "O'Po", our shortened version short for Olongapo.

The US Navy had contracted with a company out of Osaka Japan to do our major aircraft restoration work. Rick Nelson and I took three crewmen up to Osaka and dropped off the airplane. It happened to be the time Osaka Japan was hosting the 1970 World's Fair so we stayed on a few extra days to attend the event. It was spectacular to see, and the food from all over the Orient was great. The only thing was, we had to bring back our parachutes.

We boarded the Bullet Train from Osaka to Tokyo, with our luggage and parachutes. From Tokyo we went on to Yokosuka to catch a flight to Clark AFB. The problem was the MAC (Military Airlift Command) flight let us check our bags but would not allow us to check the parachutes. Don't ask, I have no idea why. So there we were, five guys walking down the aisle of the airplane with parachutes that we tucked under the seats and in the overhead bins. There were plenty of eyes watching us the entire flight.

VC-5 Det Cubi Point was a great way to start my Navy flying career. I got to visit Japan, Hong Kong, Taiwan, Thailand, Burma and Cambodia (a bit) and a lot of Vietnam and the Philippines. I even visited my old high school, George Dewey, and checked out where I lived my sophomore year in high school. Every time I traversed the road from Cubi Point to Navy Subic Bay I would pass that fuel pier where everything almost ended a mere eight years earlier. It seemed a lifetime ago, but it was all still clear in my mind.

The next month I was again sent up to Taipei, Taiwan (Nationalist China) again. This time I had one of our jet pilots as co-pilot. Upon arrival in the area, it was raining and the clouds were hanging low.

The approach into Taipei Sungshan International Airport was pretty challenging in good weather, terrible in bad. The main obstacle was that Chang Kai-Shek's palace was on approach and if you flew over the palace they would shoot you down. The precision GCA seldom was working and during the non-precision approach you had to make several severe turns to avoid flying over the palace. When you were in the clouds this meant some major changes of radio frequencies. Normally, the pilot would fly the plane while the co-pilot would tune the radios. I asked my co-pilot to tune the ADF coffee-grinder radio while I flew the plane. He was unfamiliar with the equipment and since there are mountains all around I gave him the flight controls while I frantically began tuning the radio, which was above my head. I noticed he was watching me and when I looked at the horizontal indicator I saw that we were at a 60 degree angle of bank. I grabbed the control column, leveled the aircraft and saw pinecones out the left side of the aircraft. Now, I don't have anything against pinecones but they are among the last things I want to see while flying.

I added power and we climbed back into the clouds and continued our non-precision approach to the airport.

Upon landing we were met by this staff car with several Chinese Officers. They asked if we had over-flown Chang Kai-Shek's palace. "Of course not, you are not allowed to do that," I replied.

We evidently were flying below their radar range and they lost us for a few moments. When they reacquired us we were heading away from the palace. They got back in their staff car and left.

I have chosen to exclude unnecessary negative aspects of our two OinC's, Lieutenant Commander "Holly" and Lieutenant Commander "Art." It serves no purpose for this book. Holly's end mirrored my time with him.

While Art survived the squadron, a few months after my departure from the squadron he retired from the Navy. I understand he died while flying as a crop-duster in California after a few weeks on the job.

43

WHEN I EARNED my Navy Wings there were not enough openings in the P-3 community for all of us, which is how I ended up in VC-5. It probably could not have worked out better. I accumulated a lot of flight hours, flew in several different aircraft, had my own private plane for many months and was able to visit all around Asia. I even survived Vietnam.

I arrived in VC-5 Det in March of 1970 for what should have been a 12 month unaccompanied tour. When my 12 months was completed I contacted my detailer in Washington DC and he asked where I would like to go next. Of course, I said I still wanted to fly the P-3 Orion. So, in July 1971, after 18 months in the squadron, my friends flew me back to Clark AFB for a flight to Travis AFB and from there proceeded back to Corpus Christi, this time for a quick course in celestial navigation, or as we called it, *Star School*.

When I landed in Texas I bought a new 1971 MGB and began my navigation course. I finished the Nav-course and star school, and drove out to Moffett Field, just south of San Francisco in Sunnyvale.

When I arrived in San Jose, I hooked up with three other pilots from Nav-school and together we rented a four bedroom house. There I joined the RAG Squadron, VP-31. RAG was a Navy acronym for *Replacement Air Group* or a squadron that trained pilots to fly the P-3 in this case. When we finished the RAG we would be sent to our operational squadrons.

It was a typical Navy training squadron, hours in the classroom, hours in the simulator and not enough hours in the air. To be fair, to a pilot there are never enough hours in the air.

I began this transition in November 1971 and completed in March 1972. The P-3 was designed for ASW, Anti Submarine Warfare, and was a technically challenging aircraft with four engines and a massive amount of electronic technology for hunting and attacking submarines and a few other things. Flying was relatively easy but the systems were totally more complex than the S-2 or C-45.

Soon after arriving I met Kathleen at a party hosted by a mutual friend. We hit it off right away and soon, way too soon, we were married at a ceremony at the Chapel on Moffett Field.

~~~

It is amazing how love, or something like it, can give you glasses that make all the red flags look green. My first wife was Catholic, I was Protestant; she was liberal, I was conservative; she was anti-war, I had just returned from the war and was in training to go back. Her friends thought as she did, mine were in the Navy; I wanted children, she didn't. Well, that last part didn't fully come to light until years later. Nonetheless, it is probably amazing we lasted as long as we did: six years.

Kathleen was a complex lady who tried to fit in as a Navy wife, and succeeded on the surface for a few years. She was three years older than me and, like me, had never been married. She was a good Irish Catholic girl, originally from Washington DC, and had moved to California in her 20's with a friend for a new start.

We honeymooned at the Mark Hopkins Hotel in San Francisco. I wore my Navy-blue dress uniform and I drove up to the hotel in my MGB. Kathy offered to check us in while I handled the bags. I got the bags out of the trunk of my car when this lady in a limo pulled up behind us at the front entrance.

She got out, looked my uniform over and said, *"Boy, can you get my bags?"*

"Yes Mam", I said. I took all our bags in and she gave me a $20 tip, not bad in 1972. We all went up together in the elevator. We ran into each other later at the 'Top-of-the Mark,' the restaurant on the top floor of the hotel.

In March I finished the RAG squadron and we were off to VP-4

(Patrol Squadron Four) in Barbers Point, Hawaii. While at Moffett Field I discovered that my new squadron would be deploying to the Pacific two weeks after I arrived.

I asked where they would deploy. "Cubi Point, the Philippines" was the answer.

"Oh, Great," I thought.

~~~~

I did not want to live in base housing in Hawaii so we found this house in Makakilo, a middle class development just up from Barbers Point. $45,000 seemed like a fortune at the time and my squadron mates said I was a fool for paying such a price. I said, *"Maybe so, unless I can find a bigger fool to pay a bigger price when I decide to sell."*

A normal Navy deployment is plus or minus six months. When you are deployed in and around a war zone you soon start counting the days until you return; what you pray for most is that we not get extended. After a month or two we all knew exactly how many days we had left in the deployment. When we got under two months we put together our *"short-timer's calendar."* We had it down to 'so many days and a wake-up' until we were headed home, or so we thought.

With just under 30 days left we got the news, we were extended. We had arrived at Cubi Point in early April and should have made it home by the end of September, first of October at the latest. We came home in late November. It turned out to be the highest tempo of VP operations for the entire war. I averaged 87 flight hours per month, which required a monthly waiver from the Navy to fly that many hours. The day after I arrived in Cubi we were sent to Utapao, Thailand to relieve another crew. Because I had over a thousand flight hours I was moved up to second pilot and quickly made PPC, Patrol Plane Commander.

Our mission was round-the-clock *'Market Time'*, the object of which was, to deny the North Vietnamese the ability to smuggle arms and ammunition to the south. Our P-3 Orions were armed with Bull-Pup air to surface missiles, but we normally called in surface ships to check out suspected ships or, if time was of the essence, we would call in attack-aircraft from the carriers or land bases in Utapao or Vietnam. Under normal conditions, we intercepted suspect ships that crossed inside South Vietnam's 12-mile coastal boundary. We had a maintenance detachment at Cam Ranh Bay to reduce our commute time to the zone. We seemed to be constantly flying from Utapao, Saigon (Cam Ranh Bay) and Cubi Point.

May 9th 1972 --- we were back in Cubi Point and were on the bus taking us down the hill from the BOQ to the airfield. As we passed our aircraft on the way to our briefing we noted some strange items being hung on the wings. "*Mines,*" someone said. We all knew we had the capability to drop mines but most of us had never done it, even in practice, or ever even seen a mine.

We knew from news reports that President Nixon had threatened to mine Haiphong Harbor to prevent the North Vietnamese from getting resupplied from the sea. At our briefing we were told what was going on. A-6 and A-7 aircraft from various aircraft carriers on Yankee Station off North Vietnam were about to mine Haiphong Harbor, the only logical supply route for ships coming from the Soviet Union or China. It was unknown how much resistance they would encounter. If they were not fully successful we would be launched in our P-3's to complete the mission. Things were very tense at the briefing. A few of the younger pilots were whispering they would not go if we were launched on that mission. Frankly, I was not wild about flying into the teeth of the dragon but if we were sent to do a job, I would give it my best.

We all went to our aircraft, conducted our pre-flights, which took about two hours, and discussed our procedures if we were directed to the mining mission. Then we waited, and waited. First we got the notice the A-6's and A-7's completed the mission and all had returned. There was a big sigh of relief but we were not yet off the hook. We were notified they were evaluating drop points of the mines. If there were holes we might yet get launched. At mid-afternoon we saw them removing the mines from our aircraft. We scurried back to the briefing room to be told we were to stand-down but were to be prepared to launch on a regular mission at any time. Little did we know that the long days and longer nights were just ahead.

With the mines in place, Haiphong Harbor in North Viet Nam was virtually closed. But soon, we received tasking to monitor a Russian flotilla of ships that was leaving Vladivostok in the Soviet Union. Their intention was unclear. We were tasked with relocating the flotilla every day. Once they passed the southern tip of Taiwan our tasking was expanded to 24/7 surveillance of the flotilla. An aircraft would locate the ships and loiter overhead until relieved by another aircraft. This meant flights of 14-16 hours for us. We would regularly shut down one of our four engines to conserve fuel, occasionally shutting down two engines if our relief were late. It was unknown what they would do when they approached the mine field so we just waited and watched.

As luck would have it, I was overhead when they reached the outer limits of Haiphong harbor, but by then another flotilla of US Navy ships had joined the party. What would the Russians do? Evidently their tasking was as ambiguous as ours; they dropped anchor just outside the minefield and waited. A few days later a Russian cargo ship showed up and joined the flotilla.

The mines we had dropped were magnetically activated; meaning any metal ship coming in proximity of a mine would serve to detonate it. The innovative North Vietnamese soon sent out wooden barges at night to traverse the minefield safely, unload munitions from the cargo ship and return to Hanoi. For a few days we watched as wooden barges would traverse the minefield, load up on munitions and return to Hanoi. The Russian Navy watched our ships, the U.S. Navy watched the Russians and we watched them all from several thousand feet above. We also began tracking them with sonobuoys.

Sonobuoys are ejected from the aircraft and float in the water. Upon impact, a microphone on the end of a wire (Hydrophone) is released. These buoys relay the frequency of the engines on the barges to operators onboard the aircraft. We would make a fast run closer in to the North Vietnamese coast, drop a line of buoys, and beat feet out to monitor them. Get three bearings and you had a fix of the target. This was one of the primary ways we tracked submarines and we found it was quite easy to track the barges. After they loaded their munitions we could track them inside the minefield and direct attack aircraft to sink the barges. So for the next several months that was our new mission. As you might imagine, the North was not as fond of this idea as we were.

This entire mission consisted of several layers of aircraft. The lowest was the P-3, above them were the A-7's and A-6's ('A' meaning attack) and above them were the F-4 Phantoms, 'F' meaning fighter. They were referred to as 'Eagles'. The P-3 relayed the positions of the barges to the attack aircraft, and the fighters covered our butts if the North

Viet's launched Migs our way. Above it all was some sort of AWACS (Airborne Warning and Control System...otherwise known as our, "Eye in the Sky) that kept track of the whole picture. The AWACS was apparently able to detect the Migs when they launched and track them to where they were flying.

On one particular night in this process we were on station doing our thing when we heard the AWACS say, "Migs airborne" which usually got our attention but it was not unusual. However, the next broadcast of the AWACS was much more chilling. "Be advised Mig inbound your position". What he said next was the most chilling, "Be advised, the Eagle is not on the nest." I knew what that meant: 'There is a Mig inbound to you and you have no fighter protection!'

The P-3 was a four engine patrol/ASW aircraft. Max speed was just over 400 knots, or about 460 miles per hour. The Mig 21 could reach 1,381 MPH, so outrunning the Mig was out of the question. However, if we could reach the vicinity of the aircraft carriers before the Mig found us the Navy had no choice but to respond.

So, that's exactly what I did. We had the #1 engine shut down for fuel conservation so I immediately told the flight engineer to *"Re-start #1 NOW!"* I was descending to 200 feet off the water. I had turned away from the coast and proceeded directly towards the carriers; when #1 was started I told the flight engineer, *"Full military power!"* That was one of the few times I ever used military power. We were at 200 feet and reached 300+ knots while I was telling the AWACS to let the carriers know I was inbound at 200 feet with a possible Mig. The Mig's radar was not that good, so I was betting he could not find me that low at night, and he would not take on the carrier battle group. A short time later the AWACS reported the Mig had turned towards North Vietnam. We turned south, climbed up, brought the power back and headed for home.

During the flight back to Cubi I was recalling our briefing: we had been told we would have fighter protection the entire time we were on station. We were directed to stay 200 miles from the carriers. When we got back, the briefing officer started jumping all over my case and I gave him as good as I got. From earlier experience I had resolved that, "Career be damned", I would not stand idly by while the lives of my crew were needlessly put in danger.

About halfway through the deployment my crew got a week off in

Hong Kong. Kathy flew out and we spent the week seeing the sights of the city, eating and sleeping. Flying into Hong Kong is an amazing experience. First, you have to stay out of Communist Chinese airspace which is all around and not all that easy to do. Then you have to navigate the mountains that surround the city on three sides and finally you have to navigate between high-rise apartments as you turn to the final approach to the runway. There were a few clouds and rain, just to make it all the more interesting, but we landed and another crew took the plane back.

The world is full of cities and frankly 90% of them are pretty much all alike, just big cities. Until the people speak it could be most any big city in the world. There are, however, a few exceptions to that generalization and Hong Kong is one of the glaring exceptions. It is a unique and special place. Among the others in that 'special' category are cities like Paris, Rome, New York and San Francisco. Of course, I haven't been to every city, but I have hit quite a few.

The week ended way too soon when a P-3 landed, dropped off their crew and we were the ones taking it back to Cubi Point.

44

OUR FLIGHT ENGINEER and his wife had a constant exchange of somewhat racy letters going back and forth. During our long hours of night flying he would pull out a letter and read it aloud in the cockpit. I'll save you the details, which had a rating somewhere below PG. I will share with you a series of letters that he had toward the end of our deployment. As you recall, our 6 month deployment had been extended until our replacement squadron finally began sending aircraft and crews. When one of theirs landed one of ours could return to Hawaii. As luck would have it, we were notified that our crew would be the last to return.

When our arrival date was established our flight engineer wrote to his wife, *"When we arrive in Hawaii you better have a mattress strapped to your back!"*

She responded with one of the best comeback lines I have ever heard, *"Don't worry about me, you just better be the first one off the plane!"*

My crew arrived back at Barbers Point in November, 1972; my flight engineer & his wife were reunited on the tarmac and all was rated G, or at worse, PG-13.

In early December, I was tasked to take a young man, a terminal cancer patient, to Pago Pago, American Samoa, where a Helo would take him out to the aircraft carrier, USS Ticonderoga, to observe the recovery of Apollo 17. This was well before the "Make a Wish" program, but astronaut Gene Cernan had met the boy and his dying wish was to see an astronaut return. Apollo 17 was the eleventh and last manned

NASA space mission. It was the sixth and final lunar landing and Gene Cernan was, as of this writing, the last man to walk on the moon.

Before leaving home, some friends told me there were three 'must do' things in Pago Pago.

1. Go to the beach.
2. Drink a Mai Tai at the hotel where we were staying and
3. Eat the New Zealand rack-of-lamb.

Well, we arrived in the rain and it rained most of the time we were there, so, no beach. I went to get the Mai Tai and watched the bartender pour it out of a Trader-Vic's Mai Tai mix bottle; kinda lost its charm. Next, we went to get the rack of lamb and were informed there was a shipping strike between Pago Pago and New Zealand; no lamb! Despite these setbacks we had a great time there.

We returned to Barbers Point Hawaii where I spent a few weeks home with Kathy and Ralph, but pretty soon I was off again to the Far East on a 'Special Projects' aircraft. Normally, you deploy for six months and then are "home" for a year and you deploy again. Being 'home' does not mean you can't be sent anywhere the navy feels they need you. Being on a 'Special Projects' crew meant you could go anywhere in the Pacific, Indian Ocean or Middle East on, literally, a moment's notice. Special Project tasking came direct from JCS (Joint Chief of Staff).

When I left the squadron in 1975, I was sworn to secrecy regarding what I could say about these special aircraft and their missions. So, I have done a simple Google search and I will limit my comments to what I found on the internet.

During my time in VP-4 we had two "special" aircraft that were modified electronic surveillance variants of the P-3. Normally, we would fly into a base where another squadron had deployed. We would arrive at night, pull the aircraft into the hanger where our aircraft was painted to appear to be an aircraft from that deployed squadron. The next morning we were off on our mission.

We went into some interesting areas including, but not limited to, the Sea of Okhotsk, off the coast of N. Korea and in the Tonkin Gulf near Hainan. Some of these were PARPRO flights. PARPRO, the *Peacetime Aerial Reconnaissance Program*, covered a variety of airborne missions flown by Navy and Air Force crews near what was termed "*denied territory*." This constituted hostile nations, such as the Soviet

Union, China, and North Korea, among others. While we considered them *"peacetime"* missions, many of the countries we approached did not and it could be dangerous. Several aircraft, including P-3's, had been shot down over the years, some with extensive loss of life. The most recent was the Hainan Incident in 2001. That was a mid-air between a U.S. P-3 and a J-8, a Chinese interceptor aircraft that resulted in the J-8 crashing and the P-3 making a near miraculous landing on the island of Hainan, Peoples Republic of China.

Having had my incident with a Mig, I had no interest in another encounter. I was very specific about completing our missions within the exact parameters we were tasked.

When the Russians would test their long range missiles with shots into the Pacific we were there to collect valuable data. If there were new ships or battle groups in the Pacific we would locate them and take a look, and a listen, and a few other things. It was not unusual for us to have Russian fire control radar locked onto our aircraft. This meant we were a trigger pull away from flying the friendly skies to enjoying a very long swim home.

Once, we were tasked with going to Singapore. While our official manifest said there were 14 crewmen on the aircraft, we ordered 15 box lunches for the flight, and all were eaten. The next day, when we left Singapore there were still 14 on the manifest, and we ordered 14 box lunches. I'm just sayin'…

November 1973, we were off again on what was supposed to be a six month deployment to Naha, Okinawa, and points east. As it turned out, I was virtually gone until January 1975. The squadron returned to Hawaii in June of '74 and I took the 'Project' plane and crew to Misawa, Iwakuni, Korea and a few other places I'm not sure I am at liberty to say.

When I wasn't flying the 'Project' plane, I flew one of our normal P-3's to places like Utapao, Thailand and on down to Diego Garcia. We were the second U.S. crew to land on that British protectorate.

On the way south we crossed the equator and continued on to Diego. It was after midnight and I could tell our young navigator was lost. He was not used to flying without electronic NAVAIDS. He tried to shoot some stars but he got things so screwed up; he plotted us somewhere over Russia. I had the senior TACCO keep a separate chart. Diego Garcia had a AM radio station that went off the air at midnight but they left a 45 rpm record playing all night to assist any aircraft coming inbound. On this particular night, the Seabees left the song *Dead Skunk In the Middle of the Road* by Louden Wainwright III playing over and over. So, while my young navigator was flailing around I was homing into the island via the AM radio station. I kept telling him we were running out of fuel and if he didn't find Diego pretty soon we were going to have to ditch in the middle of the Indian Ocean. Since, he didn't know where we were, we would probably never be found. He was sweating bullets. Finally, I announced to the crew to prepare to ditch and just before we reached the water I announced there was some unknown island out there and I was going to try to ditch there. Of course, we landed on Diego Garcia. For the next few weeks I made him take navigation lessons from our senior tactical coordinator. Every flight for a month I made him shoot stars and sun-lines until he could do it in his sleep. We were saved by the Seabees once; the next time we might not be so fortunate.

On Diego there was a home for the 'Brit Rep', a Lieutenant Commander in the Royal Navy who seemed, perhaps, to have been there a little too long. My crew had to sleep in tents on the beach. If VC-5 Det. Cubi was McHale's Navy, Diego Garcia was Gilligan's Island, without Ginger and Mary Ann; in those days at least. The island is actually a narrow horseshoe shaped atoll, whose only value was that it provided a base for operations within the Indian Ocean. This was 1973, the middle of the Arab oil embargo. There was very little fuel for our Carrier Battle Group in the Indian Ocean and what they had was kept in reserve for any emergency.

Our P-3's, on the other hand, were provided with plenty of fuel since it was our mission to provide ASW protection to the battle group. The only 'friendly country' we had in the area was Iran, which was under the Shaw at the time. He allowed us to fly in and out of Bandar Abbas, Iran, a southern military base in Southern Iran on the coast, adjacent to the Gulf of Hormuz. They also allowed us to purchase fuel. When we first went to Bandar, we lived off the economy until 13 members of our crew came down with dysentery. I was the only one who somehow avoided the sickness, which was a good thing, since I flew the aircraft. While we were on the ground we were allowed to roam around in the town outside the base, but we were followed everywhere by a member of the Shaw's secret police, the SAVAK.

While in a store, I ginned up a conversation with the shop owner who was rather friendly until we told him we were Americans. *"I don't like Americans"* he loudly said! At that moment, the SAVAK agent who was following us, jumped in his face with what I could only surmise were expletives not deleted, and then "suggested" we go back to the base.

My co-pilot was very interested in photography and especially photographing the local people. The locals in Bandar did not like their picture taken and shouted and cursed if you pointed a camera in their direction. So, my co-pilot used a 90 degree lens. This was a lens with a couple mirrors inside that took the picture of something that was 90 degrees left of where you pointed the camera. This worked out well and he got some great pictures but I noticed all the people in his pictures were looking to their left, probably wondering what the heck he was photographing.

Then, and in later years of flying all over the Pacific, Indian Ocean, and Middle East, I drank the water and ate the food and never got sick while the majority of my crew were not so fortunate. After that incident we began hauling water from Diego Garcia and added a few drops of clorox now and them to kill any bacteria.

The next time we were sent to Diego Garcia, Seabees had built Vietnam era raised wooden hooch's with flaps on the side and even window air-conditioners. By then, they even had a make-shift officers club that we stocked and manned ourselves, but were not allowed to open before 5:00 p.m. Occasionally we viewed 16mm movies. Everyone brought paper-backs to the island which made the rounds of all the hooch's. Normally, at a squadron's base, we had a ground job to tend to when we weren't flying. However, on Diego Garcia, in those days, there were few jobs so we spent our crew rest actually resting on the beach or in our hooch sleeping or reading. I would go through at least one large paperback per day. There was a small sailboat but someone had destroyed the sail. The atoll was known to have hammerhead sharks so swimming was limited. Except for the flying, it could have been Gilligan's Island, minus, as I said, Ginger and Mary Ann.

Along with Iran, we flew in & out of Mogadishu (Mog), Somalia, Djibouti and Mozambique, Kenya, showing the flag mostly. Mog was in its annual civil war but the city was relatively tame. The embassy gave us a car and driver but there were few places to go. We did ask the driver to take us to a local restaurant one evening and he headed out of the city and into the desert. Just when we thought things were getting a little too dangerous he stopped at this relic of a building that had a couple picnic tables out front. When we arrive they turned on some lights on a wire hanging between two trees. We sat down to a bottle of the native Somali Beer; I thought it was pretty good. While we were enjoying our beer we heard this bellowing out behind the building. Our driver told us the meal would be fresh kid goat. Soon the bellowing stopped and we realized the goat was going to be *very* fresh. It took almost two hours to prepare the meal and it was quite good. It consisted of roasted goat and couscous with some mixed unrecognizable vegetables. Because of the incidents in Bandar-Abbas about half the crew would not eat but I, along with the other half dug in and enjoyed it.

We spent a couple of nights in Djibouti while we flew missions out over the Indian Ocean in support of the carrier battle groups in that area. Djibouti is a tiny county on the Horn of Africa, bordering Ethiopia and Somalia at the very southern end of The Red Sea, where it meets the Gulf of Aden. A former French colony, the French still maintain a force of the French Foreign Legion in the country. The food is African/Middle Eastern cooked with an obvious French influence. There is very little that is unique about the capital, which has the same name as the country.

Flying out of Diego Garcia we went looking for a Russian Nuclear submarine somewhere just north of the equator. We were directed to track the sub as long as possible so we shut down two engines to conserve fuel. Then we got a fire warning light on one of the remaining two engines. We went to start #4 but it wouldn't start so we started #1 and shut down #2, the one with the fire light. Try as we could, we were stuck with two of four engines shut down and were about 2000 miles from both Utapao, Thailand and Diego Garcia. I knew we had no spare engines in Diego so I made the decision to fly with two engines to Utapao. Upon arrival at Utapao, the Air Force notified me a B-52 had collapsed a landing gear on the runway and it would be several hours before we could land. I explained we were low on fuel, had two engines shut down and requested permission to land on the taxi-way. Air Force taxiways are usually larger than Navy Runways so I didn't see the problem. The duty officer went to wake up the general to find out if we could do that. I was running low on fuel so I told the tower

I was declaring an emergency and was landing on the taxi-way, with or without permission. It was about 3:00 in the morning, I had been flying for about 14 hours, mostly on two engines, and was not in a good mood. Operations had not yet reached its normal frenzied pace so I landed on the taxiway and proceed to the Navy parking area. There was a little uproar from the Air Force but I had no alternatives and my command backed up my decision.

Kathy came to Naha for a few months and we rented a small two bedroom apartment in town with another couple from our squadron. It was a typical small Japanese apartment with the bedrooms being separated by rice paper sliding doors. Not much privacy but our roommate was on a different crew and was usually away when I was home. There were no beds and we slept on a thin mattress on the matted floor. It was comfortable enough and the wives traveled when we were away, which amounted to most of the time.

The tempo of operations was high for our crews and, since I seldom saw Kathy, she returned to Hawaii after about six weeks.

By the time I returned to Hawaii in January, 1975, things had begun to go south on the home front. I can't really blame her. We had been married for three years and the vast majority of that time I was off flying somewhere. But, I thought, I am due a change of duty to a non-deploying job and perhaps that will allow us to reconnect.

45

THE COMMANDING OFFICER of an A-6 and TC-4C squadron, VA-128, invited me to come to his squadron in Whidbey Island, Washington. The TC-4C was a twin-engine turboprop plane derived from an executive transport, which was used by the A-6 Community to train bombardier-navigators for the A-6 Intruder attack aircraft. Based on 'verbal' orders from my detailer, I flew into Whidbey and put a down payment on a house. Six weeks or so later my admin clerk called to say my new orders had arrived.

"VA-128," I asked?

"No Sir, VT-28," he said. I was disappointed at not going to the Northwest but soon it was back to Corpus Christi as a flight instructor in the TS-2A.

The TS-2A was getting old, several generations of Navy Multi-engine pilots had flown the plane to earn their wings but the breakdown rate was staggering. It was unpressurized and *hot* in summer-humid Corpus Christi heat with reflective temperatures reaching 120-130 degrees on the flight line. It was not unusual to return drenched in sweat and 5-10 pounds lighter after a flight.

As flight instructors we quickly learned the axiom, *"student pilots are all trying to kill you and your job is to not let them!"*

The cooler Northwest was a distant memory and I settled in to my new-old squadron and began a Masters Degree program at night school on base. My daily routine would be to arrive at the squadron to brief my students at 5:30 a.m., fly the flight, debrief, do my day job, fly another instructional flight in the afternoon and be in class from 6:00-10:00 p.m.

We still had Ralph and had gotten another Lhasa to keep him company. Kathy had started a nursing school program at the local community college. Saturdays and Sundays found each of us doing papers and studying for exams.

At work, the S-2 was finally being phased out in favor of a new multi-Engine trainer. The Navy actually asked a few of us instructors to fly and offer our opinions about which aircraft we found most suitable for a replacement and several companies sent aircraft to the Naval Air Station for us to review and fly. The choices came down to the North American Sabreliner, Cessna Citation, the Beech 90 and Beech 200. The first two were jets, in line with the then CNO's goal to have an all-jet Navy. The final two were turbo-prop aircraft but all were pressurized, air conditioned and with much greater performance than the venerable TS-2A, the 'S' standing for 'sweatbox'.

In our hearts we all wanted the Citation but knowing the practicality of the Navy and an understanding of the mission we selected the Beech 200. The Navy was even more practical than we anticipated and chose the less expensive Beech 90, which the Navy designated the T-44A Pegasus. It is a twin-engine turbo prop, pressurized version of the Beech King Air 90 manufactured by Beech Aircraft of Wichita, Kansas.

The aircraft was distinguished by an avionics fault insertion system used to simulate in-flight emergencies on the pilot's instruments without affecting the instruments of the instructor pilot in the right-seat. I gave this control system imbedded in the Instructors right arm rest the name, "God Box" since the instructor could play God with the pilot's instruments.

I was one of two pilots selected to go to the Beech factory in Wichita to monitor the construction of the first T-44 and write the initial flight manual for the aircraft.

While in Wichita I made quick friends with the Beech test pilots and was able to weasel my way into flying many of the Beech products as they came off the line. Beech had to put ten hours on each aircraft before they could be delivered to the customer. There were one or two test flights as they came off the production line to work out any bugs and the remainder was just to meet the 10 hour minimum. The Beech test pilots knew all the best airfields in the mid-west with restaurants so we spent a lot of time flying and eating. In total, I flew just about every aircraft in the Beech inventory during that time. I spent my non-flying time writing the initial flight manual for the aircraft.

On April 5, 1977 the Commodore from the Training Air Wing and I delivered the first T-44, number 160842, to Corpus Christi. Over the next few months I would ferry aircraft from Wichita to Corpus. For a very short time, I was the only one qualified to fly the aircraft so any time it was in the air I had to be in it, somewhat akin to my Bugsmasher days. It didn't take long though before I checked out several more pilots as instructors and we were on our way to a full transition to the new aircraft. My last flight in the TS-2 was April 29th, 1977. I remained in the squadron flying the T-44 until February, 1978.

During this time Kathy graduated from nursing school and announced she was leaving and returning to California. It was no surprise but I felt a sense of failure. Even then I knew it was much my doing, not intentionally, but the demands of a reluctant navy wife caught up in the swirl of long deployments, constant high tempo operations and numerous professional decisions, at the expense of personal ones, had undoubtedly taken its toll. I had watched many of my friends getting divorced or leaving the Navy for just this very reason.

Shortly after we met she indicated she wanted kids and I was clear that I certainly did. All I can say is, she was looking and I was looking and we found each other at the right time, or so it seemed. We jumped into marriage with all four feet and to be honest, we both worked very hard to make it work. It was just not meant to be.

Please don't get me wrong, there were many positives about being married to Kathy. I think we did love each other and while love conquers all for awhile, even it has its limitations and we stretched those limits as far as they would go. We never really quarreled; at least, I can't remember any. I learned a lot from Kathy, about myself, relationships, what love is and what it isn't. I was happy when we married, sad when it ended and I suspect we are better both people for the experience, I know I am. From that perspective it was time well spent.

— 46 —

Towards the end of my tour in Corpus Christi, Texas I contacted my detailer to let him know that I had made the decision to get out of the Navy. To my surprise, he asked what it would take to change my mind and I said I didn't want to get into that type of negotiating so I said, *"Nothing."* He then offered me to be in Command of a Navy Facility (NAVFAC) on Grand Turk Island in the Bahamas. I was floored! It was the chance of a lifetime and after a very few days of thought I accepted. *"What the heck,"* I thought, *"two years in the Bahamas and then I can get out."*

Kathy and I sold the house and made our split. She took her Lhasa and I got custody of Ralph. I told her to get a lawyer and whatever they worked out was OK by me. She left for California leaving instructions for her lawyer who called me when all was ready and I went before the judge and agreed to what they had proposed. The judge asked me if I was positive I didn't want legal counsel and I replied, *"Yes, I'm positive. No I don't."*

To this day I have never looked at the details of the action; I just wrote the amount of the check the lawyer said I owed and that was that. I had no animosity toward her, still don't. After all, marriages are like vaccinations, some take and some don't.

About a week or two before I was to leave for the Bahamas I received a call from my detailer; it had happened again. It seems there was a murder of a civilian by one of the sailors on Grand Turk Island and the Commanding Officer had botched the whole thing causing an international incident between the Brits who run the Island and the

U.S. Navy. All this ended up in the lap of the U.S. State Department. I had just been selected for Lieutenant Commander and at the time Adm. Isaac Kidd, Jr. was Commander-in-Chief of the Atlantic Fleet, on whose desk the Grand Turk mess had been dropped. The Admiral made the decision that he did not want such a junior Lieutenant Commander in that job and assigned his own man to the island. I was severely disappointed but I understood.

I asked my detailer if they still had my papers to get out and he said they had been withdrawn. He then said he had an opening in the PEP Program, the Personal Exchange Program, flying P-3's with the Australians. The only catch was I would have to stay in Corpus for a couple months.

We had sold our house, Kathy had moved to California so I bought a motor home to live in until my number came up. Then came another call from my detailer, *"I have some good news and some bad news,"* he told me. *"The Australian thing is not going to work out, but,"* he blurted out so fast before I could respond, *"I still have you in the PEP program only with the Dutch Navy in the Netherlands."* He explained I would have to go to six months of language training at the Defense Language Institute (DLI) in Monterrey, California.

"Call me in a few days and let me know if you want the posting."

I had been to Monterrey, California when I was stationed at Moffett Field so that wasn't a problem. I searched out all I could about The Netherlands and concluded I would like to do it. I called him back a couple days later and let him know I would like the job. I unplugged my motor-home, loaded up Ralph and headed off to California.

My instructor at DLI was Indonesian who grew up in his home country while the Dutch maintained their colonial power over the country which began in 1602 and lasted until WW-II, and then from the end of the war until 1949. His family was involved in the Indonesian government and they moved to The Netherlands after the colonial days ended. He then migrated to the USA and ended up in California.

There were two other families in my language class, a NFO, (Naval Flight Officer) and a SWO, Surface Warfare Officer, both of whom were going to the Netherlands as well, along with their wives.

I have to tell you, learning Dutch, especially at the ripe old age of 34, was challenging. The school brought all of the senior officers into a large auditorium the first week we were there and announced that we should expect to have much more difficulty with learning a language than the younger teenagers or the early 20's crowd. They explained it was a brain thing, not a personal flaw. It seems previous classes had senior officers who were used to excelling at everything and became frustrated when they struggled while the younger class members seemed to catch on right away.

I discovered there was some truth to this. I did well in the class but I had to work twice as hard and long as some of the younger ones. Actually, I didn't mind. I was single and motivated; the thought of living three years in Europe was exciting.

After about three months of a six month course I was notified that the Dutch wanted me three months early. I was still required to take the final exam in the class which was a test that measured one's ability to speak and read the language. The highest grade was a 4.0 which meant you spoke and understood like a native. I knew that wasn't going to happen after only three months, but I was prepared as best I could and got a 3.0 which was very high level for a non-native speaker. (When I returned from The Netherlands three years later I retook the test and got a 4.0)

I sold my RV, said goodbye to my classmates and was off to The Netherlands, arriving on a Saturday. On Monday, there I was in a classroom with a Dutch Navy instructor teaching me about the various aircraft systems of the French built Breguet Atlantic maritime patrol aircraft. I was totally and completely lost; so much for my three months of Dutch language school.

UPON ARRIVING IN Holland, I could buy cheese, a beer and get a haircut in the native language. Well, a little more than that, but I did not know the intricacies of the language enough to understand the aviation technical terms associated with the aircraft. I would feverishly take notes all day and in the evenings I would try to translate what was said. The instructor was a sergeant from a rural area in the south of the country and I think he used every colloquial word and phrase in the entire language, or so it seemed.

What I realized, but never considered before, was that instructors instruct awhile, then they just add some filler, even tell jokes. Native speakers understood this immediately and let their brains relax since this was informal chatting which would not appear on any test. After this interlude, which could last for several minutes, the instructor would continue into the meat of the lesson.

I was lost in those transitions. By the time I figured out he was telling a joke, he had told it and was moving back into the meat of the subject. Being a newbie to the language, I could not distinguish when those pauses and transitions began and ended and the instructional material was again being addressed. My mind never rested.

You cannot imagine the tension this created on the brain and the body, especially when I spent hours trying to translate words and phrases which were totally colloquial and did not exist in any dictionary or phrase book.

One of my best instructors was in meteorology, which included weather, storm recognition and their effects on flying. I knew most of the stuff in English but was having a difficult time converting that knowledge to Dutch. That instructor spoke the *'Queens English'* impeccably, and realized I knew the material, but struggled with expressing that knowledge in Dutch. He spent the entire time we had together showing me how to verbalize what I knew. He had the patience of Job and taught me more about verbal expression in the language than anyone had, up to that time.

Somehow, I made it through ground school and began flying. While flying, communication outside the aircraft was, as it is throughout the world, in English. Whereas, all communication inside the aircraft was in Dutch. It took awhile for me to reach the level of quickly transitioning from Dutch-to-English and back again without getting lost along the way. The discomfort with the language translated to my flying skill since I was not sure what my instructor had in mind. He would direct me to fly a particular pattern, in Dutch, and I would begin doing it wrong as my mind kept translating instead of comprehending.

The first level of language comprehension is to translate everything into your first language. The goal of any student is to be able to comprehend and respond in the new language without going into your native language along the way. That takes time and constant practice. It wasn't long until I could easily go back and forth rather quickly without getting lost, and I didn't look like such a dunce in the air. The entire experience gave me a new appreciation for instructing foreign students and an understanding of their difficulties in a strange language.

I did graduate from aviation training; I was even awarded a set of Dutch pilot wings, and was assigned to a crew as co-pilot, until I was more comfortable with the language. Most of my Dutch counterparts did not know I had missed half the language class and I made no excuses. I just focused on learning the language on my own as best I could.

The Netherlands is such a small country that almost all Dutch speak English and can understand German, which has a similar syntax. When I would struggle in Dutch they would just say, "Forget it, we'll speak English."

Well, that is not what I wanted or needed so I would continue in Dutch while they would be speaking English. Despite my early difficulties, within a year I had caught up and by the time I left, I was speaking like a native. I was even dreaming in Dutch.

I had left Ralph with Kathy and she shipped him on to me from San Francisco to Amsterdam. I made friends with a young neighbor and arranged to have her come over and take care of Ralph when I was gone, which, as it turned out, was quite a bit of the time.

While in the Dutch Navy, I flew to Iceland, Scotland, England, Germany, France, Gibraltar, Belgium, Denmark and Italy, some for extended periods, at least a week to each country; on several occasions even longer. As in my first squadron I made it known that if anyone did not want to go somewhere, I was available to take their place.

Since the aircraft was French built, all of our simulator flying was done in Lorient or Nimes, France. Lorient is on the Atlantic coast while Nimes is on the Mediterranean.

Everything you ever heard about French food is true. You could put some of their sauces on your shoe and it would be terrific. In my experience, everything you have heard about the French people is false. I found them gracious and hospitable and that includes Paris. In all the time I was there, I never had a bad experience.

The Dutch Navy has a union, which is not like our unions. They are actually advocates for those in the Navy and try to accommodate the duties of the Navy and the defense of the country, while keeping in mind families and individual needs. In many ways, the U.S. Navy could learn a lot from them. They had "compensation-days," which were days off for members who were taken away from families which also applied to us who were single. As a result, I would find myself with many compensation days and all of Europe at my door. I kept a perpetual Euro-Rail pass and Ralph and I traveled extensively, staying at hostels whenever possible. It wasn't so much a money saving thing, I just enjoyed the people there. We were a sight, me with my back-pack and jeans and this white dog. People seemed to trust you more if you had a dog; not too many serial killers on a train with a fuzzy dog.

I heard about the largest Fourth of July celebration outside the United States which, since 1912, was held in Aalborg, Denmark. So Ralph and I made our way up there and arrived on July third. It seems a Danish-American by the name of Max Henius immigrated to America in the late 1800's and became quite wealthy. He was interested in Danish-American relations and helped raise money to purchase 200 acres of heather-covered hills in central Jutland which he called Rebild. He deeded the land as a Danish national park with the understanding that once a year, on July 4th, they would have an American Independence Day and celebrate Danish-American friendship. And so it has been every July 4th, except during the two world wars.

As I said, we arrived on July third and I found a spot in the park next to the zoo where I planned to spend the night. As I was setting up that evening, the zoo keeper came over and told me the police would come by and chase me out of the park. I explained I was in the US military and was there for the celebration the next day. He had been a young boy when the Americans liberated his hometown from the Germans in WWII. He invited me to spend the night in the zoo instead of the park, "The police won't bother you in here," he said. Ralph and I spent the night in the Aalborg Zoo next to the monkeys, who made a fuss when we first arrived, but soon ignored us when they realized we weren't going away.

The next morning the zoo-keeper showed up with a thermos of coffee, some great Danish bread and cheese, a typical Danish breakfast. We shared breakfast with Ralph and he let us back into the park for the celebration. Ten to fifteen thousand people gathered in the park on July 4th and there were almost as many US flags as Danish. Late at night there was a fireworks display. However, being that far north it does not get all that dark at night, no one seemed to mind. The Queen of Denmark showed up; I didn't meet her but I did see her from a distance.

I suppose I could write a travel-log about all my experiences traveling in Europe; Climbing Mt. Vesuvius just east of Naples, Italy or Mt. Etna on Sicily, to meeting queens, princes and princesses, and even one king.

I found myself in Edinburgh, Scotland on a trip with the Dutch Navy and noted all this commotion down by Edinburgh Castle in the middle of the town. There was a line that everyone was jostling to get into. I joined in the jostling as well, though I had no idea what it was for.

It seems the Queen of England and the Duke of Edinburgh, her husband, visits the city each summer and greet the townspeople at least once during their two-week visit. There I was, in line to meet the Queen, which I did. It went so fast I doubt she noticed I was a foreign interloper.

I happened to be in Holland on April 30, 1980, when Queen

Juliana abdicated in favor of her daughter, Beatrix. I was invited by the military attaché at the U.S. embassy in The Hague to view the queen as she rode past in her carriage for her Investiture. Dutch royalty is not crowned, but there is a ceremonial transfer as one abdicates and the other assumes the position.

While on one of my treks with Ralph I met a Dutch girl by the name of Elly. We had a nice visit, half in Dutch, half in English; I spoke Dutch and she spoke English, a common problem for me. When the train arrived in the station at Leiden, I suggested we meet sometime for coffee. She hesitated a moment, looked at me and said, *"Just coffee."*

I replied, *"Just coffee."*

That was the beginning of a great friendship that would last the remainder of my time in Holland.

Elly knew I was determined to learn to speak Dutch like a native and we began meeting to practice the language. Knowing her was a giant leap for me in learning the intricacies of Dutch and my language skills improved exponentially over the next couple months. She was like having my own private language instructor. She was somewhat of a teacher to begin with, working with children with special needs.

Learning a language is like being a child all over again. In fact, she suggested I watch the Dutch version of Sesame Street, which actually was a big help. Every language has its own idioms and subtle phrases which you seldom learn in a class or from a textbook. The final step in learning a language is in understanding its humor.

There was this Dutch version of 'Larry the Cable Guy' whose humor was so subtle that you needed to be a native to understand it. I was determined that, by the time I left the Netherlands, I would be laughing at his rural humor, and I did.

When referring to the country you often hear 'The Netherlands', 'Holland' or 'Dutch'. Officially, it is called The Kingdom of the Netherlands. While sometimes referred to as Holland, in reality, two of the county's twelve provinces are North Holland and South Holland. Only foreigners call the country Holland. The word 'Dutch' refers to the people, the language or anything in the country such as Dutch cheese, Dutch shoes, etc.

The Dutch Empire grew to become one of the major seafaring and economic powers of the 17th century. In 1650, the Dutch owned

16,000 merchant ships. It was their Golden Age (*"Gouden Eeuw"*) with colonies and trading posts all over the world.

Dutch settlements in North America began with the founding of New Amsterdam on the southern tip of Manhattan Island in 1614. It was later changed to New York when the English influence became the dominate force. The Dutch were known for their fine cheeses and a term for a rural Dutch farmer was 'Jan Kaas,' literally, 'John Cheese', but pronounced, 'Yan Kaas'. When the English began to dominate Manhattan, they conferred upon, what they considered the less sophisticated Dutch, the name 'Yankaas' which later evolved to 'Yan-kees', and eventually became the name, the New York Yankees.

In addition to helping with the language, Elly traveled with me to some interesting places. One such excursion was taking the night train from Holland to Italy and then boarding a ship to Egypt. The ship made the trip weekly, which meant you could get off anywhere along the way, wait a week, and catch a ride back to Italy the next time around. We made stops in Crete and Greece where we could spend the day roaming around and then boarded the ship again in the evening. We arrived in Alexandria, Egypt and, from there, took a bus to Cairo/Giza. We returned to Alexandria five days later, spent two days looking around Alexandria and eventually returned to Italy on the reverse route we came in on. In Giza, we spent many hours roaming around, in and through the pyramids of Egypt as well as the Cairo Museum. We went hiking through the desert and were amazed that one could find artifacts just lying around in the sand of the desert. In a way, it was like the jungles of Cambodia, with no trees and lots of sand. Of course, it was against the Egyptian antiquities laws to disturb these artifacts. Still, one had to wonder how long they had been there and what their original purpose had been.

— 48 —

ONE OF MY duties while living, working and flying with the Dutch was SAR, *Search and Rescue*. We had a fixed-wing aircraft, the SP-13A *Atlantic* ready to launch within 30 minutes if the National "Reddings Dienst" (Emergency Service) were to tell us to launch. The *"Atlantic"* was their version of the P-3 Orion.

One thing I learned is that ships and seamen seldom, almost never, get into trouble in good weather. In fact, there seems to be an inverse-relationship there, the better the weather the less likely we would get launched. The more ice, snow, and darkness, the more likely we would be called to action. In a perverse way, I actually enjoyed flying in bad weather. It wasn't boring, it was a serious challenge, it kept you on your toes, and it meant we were actually helping someone. Besides, sitting on the base for 24 hours was boring to the Nth degree.

Our job was mostly to locate the stricken vessel and direct surface ships to help or to direct helos from the coast to the site. Occasionally, we would drop inflatable survival boats and emergency radios and other gear to the stricken sailors. We would remain above the action for hours relaying information and directing traffic. We would stay until the last survivor got aboard a ship or helo.

Occasionally, that left us searching for survivors that were not located, and we would continue searching until they were found, or we became low on fuel. We did not like leaving people in the water, but the survival time of someone in the North Sea in winter was severely limited, even with survival suits. The cold temperatures reduced their conscious time in the water to mere minutes. While we did everything possible, and the entire crew was vigilant in searching the ocean for survivors, on occasion we had to leave without finding everyone. Even if we helped rescue 20 of 21 we were not satisfied and the flight home was quiet and pensive. But the reality is, the sea can be a fickle lady, and will grudgingly return a stricken sailor and, at times, none at all.

~~~~~

The average career of a Navy pilot is to go through training, go to a ground job, back to flying and repeat the sequence for 20 or so years. My first squadron, VC-5, was a throw-away time so they sent me to a P-3 squadron as my second tour. My third was flying in the training squadron in Corpus and my fourth was flying with the Dutch. By now I was due for my second VP tour and a department head job with VP-46 at Moffett Field, California. I had been in the Navy for almost 14 years and had flown in every duty station, very unusual for a Navy career. But, first, I had to go through the replacement squadron (the RAG), VP-31, for a couple months.

When I finally joined the squadron, VP-46, we were working up for a six month deployment to Misawa, Japan. I bought a house in San José and fought the terrible California traffic for several months until it came time to head to the Far East. Shortly before we left, I was scheduled to fly an anti-submarine mission against a Russian sub several hundred miles off the California coast.

While we were in the midst of our pre-flight, an announcement came that there was a random drug test going on. I was excused from the test since we were going to fly but, in an effort to demonstrate to my men that I took these things seriously, I got in line to pee in the bottle. I flew off into the sunset and returned about 10 hours later with the mission very successfully accomplished. The next day I got a call to report to the Commanding Officer's office. I walked in and there were the CO, the XO and our legal officer.

I think I cracked a joke, but no one was laughing, as the CO began reading a legal complaint to me, that I had tested positive for something on the random drug test, that I was grounded from flying, and relieved of all duties until a court-martial could be convened.

I stood there in stunned silence. This was some sort of joke or a legal practice-session prior to deployment. The CO handed me a pen and paper which reiterated what he had just told me, and I was to sign it to acknowledge that I had been so informed. *"This is not an admission of guilt, just a confirmation that I had explained the charges and given you your rights,"* the CO said.

"You do know this is some sort of mistake," I stammered out.

His response was cold and to the point, "We are not here to discuss this, just sign the paper," he said. I read it again and signed it as directed. *"Dismissed,"* was all he said. I started to plead my case but as I looked at them I realized they would have none of it.

I returned to my office, gathered up my things and sat there contemplating my options. I was in my 14th year in the Navy. Yes, I knew about drugs in the Navy but I had never, *ever,* so much as taken a puff on a weed, let alone used drugs. I reflected on the past 14 years. I had given my heart, soul and blood to the Navy. It had cost me a busted marriage and many lost relationships and it all came down to this?

Let me be clear, there was not even an ounce of truth to those accusations. I was 37 years old, it wasn't 'till after 50 years of age that I took my first aspirin. I had probably been drunk one time and that was just to see how it felt. I didn't like it and never approached that again. Our squadron, VP-46, was known as *The Grey Knights* but I was so squeaky clean they all called me *"The White Knight."*

As I pondered all these things in my office I became somewhat angry, despondent and disappointed that the Navy could be so callous. I decided to go the base hospital and speak with our flight surgeon, a doctor who knew me well and someone whom I considered a friend.

Fortunately, he was not too busy, and sat down with me as I explained what had occurred. He just looked at me with the same incredulous look that I had. I asked if I could take another blood test or maybe a lie detector test.

After my ranting he told me, *"Larry, I might believe this of most any other officer in your squadron, but not you."* He promised he would look into it, consider my options, and get back to me. I thanked him, left, and drove home.

It was not often I would walk into my house in the middle of the day. Ralph was pleased to see me, he always was. I took him for a walk as I continuously relived the events of the day. I thought about my 14+ years in the Navy and considered the possibility it was all for naught and that perhaps, in all likelihood, it was all over. I considered the coldness of the CO and XO as they sat in their leather chairs with their steely glares, as if I had stolen their last piece of bread. I knew they had a job to do, procedures to follow; there were rules, regulations. But still, I considered their robot stares. There was a hint of perverse enjoyment, like they had caught the mouse with the cheese, and they were going to play with him awhile before they did him in. There was no hint that it could be a mistake, not even a "Did you do it?" There was just a villainous superior judgment like, *got-ya!*

I didn't sleep much for the next two nights. I didn't drink or take drugs but if I did this would be the time to do it. I did not go back to work. I reasoned that if they wanted me they would call. I imagined what it said about me not being there, but those steely looks convinced me they had made their judgments, I was guilty, and that was that.

The morning of the third day I received a call from the squadron duty officer informing me the CO wanted me in his office as soon as I could get there. I put my uniform on and drove to work. I knocked on the CO's door.

"Enter," he said. In the same chairs as three days before sat the CO, XO and the legal officer. I had no idea what to expect but was prepared for the worse.

The CO, still in his steely unemotional tone held up the papers I had signed three days earlier. *"All the charges have been dropped,"* he told me. *"These are the papers that charged you and the one you signed, acknowledging you had seen them."* He tore the papers up in front of me into little pieces. *"The issue is dropped, dismissed!"*

I stood there, just as stunned as three days earlier. He saw I was not leaving and said, *"The issue will never be spoken of again, dismissed."*

But I had questions, many questions. What had happened and why? I deserved some answers. Was I still under a cloud of suspicion? Did they think me guilty but had insufficient evidence? I was as confused with the resolution as I was with the accusation.

"Dismissed Commander!" the CO said with an unequivocal undertone of, *'This meeting is over!'*

I thought about saluting and saying, "Aye, aye, Sir." But that would have been a sign of respect and the fact was, over the last three days I had little left for the man. I did an about-face and left the room.

"Things happen for a reason!" That principle had guided me for years and I attempted to understand the reason behind these hellish three days. I was as angry at being accused with no explanation as I was with how the issue had been dropped, with no explanation.

You just cannot treat people like that. Well, evidently you can. If it were a mistake, just be a man and admit it, and at least express some acknowledgement about how I must have felt. If it were dropped for lack of evidence, say so and promise to get me next time. But nothing is, well, nothing.

The next several weeks were the most difficult. I wondered who knew, and what they knew. Things like that did not stay quiet within the confines of a unit in the Navy. What were they saying behind my back? That the Lt. Commander walked because he was an officer, or worse, because they knew I was guilty and couldn't prove it? How do you disprove an accusation that technically does not exist? I fully expected to be "randomly" drug tested on a regular basis but I was never tested again in the remaining time I was in the squadron. Sometime later, I received my annual fitness report and it was excellent. Not the signal they would send if they suspected something nefarious was going on.

Oh, BTW, sometime later, I heard someone had paid the corpsman to switch urine samples.

What this experience did, and perhaps this was the 'reason' I sought to understand, was to make me more aware about me as a person and less about me as a Naval Officer. In any career, there are many times when one must make a decision and there is consideration of the personal side or the professional aspects of that decision. More often than not, they are at odds, and I noted that almost always in the past I would decide by what was better for me professionally, rather than what was best personally. I put my career and the Navy ahead of my personal life and it had cost me dearly and often. I had to bring more balance into my life. Again, I made a huge "Course Correction," and have never looked back.

I thought about a girl I had recently dated, a divorcee of a doctor, who told me she had left her last husband because she never saw him and pointed out how she saw me even less than him.

It was Christmas Eve, she invited me over to meet her parents and spend Christmas Day with them. I was not scheduled to fly, just go into the squadron, wrap-up some reports and go home. As I was about to leave, the XO yelled at me to grab my gear. The pilot assigned to fly had a car accident, and the plane would take-off within the hour. I called the lady and explained that I had to fly that night but would be back in time to meet her on Christmas Day.

We took off on the all-nighter, deep into the Pacific, flew the mission and were about to head home when we received a message to proceed to Barbers Point, Hawaii. We landed there, slept for a few hours and were tasked to fly on another Russian sub east of Hawaii on Christmas night. I called the lady, fell on my sword again, and promised we would meet up for New Years Eve. We stayed in Hawaii for several consecutive days, flying out of Barbers Point and were scheduled to fly one more flight and return to California the afternoon of December 31. It looked like we were going to make it back in time for all of us to enjoy New Years Eve.

We finished our mission and began the flight back to Barbers Point when we got another message to proceed to Midway Island. No reason was given, just go to Midway. The crew had all gone to sleep, with the exception of the cockpit, the navigator and the radioman. I told them not to awaken anyone as we headed farther east to Midway.

As we began our approach, everyone was awakened to prepare for landing. We rolled out on the runway and proceeded to a spot in front of the tower. The ladder went down and our ordnance man came running to the cockpit. *"Sir, this is not Barbers Point; I think we landed at the wrong airfield,"* he exclaimed.

I said, *"Really, are you sure…the navigator told me this was Barbers Point!"*

He went and looked again and came back to the cockpit, *"Sir, it says Midway on the tower."*

"Tell the navigator I want to see him right away."

As I suspected, it was a med-evac situation. It seems a Navy Chief Petty Officer had nearly severed a hand and the only chance to save it was to get him to a modern hospital ASAP. The chief was stabilized on the aircraft as we re-fuelled for the flight to Barbers Point, where a helo would meet us to transfer him to Tripler Army Hospital. Though we were pushing the hours we were supposed to fly, I made the decision to take-off immediately and head back to Barbers Point, 1500 miles to the east, about a five hour flight. All went well, but I never heard if the chief was able to keep his hand. After crew-rest at Barbers we finally made it back to California on January 2. That's when my lady friend and I decided to go our separate ways. Well, she decided and I agreed.

~~~~~

We deployed for six months to Misawa, Japan. Shortly after arriving, I was notified that I had been selected for promotion to Commander, the only one in the squadron to be so selected. I did my job and flew as much as possible, not so much to impress anyone but because I truly enjoyed flying and I was good at it. My crew was number one in the squadron on any mission. That is more a recognition of each individual crewmember than of me, and there is no false modesty there. We achieved the best score in a mining exercise, ASW (Anti-submarine warfare) and in relocating ships of interest.

There was one particular Russian ship, the Nevelskoy, a spy ship in the Pacific, which the Joint Chiefs wanted located on a daily basis. The trouble was, the only crew that could find the ship was mine. We would locate the ship on one day and the next two days, two other aircraft would return empty-handed and then I would find it again, That happened repeatedly until the Commodore realized that the same crew would always find the ship. Finally, he asked me how I did it.

"It's the Nevels-koy," I joked, *"I just call my cousins and home-in on the signal they send out."* He had never made the connection of the names and always looked at me with a certain suspicion after that.

Our final major mission on that deployment was providing ASW support for two Carrier Battle Groups operating off the coast of North Korea. It was billed as a 'show the flag' exercise but with two carriers, dozens of ships, submarines and our ASW aircraft, there was little chance even the North Koreans would do something stupid. They had picked on us in the past, but only when the odds were greatly in their favor. Our mission was to fly on a line no closer than 12 miles from the coast and monitor the waters for any Korean submarines. I had briefed the navigator, the Tactical Coordinator and the radar operator to independently ensure we did not break the 12 mile line.

We were under the control of the command ship, who kept directing us on headings that would have taken us inside the 12 mile line. I assume they were upset the Koreans had not activated their Radar which would have given us "SIGINT," signals intelligence, about their capabilities. But, I wasn't about to sacrifice my crew. As I approached the 12 mile mark I would turn away, much to the consternation of my controller. He kept telling me he would keep me out of the danger zone, but I had a positive radar fix on a piece of land and refused to get any closer. In another time, I might have taken the chance, but I was briefed to stay outside of 12 miles and we stayed out. At our debrief, I had all my navigation and radar records in case I was challenged but nothing was said.

We made one final foray into the Indian Ocean for several weeks before our deployment ended. We again went to Diego Garcia where they had built large BOQ's, a Navy Exchange, new runways to accommodate the Air Force and all the trimmings. Our little Gilligan's Island had gone main-stream. I was the OinC (Officer in Charge) of the Detachment, so casually reading on the beach was severely limited.

We returned to Mogadishu, Somalia and spent several days in Muscat, the capital of Oman. It was late June, if not the hottest time of year I would hate to see it hotter. It was 130+ degrees on the tarmac. We stayed in a posh Hilton Hotel with a pool, but the water was too hot to swim. I swear, you could have boiled potatoes in there, and that's not a navy sea-story. When we left for a mission, it was not possible to calculate our take-off distance since, when you factored the heat, it went off the charts. We extrapolated a number and needed every inch of the runway to get off. We circled overhead to get to altitude and then went on our way.

On our way home we spent the night in Singapore. The entire crew and passengers spent the night in the same hotel. Shortly after we all went to our rooms, I had a knock on the door. It was two members of my crew who told me, *"Commander, there is a dead body under our bed!"* Thinking there must be a mistake or a joke, I went to their room and, sure enough, there was this dead guy under the bed. We called the front desk and they said they knew about it, but the people they called to remove the body could not come until the next day. They just could not understand our incredulous response that it was unsatisfactory, and after quite a bit of heated discussion, they moved our crewmembers to another room.

A short time later we took two aircraft to Korea and stayed in a hotel in town. At the time Korean hotels were heated with heat coming up the walls. They were notorious for having carbon dioxide leak into the rooms, and I always briefed my crews that, no matter how cold it got, always leave a window open. Two members of the other crew did not heed the warning and died of carbon dioxide poisoning.

I spent a lot of time all over the Pacific, hitting almost all free world countries. One was the Island(s) of Rarotonga, who were conducting a 10-day celebration of their constitution and had invited some U.S. participation. The State Department tasked the Defense Department, who tasked the Navy Department, who tasked CincPacFlt, who tasked our Air Wing Commander, who tasked our squadron, who chose my crew to represent the US at this event. We were treated like royalty, even offered the daughters of the King; which I respectfully declined.

I volunteered for any flight and my crew agreed.

I was a Commander and soon I was on the phone with my detailer. He started reading some places that were available for Commanders and I stopped him when he said, 'Nuclear Department, Headquarters, Allied Powers Northern European Command, Oslo, Norway'. I told him I was interested and he hesitated a bit by saying, *"Are you positive? I'm not sure how much of a career-enhancing billet this might be."*

After my experience with the drug charges, I had had my fill of *'career-enhancing jobs'* and told him, "I am positive!" Having had several bad experiences of promised orders that turned out differently, I told no one until my orders actually arrived. The more I thought about it, the more pleased I was with my decision. Three years in Scandinavia on top of three years in The Netherlands would be a fitting end to my Naval Career. I had been in the Navy for 15 years, so three years in Scandinavia and then one last job and I could retire.

I hated to leave the P-3, which by now was a close friend. Plus, I had one of the best crews in the Pacific, which made the missions more fun than work. I had told them all, *"You take care of me and I will take care of you!"* They did, and I did. When they needed strong evaluations for promotion, I gave them the best I could write; when they got in trouble I was there to defend them, I respected each of them and I think they respected me. I had achieved all the designations one could get in the aircraft, test pilot, instructor pilot, evaluator, mission commander, etc.

I had given the Navy a pound of flesh every day for 15 years and I would do the same for the next five, but it was going to be more on my terms. I had come across "short-timers", who we referred to as "retired-active-duty." They were those that still collected the pay-check but acted as if they were already retired. I was determined to never become one of those. Besides, it's much better to retire having people say, "Why are retiring?" Rather than staying on past your time and people saying, "Sure wish he would retire."

49

I HAD BEEN attending this church in the area of San Jose, California, and had met a lady a couple years younger. We went out a few times and I could see she was troubled. She had two of the sweetest young children and they really wanted a dad. A month or so before I went to Japan, while I was on one of my extended tours of the Pacific, she wrote me that she had hooked-up with someone else. She wrote glowing words about the guy and I acknowledged that she had done the right thing and I wished them the best.

My world was crazy and they needed something I could not offer at that time, stability. By the time I got back we had not exchanged letters for about five months so I didn't contact her.

About a week or two after I returned, I received a phone call from a mutual friend who said she had gone to the beach alone one night and just walk into the sea. Her body was found a few days later farther down the coast from where her parked car had been found. She had left a note for her kids.

I can't describe how that event affected me, devastated me, actually. I could not even imagine the pain she must have felt to do such a thing with her two children at home. I know she loved those kids so much. Friends told me she been on a progressive down-hill slid but the last month or so appeared to be happy, content and on the right track. I had been gone for well over six months and we discontinued our very short courtship a couple months before I left for Japan. That's when I fully understood the words, *"The pain of living exceeds the pain of dying."*

I reflected on my own encounter at the end of that fuel pier many years earlier. I wondered if she had an "out" and chose not to take it.

A few weeks later, I was serving as the Squadron Casualty Assistance Calls Officer-(CACO). One of our flight engineers was diagnosed with cancer and died almost immediately, within the week I think. As the squadron CACO, it was my duty to guide the widow through the entire process and making the arrangements for the memorial service, the cremation, all the details. I even wrote the eulogy for our Commanding Officer to read at the service. A week later, I had to deliver the ashes to the widow.

To have those two events occur back-to-back was very disconcerting for me. I just kept reminding myself, "as difficult as it is for you, think of how difficult it must be for the children and the widows". It was my intention to be the best CACO the Navy had ever seen.

~~~

When it was time to leave for Norway, I decided to keep my house and rent it out. I couldn't take Ralph to Norway, since he would have to go through another six months in quarantine, for the same reason as Hawaii. He was getting up in years and as much as I loved having him around, I just could not bring myself to do that to him again. Kathy agreed to take him which was the best fit. Kathy and I maintained a nice friendship but it was clearly over between us.

At church, before I left, I met a lady who explained that she was moving to Stockton, California. She gave me her address on a card which I put it in my wallet and we wished each other well.

In February, 1983 I said goodbye to VP-47 and, after a short visit to Texas to see how Mrs. Fenner was doing, I was off to Norway.

As we rolled out on our landing at Oslo, the stewardess came on the intercom and announced, *"Welcome to Oslo, please set your watches back 20 years."*

Judy, a Navy Lieutenant Commander, was my sponsor and had arranged for me to stay in the only hotel still open in Oslo. I thought I had landed in a Twilight Zone movie; the city was a ghost town. It seems that every Easter-week everyone, and I mean everyone, goes up to the mountains to stay in their huts or with relatives and they ski.

I settled into the Nuclear Division at the NATO headquarters, found a house to rent, and began talking with everyone about the number one pass-time in Norway, cross country skiing. Everyone in my office was into cross country in the winter and tennis or handball in the summer.

I arrived in March so I saw daylight most of the time. Oslo is about 53 degrees north latitude, a little farther south than Anchorage, Alaska, but not much. There are about 18-20 hours of light in Oslo in the summer and the same amount of darkness in the winter. I enjoyed the light and prepared for the long nights to come; *"going into the tunnel"* was the way the Norwegians described their winters.

Norway is the biggest gymnasium in the world. In the summer, it consists of endless outdoor sports such as hiking, sailing, windsurfing, sunbathing (with or without cloths) beach volleyball, and on and on. In the winter, there are all the snow sports. Even though it's dark they provide lighted and groomed cross-country ski trails all over Oslo and in many of the smaller communities.

Kolsås, just outside Oslo, was our headquarters. The Norwegians had dug deep into this mountain to construct a nuclear-proof headquarters for AFNORTH (Allied Forces, Northern European Command). From the entrance of the mountain to the actual headquarters was a little over a quarter of a mile. Inside, there were multiple giant blast doors and chemical weapon wash facilities. The entire headquarters building was built on giant springs to allow 'give' in the event of a nuclear attack. This underground headquarters served as our command post during major exercises which were conducted twice a year. During these exercises, we would have to stay locked up for a week to 10 days and it was never revealed how long the headquarters could survive totally sealed.

AFNORTH consisted of military members from the U.S., U.K., Denmark, Germany, Canada and Norway. Our basic task was the defense of Norway, and all the Baltic to include Denmark and Germany. Our senior officer was a four-star General from the UK. In previous posting, the General was in charge of all the British troops in Northern Ireland and thus had a hefty price on his head by the IRA.

As nuclear staff officers, it was our task to develop tactics and procedures to utilize nuclear weapons in the event the area were invaded by, most likely, the soviet union. Since norway was/is a nuclear free zone our job was often a bit sticky and we were required to tread a very narrow line.

The two maritime patrol aircraft in the area were the german sp-

13a atlantic and the norwegian p-3c, both of which i had flown. Nato considered creating a *maritime evaluator* and i pointed out that i was the most qualified for the job; anything to get a chance to get back into the air. They accepted my reasoning and after a few months i made my way north to fly with the norwegians and later in my tour, south into the baltic to fly with the germans. The norwegians fly two p-3's on coast-guard missions and two p-3c's as anti-submarine (asw) aircraft, keeping track of mostly russian submarines.

My last flight with the norwegians was out over the north sea and into the barents sea off the coast of russia along the kola peninsula. Th norwegians thought it great fun to head inbound to the area north of murmansk at 100 feet off the water, below radar detection, and, as they crossed the beach, would make a rapid climbing turn, into the radar detection zone and speed off into neutral territory as fast as the p-3 would go. This, of course, would light up all the radar systems on the northern russian coast and sometimes result in the launch of interceptor fighters. But, by the time the interceptors were airborne, the p-3 would be well out of their range.

On this particular flight, as best i can tell, they did not launch aircraft but the ruskies were profanely descriptive on the radios. The norwegians had turned off all electronic devices that would identify them and we were *out-of-there* before the russians could confirm our identity. I suppose they had a good idea who we were but they had no electronic or visual proof. The russians in turn would send submarines deep into norwegian fjords, often detected by the norwegians who have been known to drop live ordnance on red subs. It's almost a cat and mouse game they played to test each other's capabilities.

Since I left the European/Scandinavian area the Dutch have sold all their P-3C's to the Germans and the Portuguese. The Germans use two of their *Atlantics* for electronic warfare and the remainder of their maritime patrol aircraft are P-3C's. The Norwegians still have four P-3's which they intend to upgrade for additional capability.

There was another Brit and two Americans in the Nuc office. Lt. Colonel Dave Ford, US Army Corp of Engineers, was the senior officer and had been in Norway for about 18 months when I arrived, about halfway through his tour. He and I developed a friendship that still exists. Most weekends he and I would head off on long cross country ski treks, sometimes together, other times with others. The longest was

50km treks either in a group or in the Holmenkollen 50K ski race. There would be huts at various spots along the way that served up sandwiches & hot lingonberry juice, a native berry of the Scandinavian countries.

Being the nuclear office, almost all our documents were *'Secret'*, *'Top Secret'* or *'Top Secret Atomal.'* That meant we could not take work home, which was OK by me. Work began at 8:00 and ended at 4:00 with an hour off for lunch. The unit did not open early and did not close late, which meant those were our hours, unless we were involved in an exercise.

Late that winter I was the sponsor of a fellow naval officer, Commander Turner. I conducted the same duties as my sponsor and soon she was settled in as I had been. Often we would be invited to different social events and parties and I began inviting Bonnie to escort me and she did the same to me for her social commitments. We developed a good friendship.

During the next year I was sent three times to Oberammergau, Germany, where NATO had a Nuclear Weapons School, twice to take nuclear courses and once to teach a course. The first visit, I found myself inside the Oberammergau Theater where the most famous of passion plays in conducted every ten years .

In the 1630's, when the Bavarian town of Oberammergau, Germany, was in the depths of the bubonic plague that ravished all of Europe, the village vowed that if they were rid of the plague they would put on a play every ten years depicting the Passion of Jesus. By 1634 the plague was all but gone and that was the first year they kept their promise and put on the play. Since that time, every 10 years they have repeated the performance. There was a break during WW-II, but after the war they decided to have the play in the years ending in zero.

The particular day I was there the Bishop of Bavaria was on hand to bless the town's effort to perform the famous play. The bishop said something in German and about half the people stood. I was tired of sitting and thinking all was over I stood up as well. The German Air Force Lt. Colonel that sat next to me explained the Bishop had just asked all those who would dedicate their time and money towards the play to stand. "Well," I said. "I hope they don't ask me to be nailed to the cross."

On the return trip to Oslo, I stopped off in Paris. My senior year in high school we had a foreign exchange student from Iceland. She was a typical Scandinavian blond. When she returned to Iceland she began a career in the Icelandic foreign service and was posted in Iceland's embassies all over Europe, at various times. We had maintained a very intermittent correspondence and I knew she was working out of the Icelandic embassy in Paris.

We had dinner during an evening cruise on the River Seine. It was really quite nice to see many of the sights of 'The City of Lights' by night while enjoying an elegant dinner. It was one of those things I would never have done on my own, but I'm glad I didn't miss it.

50

EARLY IN THE spring, I was cleaning out my wallet and came across the card that I had been given by the lady from church that moved to Stockton, California. I wrote her a short note; to my surprise she wrote back. I was sent back to Washington DC on NATO business and decided to take a swing down to Texas since I had heard that Polly Fenner was not doing well. I was about to leave to fly back to Norway when I decided to give the lady in Stockton a telephone call. She said that she could not believe that I was in the States and was not coming by to see her. So, what the heck, I thought, and caught a plane to California.

Karen had two teenage daughters and we seemed to hit it off right away. When you reach my age, at the time, you have a kind of mental list when dealing with the ladies. I'm sure women do as well. My list included the usual things a guy might see in a girl, but also included all the things that had caused me to split with other ladies. I planned to be in the Navy for at least five more years, I moved around a lot, the Navy made me work a lot, I wanted children, did her children accept me, did we have similar views on things, and on-and-on the list went. I didn't give her a written exam or even ask questions, I just dropped these things in the course of the conversation and Karen hit on almost every one. I was very surprised but still not ready to say, "This is the one."

I called her before I left the country and she kept talking about what beautiful kids we could make and wanted to come to Norway!

Now, I never considered myself a 'ladies man'. I spent many, many more nights alone than I did with female companionship. At 38, I was about used to being a confirmed old re-tred bachelor and felt I was likely to remain so. While I wanted kids I wasn't willing to marry just for that. Still, I thought over all the possibilities on the flight back to Norway. I guess we had the same flight attendant because on landing she said, "Welcome to Oslo, please set your watches back five years!"

'Hmm,' I thought, 'Norway has gained 15 years since last I landed here.'

I spoke to Karen by phone a couple of times and she told me the dates she could come to Norway and we set a tentative date. By the time I got to Oslo I had a bad case of 'buyer's remorse' but as soon as she was there, that was all brushed aside. Then I did something I swore I would never do. On the whim, we discussed the issue and decided to get married. I found out the local procedure and soon we were before a Norwegian judge and, bang, we were married and had a certificate in Norwegian that proved it, or at least they told me that's what it said.

She went back to California to settle her things and get her kids. Now, I was having serious buyer's remorse! I had broken about 100 personal rules I had about relationships and rushing into things; but on the other hand, it 'seemed' so right. She left her oldest, a senior in high school, with her former mother-in-law and by early fall she was in Norway with her youngest daughter, also a teen.

Her youngest daughter and I hit it off well. She enrolled in the Department of Defense (DOD) American School of Oslo and was doing great. Karen and I were doing great, everything was great. Well, not everything.

Her oldest, who was with her grandmother in Stockton, was not doing well. Her grandmother called collect about once a week and said she could not handle her any more. There were just a few months left of school so Karen flew back to California and stayed with her until she graduated. They both then flew to Norway.

Christi was a handful. Probably a typical 17-year-old California high school graduate but a little different than I was use to. She was deep into punk, wore wild clothes by Oslo, or any other standards, and was generally a pill. One day the doorbell rang and I answered it. I went to Christi and said, "There is someone with chicken bones in his nose and ears at the door for you." She knew right away who it was. I tried to be the cool step-dad but I wasn't sure about this.

The girls were obviously not used to a male figure setting rules or policies so I explained to Karen that she should handle the discipline and I would stay out of it, unless someone was putting themselves, or the family, in jeopardy.

It was winter and Oslo was cold, I mean, really cold. The 'Trik' (local tram) stopped at 12:00 on weekdays, 2:00 on weekends. It was not unusual for the temps to reach 20 even 30 below zero. At least weekly, the local news would report someone found dead walking home in the cold. Christi had just turned 17 and the minimum driving age was 18; thank you, Norway! The girls still wanted to wear their warm weather California clothes and gloves with no fingers and reluctantly took a coat along when they went out.

Soon, Karen came to me in tears saying, "I just can't do this anymore, I have no idea how to handle teenagers, I need some help." I agreed to help but explained that we must be united and if we decided something, she had to stand by our decision. So, we all got together and set some limits, Karen agreed and the girls reluctantly accepted them.

Soon, I noted the girls were not abiding by our agreements and when I asked Karen she said they had talked her into loosening the rules.

That next summer we all went off on a weeklong tour of Norway by auto, boat and train. When I traveled, before marriage, I liked to camp but decided to upgrade by staying in these wooden huts which were typical of how the Norwegians went on holiday. These were not the Hilton but they had all the necessities and we ate our meals in restaurants.

We put the car on a ferry that went deep into one of the giant fjords of Norway. I tried to get the girls to come out of the interior of the boat to see the majestic mountains, waterfalls, glaciers, birds and animals of Norway but they chose to stay below decks, because that's where the boys were.

Karen came to me and said she thought she was pregnant. We took her to the doctor who confirmed what she had suspected. I was ecstatic; Karen, not so much. That surprised me since she had often said she wanted more children and with me.

My command sent me to Naples, Italy to brief the Admiral in charge there of the Allied Forces Southern Europe on the status of nuclear options in the North. I completed the briefing and was preparing to return to Oslo when I got a message to call home. I called and spoke with Karen, who said she just had a miscarriage. I was devastated but Karen was well-composed. She told me the baby was a boy. I flew home the next day and Karen was in good spirits and doing well. Karen broke the news that the doctor had told her that because of her fibroid tumors it would be impossible for her to become pregnant again.

I thought, 'impossible' is a difficult obstacle to overcome. I was disappointed with the news, but having children is never guaranteed for anyone and I soon came to terms with the reality that I would never have children of my own. I was 40 and I had two nearly grown step-children; I would honor all those who stood by me by being the best step-dad possible.

For the preceding 20 years I had imagined and planned to be a father someday and I knew exactly the type of father I would be. It would not be just the antithesis of my own parents. I would be the kind of dad that I had observed in those men who, with wisdom and generosity, had reached out to me in my times of need as a young man growing up. There was not one particular person I planned to emulate, but rather, like a Norwegian smorgasbord, I would take the very best of all those who had done so much for me.

Being a step-parent is one of the hardest and most demanding jobs anyone can undertake. Similar to a parent, you have to be, at the same time, both firm and pliable but doing so without the authority of a natural parent. The natural parent and the step-parent must be supportive of each other's role and must come to an agreement on how those roles will interact with the kids. It takes tons of love, flexibility and understanding. I hoped I had enough of all three and I hoped Karen did as well.

51

DURING THE NEXT several months, NATO sent me all over Europe and Scandinavia. In January, I was sent on a weeklong tour of all the military bases in Norway. At each one we received briefings on their defense plans and I would brief them on the theory, practice and procedures for the use of nuclear weapons, should that be necessary.

I suppose it would not surprise anyone if I said, "Norway is really cold in January," especially in the very northern areas. There is a spot in the north of the country where Norway, Finland and (at the time) the Soviet Union all meet and shared a common border, more accurately a common spot. We traveled to the site in a "Bombardier," a large snow mobile used by the Norwegian army to transport troops. It was -34 degrees Celsius (-34.444 Fahrenheit). We had to walk the last several hundred yards to the point, which is marked by a small metal marker with a sign in Russian, English, Finish and Norwegian warning people not to enter Russia.

There was no fence along this border but a short distance from this site, one could see a Russian guard tower with a machine gun pointed in our direction the entire time. Our military escorts warned us, "Don't even set a foot across that point into Russian territory, they have orders to shoot if you do!" We were not about to test the resolve of the Russian guards and, at 34 below zero, we were anxious to return to the Bombardier.

By the time I returned home, and much to the surprise of both of us, Karen greeted me with the news that she was once again pregnant. Together, we went to see a Norwegian doctor. He examined her and informed us that, because of the fibroid tumors, it would be impossible for her to carry the baby and that she would again have a miscarriage. He recommended a immediate DNC which would have aborted the baby. I asked if Karen's life were in danger and he said "No." Then, to the issue of ending the pregnancy I said, "Absolutely not!"

About ten weeks into the pregnancy, as the doctor predicted, Karen had some serious bleeding and cramping. I rushed her to the local hospital. The doctor examined her and announced she was having a miscarriage and again recommended an immediate DNC. Karen and I talked about it and decided to wait until the next day; if she was indeed in the midst of a miscarriage it would be easily apparent by then. The doctor said we were delaying the inevitable, but if we wanted to wait, he would schedule it for the next morning.

I went home and did some serious praying, fitfully slept for a couple hours and was back in the hospital early the next morning.

This was a hospital in Oslo, Norway. The staff spoke Norwegian and it was obvious they were not used to speaking English inside the hospital. When I arrived, I asked the nurse if I could speak with the doctor. I thought she understood as she walked away. I asked Karen how she felt and she said the bleeding and cramping had stopped and she felt pretty good. The nurse came in to take Karen to the operating room for the DNC and I told her again I wanted to see the doctor. She tried to explain to me the doctor was already prepping for the DNC and they needed to go. I stood in the doorway of the room to prevent their exit and rather firmly told the nurse, *"Please, we need to speak with the doctor."* She was not happy, but she left to tell the doctor.

A few minutes later the doctor came into the room and asked what was going on. I explained that Karen was feeling much better and we did not want to go forward with the DNC unless she was in danger. He looked somewhere between angry and frustrated as he said, "Come with me, I will show you."

We wheeled Karen, still in her bed, out of the room to a large elevator and up to the fourth floor. It was a Saturday; there was little activity in the upper floors. The doctor unlocked an exam room and we wheeled Karen into the room. He began turning on some equipment and soon he had a sonogram warming up. "The fetus is dead and I will show you why this DNC is necessary," he said in matter-of-fact tone. "I'm sorry, but you must see this."

The doctors always referred to it as, "the fetus," while I always said, "the baby," a distinction I was compelled to make. The doctor spread the ointment over Karen's belly and began going back and forth with the transducer probe over the womb area. The doctor said nothing for a few moments. I noticed a blinking light and asked, *"What is that light?"*

"That," the doctor said, "is the beating of the heart."

"The baby's heart," I asked?

"Yes," he responded, "the baby's heart."

He then proceeded to explain that while it was true the baby was still alive there was not enough room in the womb for the baby to survive with all the fibroid tumors. He said we would be back in a week or two. I told him perhaps he was right, but as long as that baby was still fighting, we were not going to end the pregnancy. I thanked him sincerely for taking the time to show us but explained that as long as the baby was alive I would not agree to a termination, unless Karen's health was in jeopardy.

We left the hospital later that morning with the doctor saying he would arrange an appointment with a specialist to try to explain to us what he was unable to explain. "In the meantime," the doctor said, "I recommend full bed rest for Karen." I thanked the doctor and the nurses and I could tell they fully expected to see us back very soon.

It took about three weeks until we could get to see the specialist. He conducted another sonogram and looked puzzled as he compared the results of the previous exam with this current one.

"The fibroid tumors are significantly smaller than in the previous exam," he explained. "When a woman is pregnant she produces certain Hormones and, in some cases, those hormones can shrink these tumors. That is what appears to be happening."

"A two-fer then," I said, immediately realizing the doctor probably wouldn't understand my low-country 'American-ism.' *"We get a baby and Karen gets fewer fibroids."*

I learned a little later that this doctor was the premier pediatrician in Norway and was highly esteemed throughout Scandinavia, Europe and certain medical communities in America. His spoke the King's English, was very sophisticated, and with an obvious deep empathy for his patients.

"Two-Fer," he said. 'I like that."

Karen was entering her second trimester of pregnancy. The doctor told us, "She must stay in bed as much as possible if you want to have a chance to have this baby. I want to see you every two weeks."

"What are our chances of having a healthy baby, Doc?" I asked.

"I have to tell you," he began, "this is going to be a long shot. First, there is not enough room in there for the baby and the tumors. The baby will most likely be very premature. There are a lot of factors and it is too early to tell but, let's just wait and see."

Despite the apprehensions of the good doctor, I walked out pretty pumped-up. As we drove home I told Karen, "We're going to have this baby!" Karen smiled but I think she was being a little more cautious, probably not wanting to get her hopes up. We had already had one miscarriage and almost a second. She had told me she had another miscarriage long before we were married. We still had about 160 days to go for a full term and the doctor did explain the baby would most likely be very pre-mature. A whole lot of things could go wrong in the coming five months.

Two weeks later we had our second visit with the specialist, who noted the tumors were smaller still. He said he wanted to do an amniocentesis, a procedure wherein the doctor uses the ultrasound to guide a needle through the mother's abdomen and into the amniotic sac to get a sample of the amniotic fluid. The chromosomes within that fluid are then examined for any abnormalities. He explained the Norwegians conducted 152 different tests on the chromosomes which could tell us not only the sex but would also reveal a proclivity for over a hundred different conditions. He then explained the risks involved, which included a rare chance of causing pre-mature birth or damage to the fetus. It is required of all women in Norway over 40 who become pregnant to have this procedure. It was up to us how much of this we wanted to know. We told him we wanted to know it all.

We discussed the advantages and dangers of amniocentesis and decided to go ahead with the procedure. The next visit, two weeks later, the doctor noted a steady decrease in the size of the tumors and completed the amniocentesis. He pointed out that in our case, as the baby grew the tumors were in decline; almost a month later the tumors were virtually gone. A few weeks later we received a letter that contained the results of the tests. In all 152 areas our baby was normal and it was going to be a girl.

241

I contacted Karen's sister and invited her to fly to Oslo to surprise Karen a few days before her due date. Despite all the warnings about a pre-mature birth, in the end, they had to induce Karen to have the baby; yet another version of "practicing medicine."

Early in the evening of April 15 Karen's water broke and we made our way to the hospital. In Norway, babies are delivered by midwives unless it is suspected there would be difficulties, in which case a doctor was always available in the hospital. We arrived along with Karen's oldest daughter and her sister. By early evening the decision was made to induce Karen to advance the process and she went into labor. It came time for the shift change for the midwives but the off-going midwife wanted to stay on, so they both helped with the process. I held Karen's hand and assisted her with her breathing until the mid-wife motioned to me that the baby was coming.

Shortly before 11:30 p.m. on April 15, Norwegian time, our income-tax baby girl was born, 100% normal, very alert and active. I cut the cord; the mid-wife cleaned her eyes just a bit and handed her to me.

I know, this event has happened billions of times, but this was my first and only time and it was absolutely amazing. I was holding a living human, having been a part in her making and having assisted in her delivery into this world. Against all odds, I held my daughter in my arms and she was perfect.

I said a quiet prayer, *"Thank you God for giving me this child; help me to be the world's best Dad."* I then looked into her eyes and said, *"God bless you, Lauren Nevels. God watch over you all the days of your life."*

We had long discussions about the baby's name and, when we knew it was a girl, we were able to eliminate half the possibilities. At the time, the only other Lauren I knew was Lauren Bacall. We both agreed "Lauren" was a good choice and eventually settled on Janelle for her middle name. *"The LJN initials make it easy to pass on the luggage,"* I observed. Little did I know that within 10 years *Lauren* would be the most common female name in America.

In Norway, new mothers and babies are required to stay in the hospital for at least seven days. It was probably for the best since Karen was very weak, and Lauren had developed a bit of jaundice. I couldn't help but think that perhaps she had inherited that from me until a nurse pointed out that about half the new babies have that condition. *"Well,"* I thought, *"I can't be responsible for all of them."*

Driving home I knew this was a day I wanted to remember forever. I was bringing my daughter home for the first time and I paid particular attention to the details of the day. This was a moment, just a few months earlier, I was told would never happen; 'impossible,' they had said. But here we were, with a mother in good shape and a healthy baby girl. There still was a little snow on the ground in Oslo. I did notice there were some spring crocus flowers that were beginning to bloom in front of our house as we got out of the car. Spring, a time of new life, the irony was not lost on me. The sky was clear as I lifted Lauren out of the car in her carry-bed, up the steps and into the house.

As I gazed into those wide, receptive blue eyes, I was struck by a thought that overwhelmed me, she already knows more than I can even imagine. My mind was instantly filled with a moment of clarity. We are born with all the knowledge our soul has learned somewhere else. At that moment of birth, or perhaps earlier, there are mega-terabytes of knowledge imbedded within us. We do not have the physical abilities to express it just yet, but there we are with all the lessons we have ever learned and all the wisdom we have ever acquired. As she looked out from underneath her blanket I imagined all the things I wanted to teach her. Yet, there she lay, already smarter than me. Over the next few days or months all that imbedded knowledge will recede into the psyche of her mind to surface over the years as a mysterious sense of déjà vu or spiritual awakening.

The wife of one of my German colleagues, older than us, was already in the house when we arrived. She had brought some food over and was about to leave as we drove up. I took the largest blanket off Lauren and she looked around to all who were in the room. Our German friend came over to see the baby and gave a noticeable gasp as she said, *"She is a very old soul."*

I knew the concept of "old souls" versus "young souls" but I had not fully come to terms with how I felt about the validity to the idea.

Yet I doubt not through the ages
one increasing purpose runs,
And the thoughts of men are widened
with the process of the suns.
Alfred Lord Tennyson

52

WHEN THE DOCTORS said Lauren was old enough to fly, we left Norway for my last assignment in the Navy, and the only one that did not involve flying. We arrived in Norfolk, bought a house in Kempsville and settled in. I worked for Admiral Frank Kelso, Commander-in-Chief of the Atlantic Fleet. I was in charge of scheduling, running and evaluating all exercises for the Atlantic Forces. I also, indirectly, worked for General Al Gray, USMC, a four star Marine general who was under the four-star Admiral Kelso. The hours were long, getting up at 4:00 a.m. and getting home between 7:00 and 8 p.m.

There was just about enough time to push Lauren around the block, get her ready for bed, and sing her to sleep. Yes, you read correctly, Lauren just would not go to sleep unless I was there to hold her to my shoulder and sing her a song as we walked around her room. I sang every song I knew and by the time I got to "Jesus Loves You" she was almost always asleep.

Karen's younger daughter went to live with her father and her older stayed with us. We had flown out to see Karen's parents whom I had never met. We also met her nephew who was finishing up his junior year in high school. He did not get along that well with his mother, Karen's sister, and was considering dropping out of school altogether. When we got back to Virginia he was constantly on my mind so I suggested to Karen that perhaps John could come to live with us to finish up his high school senior year. We invited him, and in the summer of 1987 he came to live with us and started his senior year. He had some initial difficulties since Virginia school kids were a little more serious about education than those in California. He commented to me that in between classes in California they would talk about surfing and beach activities while in Virginia they discussed math concepts and science projects.

I met with his teachers a couple times and we worked out a schedule for him to graduate and in the Spring of 1988, John walked across the stage and got his high school diploma. As they called his name I realized how John Fenner must have felt 20 years earlier and I got a bit misty-eyed. I also remembered the words Mrs. Fenner had said to me, *"Someday, someone will cross your path and need something and you will give it to them. And when you do, you will have paid us back what we have done for you."* The emotion that caused my response was probably not unlike John's, a certain amount of pride and a sense I had played a small part in making that moment happen.

John and Christi went back to California that summer and I prepared to retire from the United Sates Navy. But, before I did, the Navy sent me on one more trip; this time to Halifax, Nova Scotia, Canada. I decided Karen and Lauren should come along so the three of us boarded an Air Canada flight heading north. I held Lauren during the flight to keep her entertained. Unbeknownst to me she kept play with the hair of the gentleman sitting in front of us. When I realized what she was doing the man turned around and asked if he could hold her. I said sure and began talking with the man and his companion, his brother. They introduced themselves as Don and Phil and they were on their way to Halifax to do a concert. That's when I realized they were the Everly Brothers. The two of them played with Lauren most of the flight. They offered us tickets to the concert but, as it turned out, our return flight was the day of their concert.

I submitted my papers and the Navy said I could retire in August, 1988. Admiral Kelso, my boss, called me into his office when he saw the papers and asked why I was retiring and what it would take for me to stay in the Navy. I explained I had a two-year-old daughter and a wife, both of whom I had seen very little over the past year and the detailers were ready to send me to the Middle East for a two year unaccompanied "career enhancing" position. The admiral said he knew about the position; he had recommended me for it, it was a Captain's job and it would lock me in for promotion to Captain. I explained to him how I had made decisions for 20 years based on what was best for my career and it was time I made some decisions that were best for my personal life. He said he understood, but asked me to think about it, that there was still time to reconsider.

I admit I was flattered by what he said and the carrot of promotion to Captain was hard to turn down, but in the end, I knew it was time. I had experienced what I considered a remarkable 20+ year career. The Navy taught me how to fly and, except for the last one, flying was central or available in every assignment they gave me. I spent the first 10 years all over the Pacific, Africa and the Middle East and the second 10 in Europe, Scandinavia and the Mediterranean. I am positive I never had to back-up to a pay-window and Washington DC was always down-doppler from every assignment. I had given my pound of flesh every day for over 20 years and, quite frankly, for the most part, the Navy had been very good to me and for me; but it was time we parted friends.

Admiral Kelso insisted he be the presiding officer at my retirement and gave me a medal for my years of service "to him, to the Navy and to our Country". As I held Lauren after the ceremony he came up and said, "Larry, I hate to say it but I think you made the right decision. The Navy's loss is your family's gain."

Admiral Kelso was one of the finest officers I had known in the Navy and one of the finest people I have ever met. He was a champion for women in the Navy and it was a tragedy that a few years later he became, "where the buck stopped" following some unfortunate incidents at a Tail-hook convention that he had no part in. Senator Boxer of California shamefully and unfairly made him the target of her personal vendetta on the Navy and he resigned as Chief of Naval Operations (CNO). My heart fell when I read the news since I, and all in the Navy knew, he had done more for women than anyone else in the last 200-plus years. I was particularly upset that this was brought on by the foolishness of some fellow aviators. But, to his credit, he manned-up and took the heat; that was indicative of the gentleman he was.

The day I retired from the Navy I knew what Lou Gehrig felt like that day in Yankee Stadium when, at age 36, he gave his farewell speech from baseball after he was stricken with Amyotrophic Lateral Sclerosis (ALS), now known in the United States as Lou Gehrig's disease. At his farewell he said, *"I consider myself the luckiest man on the face of the earth."* That day, in 1988, I considered myself the luckiest man on earth as well, to have been able to serve my country for over 20 years with honor and integrity.

I have read recently about the emotions of single seat pilots in high performance aircraft and, since I have flown a few of those, I have to admit, they have their moments. But I have to say there is nothing like having other people's lives, literally, in your hands. Yes, I did some pretty insane things when it was just me in the aircraft but when I became the pilot-in-command of the lives of 10-20 crewmen with wives and children counting on my skills to get them home I changed my flying philosophy completely.

For the better part of 20 years the U.S. Navy and the Dutch Navy had trusted me with multi-million dollar aircraft and they put into my hands and my flying skills the very lives of my crews. Those crews trusted me to bring them home through, hurricanes, typhoons, severe icing, engine fires, numerous emergencies, dangerous missions, equipment failures, severe crosswinds, lightening strikes, loss of navigation aids, etc, etc. Not only did they trust my flying skills, they trusted my judgment. Many times I was placed in situations where personal judgment was necessary to make professional decisions and my experience defined, for me, just where I was willing to draw the line. I like to think that was born in the days that I played quarterback in high school and college. While lives were not put on the line, decisions, execution and leadership were demanded of the job and I strived to be, I yearned to be, in that position. Coaches didn't call plays in those days, quarterbacks did. With bands playing, fans yelling, coaches screaming it was my responsibility to keep a cool head in the huddle and convince the rest of the team that a play I was about to call would work. I treated it as an awesome responsibility and it taught me many things about myself and just exactly who I was, and who I wanted to be.

I flew through winter ice and snow over the North Sea to drop supplies to sinking merchantmen and stayed there in extreme weather as the only lifeline to dozens of sailors about to sink into the freezing North Sea. All the time directing rescue helicopters and ships to their position to snatch them from almost certain death and take them to their wives and children. And as the last person was lifted into a Helo, I watched as the giant ship capsized and sank. There we were, at 1000 feet above, with a front row seat to the entire event. We returned to base, landed in a snowstorm on an icy runway, shut her down and went home to our warm beds. For us it was just another day at the office. There were no medals, no 'thank-you's' and none was expected. Just a feeling that you did something very good that night, and that was enough.

There is a truism in aviation circles: "The difference between air traffic controllers and pilots? If a pilot screws up, the pilot dies, if ATC screws up, the pilot dies'. That is multiplied in aircraft with crews. "The pilot screws-up everyone dies, ATC screws up, everyone dies."

We handled the aircraft with daring and skill, we fought the elements and won, sometimes we fought the controllers, but mostly they guided us home to break out at the very last moment as we brought our bird, with its crew, safely down.

Still, words cannot explain the beauty in the sight of a perfect evening sunset, being thousands of miles out at sea viewing the most magnificent stars unhampered by any artificial light, brilliant shows of St. Elmos Fire, magnificent cloud-to-cloud lightening and a morning sunrise that is so brilliant that one dare not deny there is a God; and that was all in just one flight. I had crews that would fly 12-16 hours, six to eight of those hours on two engines of a four engine aircraft, land and spend the next several hours changing an engine and getting it ready to fly the mission the next day. I've flown beneath a low overcast to view a giant white waterspout coming up from the dark blue Indian Ocean and disappear into even darker blue clouds above. It's a sight that words are just not sufficient to do justice; a sight that few have the awesome privilege of beholding.

I've had crews that could track the quietest of modern Russian submarines for hours, most likely without the Ruskies having a clue we were even there. We did not do it for medals or recognition, but because it was our job and it was our country. How well we did in peacetime would tell how well we would do if things heated up, and we were ready. The greatest pacifists in the world are in the foxholes and cockpits. We do not want war, we do not want to pull the trigger or push the button. We hoped that what we were doing would be a deterrent to any aggressor but if it weren't, we were prepared to be the best pilots, the best crews and to uphold a long national tradition.

We get into those aircraft whose maintenance is completed by youngsters not long out of high school, and we place our very lives in a trust they have done their job right. Sure, we preflight the bird before we go but there is only so much we can discover in a serious walk-around. We believe they are as dedicated to giving us the best possible aircraft as we are in doing our jobs in the air.

Were we prepared to die? You are *never* prepared to die and that possibility seldom, if ever entered our minds. We strove to be masters over that for which we had control and we left the rest to whatever God we knew.

I have been sent to, or visited, 52 countries, mostly as directed by the Navy. Some of those involved combat, thankfully, most did not. Most of the missions I flew were routine, some were magnificent, a few were dangerous, and a couple were terrifying. We have a saying in aviation that it is 90 percent boring, nine percent interesting and one percent *"sheer-stark- terror."* All our training and experience was directed to preparing us for that one-percent moment and being focused enough to come out of it as unscathed as possible.

I have flown 27 different aircraft, mostly in the Navy, several while at Beech Aircraft for several months, and a few since I got out of the Navy. I seldom fly anymore. The expense involved and the knowledge of how a plane must be maintained to maximize the chances of making take-offs equal landings has limited my flying. Do I miss it? *Yes!* But I survived 8,500 plus hours flying with a clear understanding of my limits.

Let me be very clear...*I am no hero!* Yes, I served with honor for over 20 years. I was on the periphery of a few different conflicts. Flying high above, I never saw the enemy eye-to-eye. The closest I came to the Viet Cong was that sapper attack at Cam Ranh Bay and a mortar attack in the middle of the night in Danang. I have medals on my old uniform, which still fits by the way, and hangs in the back of my closet. I have citations I could put on my *"I love me wall"*, but I don't. All that I have done pales to insignificance when compared to those who gave their lives. Or those who were wounded in battle and those who survived the madness that is war. Those are our *real* national heroes and I never miss an opportunity to thank them for their sacrifice. Every time I see someone wearing a uniform or veteran ball-cap I go out of my way to offer my hand and I say, *"Thank you for your service."* Most are too surprised to respond and I just walk away thinking we both feel better for the exchange.

I am proud to have been a part of a band of brothers, the fraternity of airmen, the society of sailors who are still today prepared to defend this country from enemies both foreign and domestic. I was indeed a small part of something *much* bigger than myself.

Only being a husband and a father exceeds the pride I feel for the privilege I had to be a part of the defense of our country for a large portion of my life. I have long ago removed the accolades from my wall and what remains are the symbols of the squadrons and units I was part of over the years. I keep them up as reminders of the hundreds of men and women with whom I had the honor to serve with over the years. Together we kept the faith of those that went before us; we fought the good fight of defending this country and we have attempted to make our world a little better than we found it. Those, my shipmates, are now my accolades and I am as proud of them as is possible to be.

53

AFTER MY OFFICIAL retirement from the Navy, and at Karen's insistence, I bought a motor home and we began a year long trip that would criss-cross America from coast to coast. We began in Norfolk, Virginia, drove to DC to see friends, and headed west. It was our intent to discover a place where we could land and raise our family. I took detailed notes of each town we encountered which, unfortunately, have been lost. But we began rating each state and each town in that state with stars ranging from one to five, five being the best. Prior to this trip we had traveled from Maine to Florida and were not enamored with anyplace in particular in that area, although Maine was tempting.

From DC, we traveled through parts of Ohio and into Tennessee and Kentucky. Ohio was nice but not captivating; Tennessee and Kentucky, however had several promising towns. The countryside was beautiful, the towns were charming, several locations had four stars and a few had five. We hit Missouri, Arkansas, Oklahoma and on into Texas. We drove from Dallas down to Beeville to see Mrs. Fenner.

While in college, I had developed the habit of riding the back-roads of the Texas Hill Country when things began closing in on me at school. No place in particular, just picked a road and off I went. Turn right, turn left, eventually you ended up somewhere. I found great strength, solace and peace *in them thar hills.* I remember thinking back in 1967-68 that if I wanted to live in a large town I would chose Austin and my small town choice went to Kerrville, Texas.

We visited with Polly for a few days and decided to make a car trip up to the Hill Country and we visited Austin first. 25 years later it was no longer a large town but was a rather an imposing large city with all the headaches that went with that designation. We then drove over to Kerrville and, while coming out of those hills on Interstate 10 was impressive, the rest of Kerrville was, well, not so much. This was the late 1980's and Texas was just going into the savings and loan crisis that gripped the entire nation. Kerrville was no exception with 'for sale' signs literally everywhere. It appeared the whole town was for sale.

On the way back, we made a swing down Main Street Fredericksburg and, though I am not Mormon, I had one of those Brigham Young moments when, upon entering the valley that later became Salt Lake City he proclaimed, *This is the place!*

I have come to believe that a town, like people, has some sort of soul and, if you are keenly aware, you can detect the positive or negative vibes of a town that resonate within that soul. I have entered towns and have, literally, had the hair on my neck stand up as I sensed a negative soul. Most towns are neutral but occasionally you enter a town and sense a positive vibe, a sweet feeling, a calming nature about the town. It is a place which exudes peace for the soul. That is the feeling I had with just one drive down Main Street Fredericksburg.

Despite my positive feeling, Karen and I had made a vow to withhold our judgments until we reached Paradise. Paradise, California, that is. I always wanted to end up in Paradise so that town seemed a proper place to end *our Tour de USA.* We headed out across the deserts of West Texas, across New Mexico and into Phoenix, where we stayed a few nights with a friend of Karen's.

Lauren was two and dearly wanted to roller skate so I got her a pair and taught her how to navigate on her own. She was a quick learner, always has been, and probably always will be. We checked out Phoenix and several outlying towns and headed up to the Grand Canyon. The desert had a great appeal to me, I could fully understand why some people are drawn to what others consider as *wasteland.*

While we were at the Grand Canyon, Karen called her sister and found out her brother-in-law had cancer. We cut our touring short and made a bee-line for San Jose, California.

Karen's brother-in-law had testicular cancer, had it removed and was undergoing chemo. We camped out in the RV in front of their house for several weeks supporting them.

I'm sure a lot of people like to travel in RV's and God bless you every one. We met many people along the way that had been living in their RV for many years. With all due respect to them all, I have to say I hated almost every minute in that damn thing. I was 42, the prime of my life. I was used to long days of work and/or flying. I wanted to be doing something with my hands, in the dirt, building, anything, except being in that crazy box on wheels that got fewer than five miles per gallon. My days consisted of driving, setting up in an RV park, emptying waste-water and pumping more gas, hardly self-fulfilling.

We left San Jose and, as planned, made our way to Paradise, California. A nice place, but not paradise to us! On the way back, Karen wanted to go through her old home town of Stockton, California. As we drove into that town I had this unbelievably strange feeling. I had one of those hair-on-the-back-of –my-neck moments and the deeper we got into town it began to stand up even more. I really wanted to give the place the benefit of the doubt and suppressed my feelings by thinking that perhaps I was imagining it all. She took me to a neighborhood called Lincoln Village. It was her favorite part of Stockton and she got so excited about the possibility of living there. She directed me to a nearby school, not too far, where she said Lauren would go to, in a few years, if we moved there.

I still had this *feeling* about the town but internally admitted my prejudice for Texas may be clouding my objectivity. So I suppressed what I sensed about the place and tried to look at it with fresh eyes. By the time we left town we had Fredericksburg, Texas and Stockton, California tied for #1 on our list of places to live. As we drove over the mountains, past the wind farms and into San Jose I was becoming increasingly uncomfortable with one of those choices.

I pulled the motor home up in front of Karen's sister's house and, as we did, she came running out screaming for us to come inside. My first assumption was that something had happened to her husband with cancer. As we rushed inside she directed us to a bulletin they were having on the local TV station.

It seems that a 26 year old drifter, dressed in a shirt emblazoned with the Iranian battle cry *Death to the Great Satan*, had driven up to Cleveland Elementary School, the very school we had just visited, and opened fire on the children as they played, killing five students, wounding 29 others before killing himself.

To be clear, I know these tragedies can happen anywhere. But, the timing of this particular incident struck me as beyond mere coincidence. In fact, I seldom believe in coincidence. The level of this particular tragedy forced me back to listening to and trusting in my instincts.

Now, let me be clear, I DO NOT believe that incident occurred to show me anything. It was a tragic event, conducted by a tragic person, with tragic results for the victims and survivors.

There is, within each of us, an inner voice that may more commonly be referred to as "instincts." To be sure, that phenomenon is sometimes described in religious circles as "that still small voice." I will be honest; I admit I am not smart enough to understand everything there is to know about these things. Is this the voice of God? Or has God given us the gift of "instinct" to guide us through troubled times? I suspect the answer is 'yes' and 'yes', but to argue the source is meaningless and a waste of energy. I just accept the fact that it is there and my experience is that it will serve me well, if only I will listen and follow.

As a result of this event, and many before then, I listened to that clear voice that emanated from deep inside me, and all doubt left my being about where we were meant to be. I tried to explain this moment of clarity to Karen and she just thought I was being stubborn. So I made a deal that we would go back to Texas for six months and, if after that time she was not convinced that town was where we were meant to me, I would be willing to revisit that decision.

She eventually, albeit with great reluctance, came around to accepting my proposal. I drove the RV south to Interstate 10 while Karen drove our car. She cried all the way to the Arizona border.

We reached Fredericksburg, rented a home, and after six months, I reminded her of our bargain and she agreed; Fredericksburg was where we were meant to be.

This was 1989 and the country was in the midst of the 'Savings and Loan' debacle. While it reached Texas, it was slow to come to fiscally-minded Fredericksburg. I made a purchase offer on a property on Franklin Street, but the deal fell through when the bank insisted on strings that I felt were not in our best interest. A few months later the bank went under and all their assets became the property of the US government. It took almost a year before that property finally came up on the government list to sell, but when it did, I made a 'low-ball' offer and to my surprise it was accepted. On April 1, 1990 we moved into our new home on Franklin Street.

After living in an RV for over a year, and before that being consumed with a very cerebral job in the Navy, I was ready to roll up my sleeves and get my hands dirty working on our new property. I surveyed the property and determined the 1855 rock house was the best candidate for immediate renovation and a source of income as a Bed and Breakfast.

That spring, I began teaching at the local junior high school during the day and working on the house at night and on weekends. When school ended I worked all day and long into the night on the renovation and opened *The Commanders Place B&B* on the weekend of Fourth of July, 1990.

That fall I began teaching at the high school and turned my attention to the third house as a second B&B.

<center>~~~</center>

Middle school, or junior high school, had its own set of challenges. The students were, as the term implies, somewhere between elementary and high school level. I noted the girls at that age were notoriously fixated on power and control, and enjoyed ejecting some individual from their circle of friends for no other reason than, *they could*. There was almost a daily set of tears from a young girl who had been expelled by her former friends, and no amount of consolation from me would convince her that her entire life had not just ended.

The next year I had the exact same kids in high school and I was amazed that they had miraculously become human again, and a joy to teach.

<center>~~~</center>

While teaching during the day, and working late into the night, I was making progress on the two restorations. I contracted the difficult things and did the "no-brainer" work myself, laboring in the afternoons and deep into the night. By Thanksgiving, we opened the second house as two additional B&B's. While it was nice to have the income, that meant quite a bit of additional work and time, but that was all calculated into my new business plan for "retirement."

In 1991 I applied for and was chosen the first Director of Economic Development (ED) for Fredericksburg and Gillespie County. Shortly after that, I was asked by the County Judge to take over as Airport Manager of Gillespie County Airport and project manager for the redevelopment and renovation of the airfield. Both those jobs made it impractical to continue teaching, so I devoted my full attention to ED and the airport.

You may recall, as a young boy in a foster home, how I had to listen to Arthur Godfrey at lunch. Well, our airport had a connection to the man as well. It seems in the late 1940's, Godfrey was flying in the area and it was getting dark. He needed gas but the airport had no landing lights. He contacted the airport manager on the radio, who called all his friends in town to drive their cars and trucks to the airport. They lined up on either side of the runway with their lights on, in order for Mr. Godfrey to land. He was so touched by the rapid response of the townsfolk of Fredericksburg that he purchased a set of landing lights for the airport runway.

I took over as manager in 1991 and they were still using those late 1940's Arthur Godfrey runway lights. With the new renovation of the airport, they changed out those lights, extended and repaved the runway, and put in a new rotating beacon light along with several other needed improvements.

I got to fly again with several who had planes at the field and it was fun getting back into the air. I toyed with the idea of getting my own plane but the cost of the plane, maintenance, insurance, etc. brought me down to earth. I did notice that I was hanging out at the airport more and more and could feel the tug of becoming a hanger-bum pulling on me. If I did not have my family responsibilities I probably would have. When the airport redevelopment program was complete, and as the lure of the air steadily increased, I decided I should quit the airport job before I was totally sucked-in and concentrate on community economic development and our B&B's.

54

Who knows exactly where, when or how a relationship goes bad? I suppose it is more progressive than instantaneous. If there were something or someone to hang the blame on it might be easier, but I doubt it. I know it was over a period of time but it seemed that one day this one just dissolved. I suppose it was obvious to some and looking back, I probably should have seen the warning signs. But still, it came as quite a shock to me. In hindsight, I suppose I could relate a litany of issues, but that does not fit the purpose of this effort, and there seems no socially redeeming value in doing so.

If I learned anything from that experience, it is that *hurt people, hurt people.* The end was not quick in coming and certainly not without casualties. In fact, it was the darkest time of my life, my *Annus Horribilis.* I know what you are thinking and you should be ashamed of yourself, that means, *horrible year.*

My greatest fear was that I would not have an impact in my daughter's life. I absolutely believe children need both a mother and a father in their lives. Can they survive with one or the other? Certainly they can, but without both, they miss necessary elements that complete their emotional and moral maturation.

To be sure, a good father confirms the femininity within a daughter and a good mother confirms the masculinity in a son. You may consider this proposition counter-intuitive and think it diminishes the impact of same-sex parents but that is not the case. Certainly, children need both a mother and father but a good father completes a daughter and a good mother completes a son. There is more than a biological reason for fathers and mothers. The emotional impact on the maturation of a child is just as important, and there is a missing piece to life's puzzle when the nature of things is disturbed. Having said that, whatever life gives us we can overcome, and thrive, and we can all be mentally and emotionally healthy. But outside the natural course of events we have to learn these things on our own.

This was a terrible divorce, as if there is any other kind. Some are just more terrible than others. If you have been through one you know what I mean. If you haven't, you should thank your lucky stars and hope it never happens to you.

In my grief and desperation I went to my Episcopal priest who listened intently to everything I had to say and offered the dutiful advice. At the very end he told me, *"Larry, what a beautiful blessing all this is for you."*

I'm sure I looked at him like he was nuts. He must have read my thoughts or my expression as he said, *"What a great opportunity this is for you to grow and to learn so much about yourself. I know you can't see it now, but there is a purpose for all that is happening to you. If you seek to understand that purpose you will find that happiness and contentment will return to your life, and you will eventually be in a far better place for it all."*

I'm not sure I went away fully convinced, but in the end, he was right. As painful as that period of time in life was, I came away a better and stronger person with a much clearer idea of who I was, and what I wanted to be. In a strange and sometimes seemingly perverted way, that rocky road paved the way for my future happiness. It took quite awhile longer and a few short encounters to fully learn what I needed to know but, in the end, I got it! That priest was right, what a wonderful blessing that was; though I honestly hope I am not so blessed again.

It took well over a year but eventually things were resolved and we settled into the routine as divorced parents with a common child. I grieved terribly at not being a daily influence on that young girl, my only child, but it was-the way-it-was, and grieving would not change anything. I worked and ran the B&B's by myself and lived in anticipation of picking up Lauren on Fridays every other week. I tried to squeeze as much quality time from Friday evening until I took her to school on Monday morning. We maintained that routine throughout the remainder of elementary school and soon Lauren was about to go into junior high school. It was one of the darkest times in my life and I spent more than a few evenings screaming at God in the middle of our acreage. That was when I realized that God has big shoulders and He can take the verbal abuse of a heart in pain.

55

It was October 1997, about 4:30 in the afternoon. I had a question about my IRA and went to my insurance, investment company in San Antonio and requested to speak with a representative. Out walked this stunning brunette who introduced herself and led me into her office. At first we talked about why I was there, but soon the conversation seemed to take on a life of its own and it began to ping-pong off the walls about all sorts of things. I explained I was from Fredericksburg and she asked, *"Do you raise pigs."*

"I've heard that there are a lot of pig farmers in Fredericksburg," she commented.

"Well no, I don't raise pigs but I do raise Texas longhorn cattle," I replied.

She pointed out that she was a Texas Longhorn, Class of '72. I think I told her that she was much prettier than any of mine in Fredericksburg.

We talked for about an hour, very little regarding my IRA, but that was probably mostly my fault as I would continuously change the subject. Despite the semi-personal banter, we did manage to discuss some financial issues but not enough to dissuade me from scheduling another face-to- face visit. I realized she knew much more about me than I knew about her, since much of my financial and a lot of personal data was on file inside the company computer. She was friendly, but totally professional, and gave no indication otherwise, despite my attempt at directed humor.

I thought about her off-and-on over the next couple weeks but reminded myself it was probably nothing. Though my painful divorce was four years back in my rear-view mirror the sting was still there. I wasn't sure I was ready to start looking seriously. Still, I could not get her out of my mind.

A few weeks later, I went back to conclude our business, this time with Lauren in tow. We conducted our business and as I was about to leave I suggested she should come up to Fredericksburg sometime and I would show her there was more to the place than pig farmers. She explained that she was going on a vacation and then there were the holidays but, perhaps, sometime.

As I drove back to Fredericksburg I convinced myself, "Just as well, I suppose, I'm really not ready to dip my toe back into the serious relationship pool."

About four months later, in February, I got an unexpected call from her. She told me she was considering coming to Fredericksburg on Saturday to do some shopping. I told her to call when she got into town and I would meet her for lunch.

Saturday came and, with it, the most intense ice storm in many years to hit the area. I had heard they closed Highway 87 into town because Steeler Hill, coming up from Comfort, Texas, was iced over. I just assumed that Linda would not be coming.

Lauren was invited to a birthday party so I helped her get ready and delivered her to the kiddo's soirée. I was very surprised to come home to a message on the answering machine that Linda was indeed in town.

I jumped into my pick-up and drove up and down Main Street, but it was so cold and icy that anyone down-town would probably be spending most of their time inside one of the many stores or wrapped around a hot cup of coffee. There were few cars parked on the usually busy street, so I decided to see if I could identify one, even though I had no idea what she drove. I found a car with a parking pass from the insurance company where she worked and noticed a Trisha Yearwood cassette tape on the passenger seat, a singer we both enjoyed. I took a chance and left my business card with a note in the window and went back home. Sure enough, a few minutes after I arrived back home she called.

We agreed to meet at a specific intersection downtown. It was freezing cold with lots of ice as I pulled up to the intersection, honked the horn and she jumped into the cab of my warm pick-up and we drove off.

We each had a cup of hot tea and talked for some time. I asked how she made it up to Fredericksburg with all the ice on the roads. She said she just went on to Kerrville and came up on Highway 16 where the road was still open. It occurred to me that, that indicated a certain level of determination, but I wouldn't let myself think too much into it.

I explained that I was a little uncomfortable that she knew so much about me and I knew so little about her.

"Well, what do you want to know?" she asked, and she proceeded to fill in the blanks about her life. She told me about her daughter who was entering The University of Texas, of her personal passion was for music and that she had been in different choruses since high school, where she earned all-state honors as a tenor. When I asked about hearing her sing sometime she invited me to come to a show her women's chorale was giving in Austin in a couple weeks.

We talked for several hours, that went by way too fast, for both of us, I thought. But, soon it was time for her to try to find her way back on the icy roads to San Antonio. I reflected on our long conversation and realized it was detailed but not too personal. I wondered if it meant as much to her as it did to me.

A few weeks later, I made my way to Riverbend Church in Austin to listen to her chorales performance. There were 70-80 ladies in the group, but I quickly found her in the top right corner of the risers and had great difficulty taking my eyes off of her. At intermission she came out to the lobby to see if I had actually come to the concert. We saw each other across the large entry area and gleefully made our greetings. We only had about ten minutes, but agreed to meet after the show.

I suppose it was a great show, or so they tell me. I was focused on one thing and cannot remember much of the performance. At the end of the show we hooked up for a short while in the parking lot. She had to get back to San Antonio and I needed to get back to Fredericksburg. We both had over an hour on the highway to make it home. But, I invited her to come up sometime and hike up Enchanted Rock. A couple weeks later that is exactly what we did.

Enchanted Rock is a huge, pink granite monadnock dome located north of Fredericksburg and south of Llano, Texas. It is the largest such pink granite dome in the United States; hundreds of visitors show-up to climb the rock every day. It rises 425 feet above ground, 1825 feet above sea level, and covers 640 acres. It is one of the largest batholiths (underground rock formation uncovered by erosion) in the United States.

We both had climbed the Rock several times with our daughters, but never with the laughter we shared that day, hiking up the face of the edifice.

Every relationship has its predictable stages. If things go well at *the introductory stage*, a relationship will enter what I call, *the giggle sage."* The title pretty much sums up what is going on; giggles, laughing, smiling, beaming, anticipation and it is hard to hide. It's a very fun stage and while lasting relationships inevitably move to subsequent stages, great relationships always keep a bit of the giggles there as a reminder how they felt in the beginning.

A month or so later, we met for lunch at Los Patios, Restaurant in San Antonio, Texas. We were certainly still gleefully mired deep within *the giggle stage* as we had lunch. Afterwards, we sat out on a cement bench underneath some hanging Texas live oaks along a path that ran beside the restaurant. As we sat there just looking at each other a young couple walked by. The girl was probably in her mid to late 20's, about thirty years junior to us, and made a telling comment as she asked, *"Are you two in love?"* She walked around the corner before we could respond but we both just looked at each other and we both confessed, *"Yes, I guess we are."*

We dated for two more years, both having been hurt before and each of us wanting to be sure before we jumped into anything serious.

Another reason we waited was our two daughters. We wanted them to be as willing as we were to make a family together. Lauren came around rather quickly and thought marriage would be a good thing. Stacey, Linda's daughter, understandably was a little more hesitant.

56

I VERY QUICKLY realized I had a natural affinity for Stacey. While that feeling wasn't always mutual, I made the choice not to be offended. (Being offended or not being offended is *always* a choice.) For me, looking into Stacey's eyes was like looking into a mirror. I saw myself, many years earlier, in her reluctance to get close or risk her emotions on a stranger. She had been disappointed during her early years and those scars were fresh. People would be there and then they were gone. To her, I was just another man who was going to leave her. I understood all that very well, been there, done that, many times.

There have been some times in my life when, what I can only describe as, a circle was drawn around me and nothing negative could penetrate that circle. That is exactly what took place between Stacey and me. This particular time was not the first and it would not be the last. While being offended is always a choice, the choice to reject an offense is not always easy to maintain. But this came easy for me. I realized it was out of my hands and I would leave it to other forces of the universe to bridge the gap that separated us.

I helped Stacy move three or four times while she was a student at the University of Texas at Austin, and Linda and I would attend every honor function she was involved in, and there were many.

Stacey is a bright and talented young lady, at <u>so</u> many levels. She was in the Plan II honors program at the University of Texas and flourished in that challenge. While she chose to avoid sororities, she was involved in several service organizations, at least one of which benefitted children.

Linda and I attended football games on parent's weekend at UT Austin, and we always tried to bring Lauren along. I did have an ulterior motive, several actually, but our principle motive was to support Stacey. An extra added benefit was that I wanted to plant within Lauren's mental-being the concept of college and all the trimmings surrounding higher education.

Lauren had lost her self-confidence in the classroom and I had to do what I could to help her get it back. Including Lauren in all of Stacey's honor events was not without risk. Lauren was academically fragile and I did not want her to be so overwhelmed with Stacey's success that she felt she could not live-up to that expectation. Personally, I believed in Lauren, and that she could and would do quite well, but I never wanted her to think there were expectations for her to live up to someone else's standards. I was fully aware of the risks involved here, but it was a risk worth taking. Still, perhaps it wasn't so bad to have an *older sister* as a model to follow.

Each time we went to Austin I made sure we went a little early. That enabled us to roam around the campus for a short time, and just sort of let nature take its course with Lauren. There was no intent to vector her into Austin or the University of Texas. In fact, I fully expected her to go elsewhere, if for no other reason than to make her own way.

My *mother*, Mrs. Fenner, had gone to UT Austin, as did Linda and now Stacey. My *father*, John Fenner, went to Texas A&M. They were both great schools with long traditions. There were other schools that Lauren considered: Texas Christian & Texas State among them. Honestly, it really did not matter to me. I wanted Lauren to go where she felt most comfortable, just as I had done many years earlier.

I was as proud of Stacey as her mother and could not have been prouder if she were my own natural daughter. It didn't bother me that my expressions of pride seemed to fall on deaf ears; it was that circle thing. Sometimes her Dad would attend, sometimes he missed them. When he was there it was not always pleasant. Frankly, I wanted to punch his lights out for not expressing the same pride I felt in her accomplishments.

When I first moved to Fredericksburg I did some substitute teaching at the middle and high school. I discovered that teacher's lesson plans were, more often than not, insufficient to keep the kids busy for the entire class time. Since the quickest way for a sub to lose control of a classroom was when the kids had nothing to do, I would come prepared to fill in the empty time with other activities. One of the things I discovered was that the kids really enjoyed taking surveys and discussing the results. One of my surveys asked the question, "*What are the five things you want to hear from your parents?*"

In my generation the number one answer would be, *I love you.* It seems that was lacking from parents in the 40's and 50's. But, after the 'love movement' of the 60's, it seems we were almost overwhelming our kids with expressions of love, and they were missing something else.

Let me be clear, I am aware that my surveys of a couple hundred kids may not be reflective of an entire generation. Still, on the average, *I love you,* came out at number three. The #1 response was, *I'm proud of you* followed by *I trust you.* FYI, *I understand you* was number four and *I hear you* came in a number five.

Past experiences have a great influence on how a person handles future situations. That greatly applies to how we deal with our children. We usually give them what we lacked as a child when perhaps that is not what they need the most.

While my mother did say in later years that she was proud of me, I do not ever recall my father or mother saying, I *love you.* In raising Lauren, I was very intentional in letting her know how much she was loved. I believe that once a child is secure in that knowledge there is one more thing they desperately need. That is, they yearn to hear from their parents how proud they are of them. Expressions of *warranted pride* validate a child and, along with love, complete them.

Many years ago, when my father left me in that cell in Long Beach California, his last words to me were, *You will never amount to anything!* Over the next many years I would recall those words and use them as inspiration to work even harder. When I wanted to be quarterback of the football team, a class officer, a college graduate, a pilot in the Navy, two Master's Degrees, achieving the rank of Commander and when I had a child of my own, I used those words to inspire me to keep going and keep achieving, and made it my goal to be the best at everything I tried. Words are powerful, especially to children. Parents can build up their children and give them a validation that is difficult to emulate. Or they can shred their children to pieces by withholding their affirmation. I do not fully understand how words can destroy one person and to others the exact same words can be what inspire them to prove something, to succeed. In the bible, these affirmations are referred to as, *the blessing*. It is just as important now as it was in Old Testament times. Our children desperately need our blessing and they get it when we say how proud we are of them, how much we love them and that they have earned our trust.

The natural affinity I had for Stacey was that I could see in her the heartfelt desire to hear her father tell her, *"I'm proud of you, Stacey."* She was an honor graduate at the University of Texas, Phi Beta Kappa, a great dancer with a Law Degree from NYU (New York University) and a damn fine person with a heart that is bigger than the Big Apple itself. Perhaps her father did say something but I was there for most of those recognitions of her achievements and I never once heard him say that he was proud of her. That was another reason I had to resist the very real temptation to punch him out.

My father didn't know it, but those words of his to me when I was in that cell in Long Beach were almost like the Johnny Cash song, *"A Boy Named Sue."* The father in the song gave his son that name to make him tough and it worked. My father unintentionally inspired me to succeed at almost everything I tried, sometimes just to prove him wrong. Perhaps, not the most pristine of reasons, but in crunch-time, it seemed to work.

Over the years and after many successes never once did my father tell me, *I'm proud of you, Larry.* He's gone now and I have come to terms with the fact that will obviously never happen. Actually, I came to terms with that reality many years before he died. More importantly, I have come to terms with the fact that I will no longer allow myself to be held hostage by what someone may have said to me or may have refused to say. Expectations and inner-need for such a validation only grants control of a part of me to someone else and I *will not* grant that control anymore. I have learned that I can get all the affirmation I need from many other sources. But the most important source is *me.* I decided to achieve for myself and because I believed it was the right thing for me; and that was/is enough.

I am so incredibly blessed to be the father of two of the finest ladies on the planet and I am bursting with pride to be their father. Notice I don't differentiate between daughter and step-daughter and that is intentional. For me, there is no difference and the pride I feel for them both is incredible and genuine. Not so much for all they have accomplished, as it is for the pride I have in the women they have become. I am incredibly honored, blessed and constantly humbled to be their father!

I suppose patience, sometimes, truly does pay off. In early 2010 I received an email from Stacey. She let me know she was in training to run a marathon, The San Diego Rock & Roll Marathon. She explained that it was a fund-raiser for leukemia and she wanted to know if I would mind if she ran in my honor. I told her I would be honored. She will probably never know how honored I was.

Stacey ran and finished that marathon, her first. She raised over $3,000 of the $8.2 million that was raised for Leukemia and Lymphoma that day.

When Stacey crossed the finish line, unbeknownst to her until that moment, her mother and I were there to congratulate her for her efforts. It was a very emotional moment for us all.

The next day I thought we were going to the San Diego Zoo. I know how much Stacey loves animals and that is one of the best zoos in the world. But, the next day, she informed us they would like to visit the floating museum that was the aircraft carrier, the USS Midway. I'm not sure if she realized it at the time, but that was one of the aircraft carriers I had landed on during Vietnam. I was able to share a little with them about how naval aviation had affected about one-third of my life.

Shortly after Veteran's Day Stacey sent me an email and made the comment, *"It was evident from being in your company on the Midway back in June that you were part of something bigger than yourself, a brotherhood of bravery and respect. Happy belated Veteran's Day!"*

I look up from reading that email, admittedly misty eyed, and smiled as I whispered a quiet, *Wow!*

57

It was the summer before Lauren started in middle school that I received a call from a friend informing me that Karen had been diagnosed with Stage 4 uterine cancer. I tried on several occasions to let Karen know how sorry I was and that I would continue to pray for her. Sometimes those efforts were well received, other times they were not, That was the nature of our relationship.

The next three years Lauren had to deal with fact that her mother had the big "C" and might not make it. Karen's oldest daughter, Christi, came to live with them to be the primary caregiver which took a lot of the burden off Lauren. But still, it was a great deal for both of them to endure.

Lauren was 12 when her mother was diagnosed with cancer, just 14 when she died. Christi, Karen's oldest daughter was about 20 years older and became the primary care-giver. Dealing with such an issue at any age is terrible. Dealing with it as a pre-teen must be horrific. Being a care-giver means one must care for two people, the one who is ill and yourself. Many people forget to care for themselves; the very thought of that seems selfish and can easily lead to guilt issues. It is common for care-givers to feel the extremes of sadness, anger, grief, guilt, loneliness, and feelings of inadequacy. The younger one is, the more magnified these emotions may manifest themselves. If not confronted, these emotions can linger long into adulthood.

One must understand that there is only *so-much* anyone can do and that the human body and psyche has its limits. When one is young, one reaches that *so-much* level rather early on; it is only simply logic.

Processing all the dynamics of dealing with approaching death that young are complex and can leave lasting scars.

Viewing someone much older who seems better at coping only complicates the matter. But the reality is, we all do the best we can in these issues. We should *never* compare our efforts with anyone.

Finally, where there is guilt or feelings of inadequacy. Simply, it is imperative that we genuinely forgive ourselves. The entire basis of the Christian faith is forgiveness. It is ironic that we can often readily forgive others but struggle in forgiving ourselves. Others forgive us, God forgives us. Why do we struggle so mightily when it comes to the most important act of all?

It was during those early teen years that I realized that Lauren had somehow lost her self-confidence in the classroom. Part of that may have been that primary school did not require much effort on her part to make straight 'A's. She now needed to study and that was new territory for her.

Successful people learn that *life is a series of challenges* and there are steps and plans that can be implemented and carried out to achieve the things we want and need. It sounds simple enough when stated in a short concise sentence like that but, it should be no surprise that there is an astonishingly large number of people who never seem to figure it out.

During the spring of her final year in middle school, 8th grade, she was still living with her mother and went to register for classes for her first year in high school. Her mother took her to register and I met them at school to be a part of the decisions she would have to make. She chose her classes and I looked them over noticing that she had taken the basics but no AP classes. I spoke to her explaining that she needed to take AP classes if she wanted to get into the college of her choice.

"Dad," she said, "I am not smart like some of the other kids. I know you want me to be, but I'm not."

I stared at her...dumbfounded. How had this self-confident, high achieving young girl fallen to these depths? More importantly, what words could I say that would make her see the image she had of herself was just simply untrue? I quickly realized I needed to choose my words carefully, and that it was not going to be an easy task to assist her in changing her self-image.

"*Lauren,*" I started, "*You are just as smart as anyone in this school.*

But, if you don't feel you can take a full load of AP classes we can certainly talk about it."

We discussed it for quite awhile and in the end I convinced her that she had always been good at language arts and I knew she would do well in AP English. She reluctantly agreed, but insisted on the caveat that, if she was not doing well by the end of the first six weeks, I would allow her to revert to a regular class. I knew with near absolute certainty that the only thing that could hinder her success was her state of mind.

About two weeks before Lauren started her freshman year in high school her mother died. It had been obvious for some time it was coming, but the stark reality still serves up quite a shock and sense of loss, along with a big dose of, *what now?*

That next year, Lauren's freshman year in high school, was tough for her. There certainly had been the lingering and recent memory of her mother's death, an event no child should have to go through that young. But there was also a complete change in her circle of friends. It started in AP English.

The top ten per-centers all were in her AP English class. It did not take long for her to realize that she did just as well as any of them and better than most. This gave her self-image a needed boost and soon she was convinced she could do anything they cold do.

I had engaged a counselor for Lauren when her mother was diagnosed with cancer and realized it was even more necessary, after the funeral, for her to continue those sessions. While they were very helpful, Lauren had become emotionally stuck.

This it was not apparent to her, but it had become increasingly obvious to me. Lauren was not able to move beyond her anger and guilt over her mother's death. She was angry with God, with Linda and especially with me, her Dad. While those feelings are not unusual, they can be roadblocks to emotional progress following such a horrific event.

It has been my experience, and one of my major life lessons, that the two most dangerous and destructive emotions are *anger* and *guilt.* Taken to the extreme, either, or both of these deadly emotions, can literally kill you, if you cannot get beyond their grasp. To a survivor, these two can often linger together, and can easily inhibit the growth of a healthy personality. These emotions are insidious, because people rationalize them as based on truth, and subsequently convince themselves they are actually entitled to be angry and/or guilty. In reality, this is an emotionally unhealthy rationalization. The stages of grief are healthy and necessary and while people should be allowed to progress through those stages at their own pace, it is possible to get stuck in a particular stage, and to become unable to move on. Anger is often the emotion that consumes one in life and in grief, and the consequences to the individual can be catastrophic. I remembered the anger my own mother carried with her all the days of her adult life after the loss of Robert in that road house outside Pittsburg, Pennsylvania.

I knew that much of Lauren's loss of confidence in herself, as well as her constant fits of rage, were all tied to the lingering emotions surrounding her mother's death. There is no specific or predictable timetable for going through the established and accepted stages of grief, but it was becoming clearer to me that, if we didn't have some sort of breakthrough, she was going to remain stuck in the muck of anger, and it could become an addiction, not unlike substance to a druggie.

I had to do something but I did not know when or what, and prayed every night for patience, wisdom, clarity and inspiration. I waited for my opportunity and prayed that God would make me smart enough to see it when it presented itself, and wise enough to properly implement it.

It was a few months after her mother died when Lauren came home one afternoon in her usual hostile manner, slamming doors, making surly comments, and being generally disagreeable. I followed her into her room and exclaimed, *"Lauren, get into the truck!"*

"What for," she gruffly asked?

"Just get in the truck!" I firmly said in a tone that she knew I meant business.

In better times, I had taken Lauren out to practice driving through the Texas hills, much for the same reason I traveled those same roads as a student in college. She still did not have her license, but I wanted her to have as much experience behind the wheel as possible before she set off on her own. Unbeknownst to me, she began to feel the same healing powers of the Texas Hills that I had experienced many years earlier.

I was driving as we left the driveway and turned onto Texas Highway 290, heading east. At first she just sat there looking out the window. Then I asked her what she thought about me. She just looked at me with suspicion so I asked her again, *"Tell me, Lauren, what do you think about me."*

"Honestly?" she asked.

"Yes, honestly," I replied.

She hesitated a moment and then blurted out, *"I HATE YOU! I HATE YOU!"*

She waited to calculate my response and when I said, *"Tell me why,"* it all came out. She began crying and screaming and giving it to me with both barrels and then reloadeded several times and fired again.

To be clear, I had been in the Navy for over 20 years and I can tell you, sailors have earned the phrase, *"Cussing like a sailor"* for a reason, and I thought I had heard them all until that afternoon on that road in the Texas Hills. When she would begin to slow down I yelled back at her, *"Is that the best you can do? Is that all you have?"* Then she would start in again. I gave her the freedom to say everything and anything in any way she wanted or needed, and she did.

The amazing thing about that event was, I was not offended by anything she said. In fact, I rejoiced in listening to her as she released the poison that had been pooling up inside her, from deep within her being. I kept pushing her to say more and encouraging her to say it all. I wanted to exorcise her demons of anger that had come to control her life and I wanted nothing left inside her. With each horrible thing she said I rejoiced. God had given me the wisdom to see this was exactly what she needed to do in order to rid her of the anger that had come to control her being. And he gave me the patience to endure her very personal ranting. It was as if the circle had been resurrected around me and nothing evil could penetrate that barrier.

After about an hour she began to weary but I still encouraged her to continue until she had nothing more to say, and sat there like a limp rag. We drove awhile more while she cried and looked out the window. I pulled into a gas station along the way, bought two colas, some gas and asked her if we needed to continue driving east, or turn around and go home. She was silent and I could clearly tell, she was totally spent. We turned back on the road and headed west to Fredericksburg.

We pulled into the driveway and both got out of the truck. She went into her room and slammed the door. I waited a moment, went to her door and could hear her inside her bedroom, sobbing with great intensity. Something told me to resist my instinct to go in and comfort her. I left her there, sobbing and crying.

About an hour later I went to her door, knocked and went in. I sat down on the side of her bed, gently pulled her to me for a fatherly hug and said, *"I love you, Lauren!"* She looked at me, somewhat dumbfounded. I then told her, *"There is something you need to know...there is <u>nothing</u> you can ever do or say that will keep me from loving you, ever!"*

I held her for a few moments, gave her a fatherly kiss on her forehead and left the room. From that moment on, *everything* was different. I had my daughter back and she was healed.

Anger is as much an insidious sickness as any there is and it will destroy you if you let it...it will consume and control your every moment unless you can find a way to expel it from within the depths of your soul. That evening, Lauren let her anger go, and the changes within her over the next few months were dramatic.

I would like to think I was this wise old sage who knew exactly what I was doing that afternoon and evening, but that would not be the truth. I was searching for answers as much as she. The truth is, I turned the entire event over to God, and it was His power that directed her actions and that prevented me from being offended. Some, not so unknown, force took control of me, as much as her, and took us both on an exciting ride across the Texas Hills and into a new and better place for us both.

After that, Lauren began, rather quickly, to change her circle of friends. She began to hang with her AP English classmates much more, most of whom had been her friends since pre-school. Somehow, in middle school she had pulled away from them. That factor cannot be underestimated, and it did not come without some cost. She made an A that first six weeks in her AP class and mostly A's in her other classes. Her confidence in the classroom was coming back.

By the end of the year she was doing well. I was teaching her to drive and we headed off into those healing Texas Hills as often as we could. There is a unique dynamic when there are only two people in a car. The scope of the conversation is dramatically different than if there are three or more riding together. It is much more intimate and honest.

One of my jobs in the Navy was as Safety Officer in a squadron. A study came across my desk that was developed by the Naval Safety Center that documented that the odds of being in an accident went exponentially down after a pilot had been flying more than 1,000 hours. The vast majority of accidents occurred to pilots with fewer than 1,000 hours in the cockpit.

I explained to Lauren that I wanted her to have 1,000 hours behind the wheel before she went out for her first solo drive. We did not keep a logbook, and I cannot accurately say how many hours she actually had before her first drive alone, but we were both confident her skill level was sufficient to the task.

It was towards the end of her freshman year that she came home, obviously depressed. We went for a drive through those healing Texas Hills. I asked what was wrong and she explained that she and a few of her friends went to the counselor to check their class standings.

There were around 257 in her freshman class and she was ranked number 57. I told her that wasn't bad, and she replied, "Dad, Meredith and Allison were both in the top 10. I could not believe it, I thought I was doing so well. I have never been so embarrassed in my life."

I have to admit I silently rejoiced at her 'embarrassment' comment because I had long observed that, for her, a personal embarrassment was one of her most effective motivators.

"Lauren," I explained. "First, being number 57 out of 257 is not bad. The second thing to keep in mind is that you have had a very serious loss this year. Those ahead of you have taken more AP classes than you and they count for more points than regular classes".

"But Dad, I want to go to the University of Texas or Texas A&M and I can't be sure to get in unless I am in the top 10 percent."

I measured my response carefully before I spoke.

"It's true that, in Texas, the top 10 per cent are guaranteed entry to the state college of their choices. But, that doesn't mean you can't get in if you are not ranked that high."

She looked at me for a moment and I assumed she was contemplating what I had said. Then she responded, "Dad, I want to be in the top 10 per cent. What do I have to do to get there?"

It has been my experience with Lauren that once she focused her sights on a goal she would not quit until she achieved it. I remember when she wanted to learn to whistle and almost passed out from hyperventilation in her effort, but she got it. Another time she wanted to be first chair in band and stayed up all night for several nights practicing until she was the best flute player in the school.

"*Well,*" I said, "*It's not going to be easy, but if anyone can do it, that would be you. First, you have to realize how much easier it is to go from 200 to 100 than it is to go from 57 to 25. Those ahead of you have taken more AP classes than you, and they will be taking AP classes for the next three years. If you really want to do it you will have to sign-up for every AP class you can take for the next three years and you will have to make A's in almost all your classes.*"

"*Then that is what I am going to do!*" she said.

For the next three years Lauren indeed took every AP class available to her and she slowly moved up in her class standings. She did not make all "A's" every time but she did so in her AP classes.

Our mail at home was delivered at about 10:00 am each day. Once or twice, I got a progress report on Lauren in the mail. I would jump in my car, drive up to the school, call her out of class, and ask her what was up. She usually explained that it was some paper she forgot to turn in or something innocuous. I would remind her of her goal and before the week was up, everything was current and she was back on track.

I could see the same determination in Lauren that was in me when I read what the doctor had written in my record over 30 years before. I could not help but smile; the apple had not fallen too far from the tree.

For several years I had served on the high school Campus Improvement Committee. One of the issues we tackled was the problem of high school dropouts. We came up with many suggestions, but the one that reverberated was starting a high school Junior Officer Training Program. Our rational was, teaching discipline and leadership would be a major leap for all our students and would be critical skills for students at risk for dropping out.

Fredericksburg is the birthplace of Admiral Chester Nimitz, the Commander of the Pacific during World War II, and it was logical to apply to the Navy for a Navy Junior ROTC program for Fredericksburg High School. The application was accepted and the school district began a search for a senior naval officer to lead the program and a NCO (Non commissioned officer) to help administer it.

I was approached about applying for the senior officer position, but when I reviewed the requirements I realized I had been out of the Navy much too long to qualify. The best candidate for the position was the commanding officer at the ROTC program at the University of Texas at Austin, but he was not available for another year.

We had two options; postpone the start of the program or find someone who would be willing to do it for one year. I made some inquiries to the regional program director and explained that I would be willing to do it. He felt confident he could get a waiver from the Navy for me to start the program for a year and hand it over to someone else after that time.

I was still the Executive Director of Economic Development (EDC) for the city and county and proposed to my board of directors that I was willing to do both jobs. One of my retired directors agreed to fill in for me if needed. I don't think they were too excited at the prospects of me doing both jobs, but I made it clear that I believed very strongly in the benefits of the JROTC program enough to offer my resignation from the EDC.

That summer, a Marine First Sergeant and I began recruiting students and preparing the program for its initial year. As the school year started, we had about 125 signed up for the program. The Navy required 10 percent of the class or a minimum of 100 students, to be in the program. We were pumped about our prospects.

I won't spend a lot of time on the details of that first year, only to say a couple of things. First, Lauren was not wild at all about me being at her high school for her junior year. But, when she realized I would be away from her classes and too busy to interfere with her issues, she accepted my close proximity. Besides, if she ever forgot lunch money I was just a building away.

The first year of any program like this is one of the most demanding. The kids could not spell JROTC and there were a few of my fellow teachers who were not always agreeable to the program. Some of the parents were not sure if I was a teacher or a military recruiter, which I was not! The learning curve for everyone was vertical.

It became my routine to go to my EDC job at 5:00 each morning and take care of any administrative issues. I would return during my off period at school and after school at about 5:30. That meant that I got home between 7:00 & 8:00 pm, petted my wife, kissed the dog, ate dinner, spoke a few words to Lauren, and went to bed only to repeat the schedule the next day.

By the end of the first semester, I had begun to feel extremely tired but I attached the blame to my crazy schedule. More significant to me at the time, I began to have these episodes of rather severe chest pains.

It was a Saturday that fall; Linda had gone to San Antonio to do some shopping. I decided to do some trimming of the many Texas live-oak trees we have, and rented one of those extension chain saws in order to reach limbs up high. Being a cheap bastard, I rented it for half a day. Actually, I figured I would run out of gas and energy by 1:00. As I was trimming, I suddenly had one of my episodes of chest pains. It got pretty severe, so I went inside and sat down for awhile and eventually the pain subsided a bit. I went back out to finish trimming and the pain came back, only much more severe than before. There was chest pain that radiated up and down my left arm, sweats and dizziness, all typical symptoms of a cardiac issue. I began to get a little concerned as all the symptoms continued. There was no one home if I were to pass-out and there were no neighbors nearby. I went inside and sat down again, hoping to relieve the pain as before. But this time it would not go away. I took two extra strength aspirins and decided I better get it checked.

I jumped in the truck to drive myself to the emergency room but, being the cheap-bastard, decided to return the chain saw on the way. I walked in the tool rental shop and it was obvious I was in a hurry. They thought there was something wrong with the saw so they took way too much time checking it over. Eventually, it was all taken care of and I was off to the ER.

By the time I arrived I was in severe pain and when I described my symptoms they rushed me out of triage and into a special section. They put needles in both arms, oxygen up my nose, and monitors on my chest. I managed to reach my cell phone, call Linda and say I was in the ER when the nurse took my cell phone away. She said it was interfering with the sensors.

Linda was about to checkout of the store in San Antonio and dropped everything she had selected and made the hour drive back to Fredericksburg. I only had time to tell her I was in the ER and she had no idea if I had cut my arm off, or what possibly was the cause of my being there.

After they had run all the major tests they gave me some Toradol in the IV which began to ease the pain a bit.

Linda arrived and I spent about four more hours there until I was stabilized, the pain had subsided, and they had determined it was probably not cardiac-related. They noted however, that my platelets were extremely high. I left the ER as baffled as the doctors, but at least all other indications seemed back to normal.

I had my annual physical in January and my family doctor noted an even greater increase in my platelets.

My platelets began a steady rise until they approached a million, normal being below 400,000. My doctor set me up to see an oncologist/

hematologist. That doctor did a bone marrow biopsy and announced that I had a rare form of leukemia.

I was bummed out for a few days, but refused to miss any work or to tell anyone other than Linda. I knew the impact it would have on Lauren, who was just recovering from her mother's losing battle with cancer, so I delayed telling her for as long as possible. It was then that I remembered making the bargain with her that I would always tell her the truth and that I would never keep anything from her; she deserved to know.

There is a certain mutual confidence in that agreement and I would recommend it to any parent. I think we give our children too little credit for what they can handle, and there is a certain confidence within a child when they understand their parents are always going to be honest with them and not wondering what they are holding back. Of course, there is always the issue of "age appropriateness," but we should not let that be an excuse to keep issues from our children. Lauren was 17, a junior in high school. I felt she could handle it and she did. It was not met without some trepidation on her part but when I told her I was doing fine and I would keep her informed if anything changed, she accepted the issue.

I began a regimen of high doses of oral chemotherapy in an attempt to get my platelet count down under 600,000. It seems the incidence of stroke is exponentially greater with a count nearing or exceeding one million. The chemo seemed to interact with my red blood count and my energy level was greatly impaired. However, once my body adapted to the medicine, things seemed to level out; still way out of normal, but tolerable, and considering the alternatives, I learned to live with it.

By the end of the school year I was exhausted, but gratified by the acceptance of the program by my kids, their parents, the school administration and the entire community.

We had our annual inspection by the regional director and were selected, *"The Best New Program"* in the eight-state region.

The major hiccup during the year was the first invasion of Iraq. Despite my assurances, many parents had the idea we were recruiting for the armed forces and their kids would be shipped off to fight in Iraq. As a result, we did struggle to meet the same numbers as we did that first year, but we still exceeded the Navy minimums.

On top of everything else that was going on that school year, in January, I was diagnosed with prostate cancer.

I went through the usual stages of grief when I was informed I had the Big "C."

I had injured my back while I was in the Navy and it began to get progressively worse. After living with it for several years, it deteriorated to the point that I was a walking cripple. I had tried several alternative treatments but finally came to the conclusion that surgery was my option of last resort. My doctor had explained the risks a few years earlier and they seem so ominous. I decided to attempt even more alternatives. But, there came the day that the pain was so overwhelming that I felt the risks were worth taking. I had the surgery and found immediate and dramatic relief from the pain. The doctor wanted to keep me in the hospital one more day but Lauren was going to her Junior Prom that night and I wasn't about to miss seeing her off. I was released and did just that.

I check out of the hospital and, about two days later, I came down with this incredible pain. I assumed it was associated with my back surgery and feared it was some sort of aneurism. When the pain became intolerable, I agreed to go to the ER. There, they determined my gall bladder was the culprit and they removed the thing that night.

So, there I was, a zipper on my back and two on the front. The pain relief from the back surgery was so dramatic that I regretted not having the surgery earlier. But, for a guy who never took even an aspirin until I was over 50, to having all this medical intervention in the space of a year, well, I feared my body was falling apart. I did have one other surgery on my foot but I recovered and within a year was back to normal. I had spoken to several people who have had surgeries similar to mine and the common thread in all their comments was, "Follow the doctor's instructions completely." That is what I did and the recovery was close to perfect.

I was a runner from the time I was in junior high school until just recently. While I did quit for awhile after my surgeries, I picked it up again and worked up to a 5K per day. But, in the last few years, I could see an end to my running days and I was not happy about that. In my early days of running it was to get into, and stay, in shape. An added bonus was the emotional high that runners get. I think it was that endorphin rush. But, running was also a time to keep my head grounded, and to sort out issues I might be facing.

I dreaded the day when I could no longer run and the thought of walking seem boring, almost depressing. But now I walk, only about 10-12 miles per week but mostly on a daily basis. I have learned to enjoy that time almost as much as running. I walk mostly with my wife and we consider it to be our "quality time."

It took awhile but finally I accepted the reality that I have health issues and probably always will. I did the chemo thing and had the prostate removed and I'm doing well, for my age and issues, or so they tell me.

We are not promised anything coming into this life and are certainly not promised a life without issues. It's perhaps trivial to say, *"It is what you do with the challenges that come your way that proves the mettle of your character,"* but that is the truth.

I began to learn the value of perspective. My doctor would look at my blood count results and say, *"Well, Larry, these look pretty good."*

"But Doc," I countered, *"they are all out of normal".*

"Yes, they are," he reminded me, *"but they look pretty good for you."*

Things aren't going the way you planned or want? Get over it and adapt. Look in the phonebook...how many "dinosaur exterminators" can you find in the yellow pages? None! Now look up "cockroach exterminators," plenty of them are there. The dinosaurs and the cockroaches were here together; roaches adapted to changes in the environment and they are still here; dinosaurs didn't and they are gone. So, are you a cockroach or a dinosaur? Tough choice.

60

By the end of Lauren's senior year in high school she had taken virtually every AP course she could for the last three years and she was very near the top 10 per cent.

Then reality served up an uneasy blow. She was working on the assumption that there were still 257 students in her class and she had to be in the top 25 to make that top 10%. When she checked her standings in the middle of her senior year she had jumped to #23 and she rejoiced until it was pointed out that there were now 220 students in her class and there may be fewer still by the time graduation came along.

I told her not to be too bummed out until the final numbers were calculated. As it turned out, she missed the Top 10 percent by one.

That was a bummer to her until I reminded her she had a tougher freshman year than anyone in the school and she had overcome it all to be where she was. I also reminded her she had reached her original goal, that the numbers had changed and she should be proud of what she has achieved.

Finally I told her, *"Lauren, I would not have been more proud of you if you were valedictorian for what you have accomplished!"* And that was the absolute truth.

I explained that, in addition to grades, she had to submit an essay with her college application and that writing was her strength.

Lauren submitted a killer essay along with her grades and was accepted to all five of the universities where she applied. While earlier in the year she was leaning towards Texas A&M University, as the deadline approached, she chose the University of Texas at Austin.

Lauren completed her degree in psychology with a minor in Business from the McCombs School of Business in three and a half years. She made Dean's List throughout, an honor graduate, and like her older sister, Phi Beta Kappa.

What did I ever do to deserve two such gifted and talented daughters?

61

You may notice I have not been inclined to name these chapters. But if I were to do so, this one would be, "On Happiness."

I look at my family, my extended family and my friends, and what I see them seeking most is happiness. I am pleased with that since they are not necessarily seeking material things as their source and are looking beyond themselves to find the happiness they seek. They are looking into themselves, their relationships and their faith to provide the joys they seek.

As I write this, it is almost Thanksgiving Day, my favorite of all holidays. To put it in the simplest of terms, "If you want to be happy, *be Thankful!*"

"Hey, that's too easy," you may say. Well no, it is *just that easy.*

Upon reading these pages of my missive, you may have perceived a life of desperation. That could not be farther from the truth. It has been a life of constant gratitude for all the daily necessities and occasional 'wants' that have been bestowed upon me.

I have a few friends who have recently come to know some of these stories. Often the comment I hear is, *"I wish we knew, so we could have been some help."* In truth, I did not want anyone to know. Perhaps it was shame or embarrassment. People had no idea these things were going on, and that is the way I wanted it. People didn't know I went to study hall during lunch because I did not have the simple change to get a meal ticket. The second half of my junior year and all my senior year in high school I got a job selling lunch tickets at the cafeteria. There was no pay; only a free lunch, and that was fine with me. I was VERY thankful for that arrangement.

In the midst of the turmoil that was my life, I maintained a 'happy-go-lucky' exterior which wasn't entirely a facade.

In one of the assemblies at the end of the year, I was awarded the "School Spirit" award. That meant a lot to me, because I was proud to be a "Fighting Beeville Trojan" and it pleased me that others recognized that, being around my classmates made me proud and happy, very happy.

That is the way I wanted people to view me. Not a pitiful case with a terrible home life. Over my lifetime, I got very good at projecting a conjured-up image and coming up with excuses about things. I would just make a joke, laugh and, more than likely, change the subject. I did not lie very often. I hated doing that. But I was good at diverting the discussion and vectoring my comments to something much happier.

It became my survival mechanism. In the midst of all that happened, I became, like my grandmother, thankful for what I had and did not dwell on that which was financially or otherwise beyond my grasp.

Truly happy people are seriously thankful people. You do not need "stuff" or the latest gadgets, clothes, cars or homes to make you happy. Those things are more like drugs; they may bring a temporal 'high,' but that addiction needs to be constantly fed in increasingly higher doses to maintain that sense of euphoria. Eventually, there is the predictable downer as the addict comes crashing down, often when they run out of money to buy more stuff or their credit card is rejected. You all probably know a 'shop-a-holic' and you have undoubtedly heard the joke or have seen the T-shirt, *"when the going gets tough, the tough go shopping."* There is more comfort and more lasting truth in, *"When the going gets tough, the tough find something to be thankful about."*

I have a mother- in-law who is one of the happiest people I know. She will spend this Thanksgiving Eve getting things ready for the next day, and all Thanksgiving morning she will be making all the special things the family enjoys. All she expects in return is, on that Thursday, seeing her children, grandchildren, great-grandchildren, even her son-in-law, gathered around the table enjoying the bountiful feast she prepared.

What I have noticed most about her is her constant state of thankfulness for the people in her life. For her birthday or Christmas she asks, "Don't give me anything I have to dust." She doesn't need 'things' to make her happy, only her friends and family. She spends much of her time helping others, and she NEVER complains.

She constantly tells me I am her favorite son-in-law, disregarding the fact that I am her only son-in-law. But that does not diminish the sincerity in her comments. She is genuinely thankful that I am in her daughter's life and that 'thankfulness' makes her happy.

If things are tough, find something to be thankful about and, if your thoughts are genuine, you will notice the rough edges will fall away. It's such a cliché to say, 'develop an attitude of gratitude,' but the truth is, it works.

Many years ago Polly Fenner gave me a "Worry Stone." It was a smooth rock that you were supposed to rub with your thumb and, supposedly, it would diminish your 'worries'. Instead, each time I reached into my pocket and felt my stone I was reminded to be thankful for something.

Oh, when I did this, my 'worries' seemed to fade away as well. I guess it was my multi-tasking stone.

62

OVER THE YEARS, I have been both blessed and cursed with an enormous energy level. I have always been on the run, in play, in track, football, one marathon, a couple half marathons and countless 5K's and 10K's. I devoted that energy level to succeeding in the Navy and to the various careers I pursued since I got out. I used to run to keep in shape; in college for football and track, in the Navy for my annual physicals, and during my post Navy career, because, I suppose, by then it was a habit. One of the side effects I noted was this mental healing while running. Running longer distances gave me plenty of time to think. Add into the equation the 'endorphin high' that runners get and I guess I was somewhat addicted to running.

I have always loved the challenge of a new venture and I seemed to have an endless flow of ideas which I tackled with focus and determination and most were brought to fruition. While I was in the Navy I had limited time to devote to my community and that disappointed me.

While in my squadron, VT-28, as an instructor pilot I was tasked with coordinating a gathering of all our squadron mates and their families for a Thanksgiving celebration a week or so before the actual day. Mrs. Polly Fenner was a great supporter of The South Texas Children's Home, a place for orphans or unwanted kids. So I came up with the idea to invite the kids from the Home to our squadron party. They brought a bus load of kids from the Home and everyone had a great time and they mixed right in together with all the other children there.

There was this one kid, a tow-headed blond that looked so much like me at that age, he could have been mine, but I'm pretty sure he wasn't. I led him on a personal tour of our aircraft and arranged for him and a few other kids to get a ride on a helicopter.

In the middle of all this I had the idea of inviting these kids to join families from within the squadron for Thanksgiving Day. The next Monday at our AOM (All Officers Meeting) I presented the proposal and the response was overwhelming. I spoke with the administrators of the Children's Home and they were just as excited as we were. So, on Thanksgiving Day each and every child in the school was matched with a family from our squadron, and a few from our sister squadron on the base. These kids were able to enjoy a Thanksgiving Dinner with a real family.

It was such a moving experience that I proposed to the Home that we do it again at Christmas. Word had spread to a couple other squadrons about the program and pretty soon I had more homes than kids. It was then that I remembered another children's home near Beeville and soon I had more kids than homes. So I contacted a friend at Chase Field Naval Air Station in Beeville and asked him to float the idea around and quickly I had more families than kids. I realized that was the best place to stop and it ended up that all the kids from two Children's Homes had families to be with at Christmas. The stories I heard from the hosts were mind numbing. It reinforced my belief in people and their ability to assume the role of 'angel' if only someone would give them an opportunity.

While in The Netherlands I took a couple gloves and a bag of baseballs to a local park by my house and began playing catch with some of the kids. They knew of American baseball but were not sure what it was all about. Eventually, I laid out a diamond and gave them a Baseball 101 lesson. They would hit the ball and run to third and a few got hit in the nose trying to catch the ball, but they eventually got the hang of it. Probably shoulda started with a softball.

When I came to Fredericksburg you would have been reminded of the old joke, *"What is the difference between me and a parrot?"* You could teach a parrot to say *"No!"*

I do not intend to create a self-grandiasing list of all the places I have volunteered over the years here in Fredericksburg. I do, however, want to thank those who gave me the opportunity to be a servant-leader in my community.

Over the last few years I have had to quit running due to health issues, mostly involving the effects of a broken foot while running in a NATO track meet in Norway, but also the effects of two types of cancer. Even before I quit running I could see the day was fast approaching when I could no longer run for more than a very short distance. I bought a Precor elliptical runner, which has facilitated my transition, and my wife and I have become known in the community as "The Walkers." If someone does not know our names they say, "Oh, you are the walkers!" I dreaded the day when my primary exercise was walking through town, but I must admit I have learned to enjoy that less exciting life. It has become a great 'quality time' for us and we are our own captive audience for talking and sharing.

I have a 14 year old Yellow Lab. When I got him as a puppy I was still running and we both had energy to burn, and burn it we did. He would run-away with anyone who walked by or would throw a stick for him. I spent many a day/night running around the neighborhood trying to find him. But things improved dramatically when I gave him a few jobs to do around the house. He carries the mail back from the mailbox, retrieves our newspaper and brings it to the back door and he carries the trash, in those plastic trash liner bags, from the B&B's to the trash bin. He is so proud of his jobs and waits anxiously to serve his purpose. My experience with dogs has been, *if you have a dog you best give him a job. If you don't, he will find a job, and the job he finds you won't like.*

The reality is Toby and I seem to have aged together over the last 14 years. In dog years he is now 98 years old. He still does his jobs but he sleeps a lot more than he did as a pup. I suppose I sleep a little more as well. His energy level is obviously waning, as is mine.

But, I think we both have a few miles left on us, despite the obstacles that come with age. *Growing old, it's not for cowards.*

63

IN THE TELLING of the elements and events that shaped my life, it would be incomplete without the mention of the influence of music upon me, and within the world I have known. I was born side-by-side with Rock & Roll and have listened to its every twist-and-shout over the last six decades. In the early years I admired the beat and reveled in the uniqueness of the sound. In the second decade of R&R, the 1960's, I began to be drawn more to the writers and the lyrics they composed. I sat in awe as I read the words of Rod McKuen and Leonard Cohen and was blown away at their ability to put those words to music and create the very mood I was feeling at the time. I was captivated by the stories of Harry Chapin. It was literal magic to me as I had a constant flow of, *"I wish I would have said that"* moments. I was amazed how those songs could express the exact emotions I was feeling at the time.

Phil Ochs had a great song, *"Crucifixion,"* (best done by Glenn Yarborough, and is included in my yet to be published book, *"The Gospel According to Rock & Roll."*) It is a magnificently written tribute to the rise and fall of any hero from Jesus to John F. Kennedy, not that JFK is close to comparable to Jesus.

In the late 60's, early 70's it was the words and melodies of Kris Kristofferson and Jim Croce. Kris wrote the words and Croce was a switch-hitter, being able to both write and sing, a somewhat rare talent it seems. I was as devastated by his demise in a plane crash as Don McLean was at the crash of Buddy Holly and friends 14 years earlier.

I suppose I *must* include Paul Simon's *Bridge Over Troubled Waters,* an exquisitely written song that so moved me that I had to pull my car over to the side of the road the first time I heard it on my radio.

Because You Loved Me, written by Diane Warren as a tribute to her father, and sung by Celine Dion, is one of my all time favorites and one of those *"Gospel According to R&R"* songs. Change one word and it's probably one of the greatest "praise" songs ever written.

As I reflect on all these artists and their songs, I come to the conclusion that I have been moved by the chords of love and I aspire to be saved from the chords of sadness. But still, I find myself being equally drawn to both as a means of fully understanding my own emotions.

~~~

So, why did I write all this, the details of one man's life? It is, after all, unique only in the fact that *each* one of us is unique. Every one of us is the sum of all the parts of our lives. To know me without knowing my past is an unpainted picture, and I have hidden that past far too long.

This work is a confirmation to the statement: *"Everyone has a story and every story deserves to be told."*

But even more than that, it is one person's attempt to come to terms with who he is. Living is like driving on the autobahn in Germany, no matter how fast you go someone will pass you. No matter how bad you consider your circumstance, someone else has had a more difficult time of it. *The Little Match Girl* comes to mind.

There is something magical in writing. It forces you to have thoughts that you are sometimes reluctant to share, but are never-the-less compelled to canonize. It requires you to visit the hidden resources of your soul and put what you see into words. It impels you to compel your thoughts to come alive on the pages before you.

For me, the sharing of this story is one of personal redemption; a story of one person coming to terms with his past and a statement of thankfulness for all who were part of that past, and the redemption that occurred. I had a lot to learn with limited helpful role-models early on. From my early years, I learned more what I wanted to avoid than what I wanted to be. As time passed I began a thoughtful quest to discover what I wanted to become. I had the opportunity to choose my role-models and I was intentional to select them very carefully. Life was my personal smorgasbord; I knew I could not eat it all so I went for only the very best.

I admit there is something a bit more vainglorious for this, my expiatory offering. I have dreams, often extremely terrible dreams perhaps more accurately, *night terrors*. They are mostly about flying in the Navy, and almost always contain the faces of those whom I have known that have been killed. In the midst of many of these frightening dreams, I have screamed and flailed my arms about, occasionally hitting my wife. A doctor or two have helped me to cope with these night issues a bit but I am resigned to the fact I may have to live with them for some time, perhaps the rest of my life. Some refer to it as "survivor's guilt," to others it is a form of PTSD. But in reality, those are mere names and phrases. I find nothing guilty about it at all. I suppose it has crossed my mind to wonder why I am still living while so many others I've known are not around anymore, but I consider that fact divine providence more than mere good fortune.

For my friends, shipmates and fellow pilots, the list of culprits for their demise is long, be they enemy action, illnesses, suicides, accidents, both in the air, on the seas and the highways, or merely silently at home. Most of those can happen to anyone and they eventually do. Living close to the edge, as we did for many years, may increase the odds a bit but life has a way of defying the odds at times, no matter your profession. In the end, we all end up staring into that dark abyss.

My first inspiration to write these words was when my daughter commented that she knew noting of me before she came along and wondered about those 45 years. Now, that I am about finished, she cannot remember making that comment.

I expanded this writing project as an effort for me to be able to come to terms with the many issues and memories that haunt my sleep. I still have the dreams but I feel they are becoming less intense, certainly kinder versions of established issues. I hope writing continues to be my savior from myself and a door that waits for me to open in the coming days and years.

My life has seen some amazing moments and given me some fantastic memories, but it is the people I remember the most. The concept of people showing up for a reason, and leaving for an equally compelling reason, can be a blessing and a curse. The first part is benign and rather easy to accept, while the second part becomes problematic in its acceptance and sometimes painful.

Still, I have a few wishes; I wish I were a better speller, had paid more attention in some classes and had been a little kinder on a few occasions. But I know I did the best I could, based on what I knew at the time, and I think that is what God expects of us all.

I am very proud of the years I served my country, but I am most proud of my family; to me they are the three most wonderful women on the planet.

As much as I like Somerset Maugham, I am compelled to take some issue with this comment…*"It's no good trying to keep up old friendships. It's painful for both sides. The fact is, one grows out of people, and the only thing is to face it."* I suppose it is true that we do *"grow out of some people,"* and they grow out of us, but I cherish my old friends. With that in mind, I tend to gravitate to Harry Chapin who said, *"Old friends, they mean much more to me than new friends, 'Cause they can see where you are, and they know where you've been."* (From *"Let Time go Lightly"*)

With this epistle I have attempted to be fair without being boastful or self-deprecating, and I have arrived at my conclusions after long and careful introspective evaluation. I know from where I come, and I accept the choices I have been compelled to make. I am also keenly aware of the many *Course Corrections* I have made along the way; some dictated by circumstance, but most my own personal choices. I hope all divinely inspired. I have been at the same time firm and pliable, determined to lead but willing to be led. I have listened to that still small voice in the valleys and I have shouted my stubborn convictions among the mountains and the clouds. Mine has been a fantastic journey of an outward man attempting to come to terms with his inner spirit. Let there be no doubt, I have been guided on this journey by forces I do not fully understand.

I have cried a bit but laughed a lot. Looking back, I note my losses have been temporal; my victories have been eternal and made possible, sometimes in spite myself. I have loved and lost and, in the end, loved and won. But most importantly, I have no regrets about either. I have equally embraced my failures and my victories, for both have taught me eternal possibilities.

I go forward from this place loving my wife and daughters with all my heart, for they are a part of me for all eternity. I love being a husband and a father, and I hope I have given to those I cherish something to hold onto when the days get dark and the path ahead becomes uncertain. To them I say, *"Know full well that I have been there, too, and if I can make it, you can surely make it. For you are equipped much better than I."*

While following my heart has been perilous at times, it has always guided me from darkness to light. Even still I am compelled to make the occasional *course correction.* I used to get upset with myself for some stupid choices I have made. But, I have come to terms with the reality that life is just one decision after another and no one leaves this sphere batting a thousand. Hindsight merely means you have additional information and it is easy to be critical but not always productive. I may have learned more from bad decisions than I have from the good ones, but, I have not kept score.

I have come to embrace my *"Course Corrections"* as 'markers' along my way. In ancient times, the Byzantines, and later the Romans, created a system of roadside markers, originally to advise their legions how far they had traveled. We know these today as "mile-markers." The distance of the Roman-mile was a thousand paces (one pace equaled two steps), or *mille passuum* in Latin. The 'Roman mile' was 1,617 yards while our 'statute-mile' today is 1,760 yards. I don't know why the difference, perhaps it was a taller man who stepped out those 1,000 paces when the statute-mile was codified.

Looking back, I see my markers are not so equally sequenced, but they are no less important to me as being spiritual, personal, mysterious, and yes, a bit magical. I admit I have ended up on a few dead-end streets, and have had to retrace my steps from time to time. But, those were some of my greatest lessons.

I'm not Presbyterian enough to think all this is pre-determined but I'm not naïve enough to discount any possibility. I do believe there is an intelligent order-of-things and our lives are a journey towards fitting into that order. While perfection is not likely, each event and each person in our lives leads us forward towards that blissful balance we all seek.

To Linda, my soul-mate, I say: Before you, I was drifting. I allowed the tailwinds of life to carry me with little understanding that they would eventually lead me to you. I landed once or twice along the way, but eventually I always continued my drifting. Since I met you we have flown together, intentionally, and with a common purpose. The way forward has been clear; the skies have been mostly calm. Occasionally, we have seen a few storms along the way, but we navigated around them easily, together, always with the knowledge that flying together was so much safer than flying alone. No matter what our future may bring, I will *never* leave my wing-man.

Finally, to my children let me say, I hope you never lose, *"the light and vivacity that laughs in the eyes of a child."* (Charles Dickens). Embrace your own *'Course Corrections,"* not as failures, but as victories of the soul, for those corrections will take you to new and exciting places and result in meeting many interesting people.

That vivacity is a place of contented acceptance that, whatever we are lacking will be revealed in due course and being open to that revelation and accepting of its lessons, allows each of us to become better people.

After all, isn't that what life is all about…becoming better?

Quandaries of Love

Perhaps it's your eyes I miss the most,
Or maybe it's your touch.
I know it's not your words
Or promises you could make.
I've heard too many words
And seen too many broken promises
To put much trust in either.
One smile from you does more
To convince me you'll stay
Than all those words we first shared.
And that one warm touch today
Is worth a thousand promises of tomorrow.
Please don't think me unkind
If I don't tell you I love you.
It's not that I don't…It's just harder for me to say.
I can't help but love you.
The moments we shared won't allow anything but that.
I know you wonder at the silence in my eyes.
I wonder too at times.
Perhaps I'm content to be near you
And words seem unnecessary
Or perhaps it's just that the feeling is yet too new,
Not ready for words.
And maybe I'm still unsure
Wondering at how and why it all happened.
Afraid to close my eyes for fear that when I looked again
You'd be gone.
Or if I spoke I'd wake from some sort of dream
And find you were never there at all.
So, for now, I'll touch you when I can
Content with the few moments we can share today
Expecting little of tomorrow
But still hoping morning finds your smile close to mine.
LJN

— Postlude —

February, 2011

Most of the previous was written in 2009-2010. I did not intend to have a postlude to this endeavor but life sometimes has a way of interfering with our plans.

I became semi-retired a couple of years ago and today my soul-mate, Linda, began her official retirement. These are the days we have looked forward to all of our lives and, yes, sometimes with great trepidation.

We are both extremely active people, we love mostly the same things and we have a modest retirement. We have financially and mentally planned for this new phase of our lives for a very long time, all of our lives, actually. We have had a vision that retirement would be a pleasant reward for a life of hard work and years of financial abstinence.

But, as the saying goes, *"If you want to see God laugh, tell him your plans."*

I have been dealing with the effects of a blood disorder for some time. For so long that it has come to be more of a minor annoyance than any sort of threatening issue. I have come to accept my hematologic abnormalities as merely a part of what I am and I just ignore the swings that show up in my blood-work.

But then my hematologist decided I needed a bone marrow biopsy, *"Just to see what is going on."*

I won't go into the grizzly details of that sort of biopsy except to say that he made several attempts to get a good sample of my marrow and he was unsuccessful. He did, however, get a bone fragment which he felt had enough marrow on it to get a sufficient result.

A week later, the first day of our long awaited retirement, we were in the doctor's office and he opened the conversation with, *"We have a lot to talk about."* Probably not a good omen.

He continued with, *"Your biopsy revealed that you have myelofibrosis." This is a disorder of the bone marrow, in which the marrow is replaced by scar tissue and eventually inhibits the marrow from doing its job. As you are aware, bone marrow produces red and white blood cells along with your platelets. There is no set cure for this condition and few medications. The only possibility for a cure is a bone marrow transplant, which itself is fraught with danger and extreme risks."*

He went on with quite a bit more but my mind kinda got stuck in the mud that was, *"there is no cure."*

But, as we all know, there is a reason they refer to it as *"practicing medicine."* I have been here many times, from that initial diagnosis many years earlier of rheumatic fever and a bad heart, to liver cancer and six months to live, in 1972. At least three times being diagnosed with hepatitis, being put into isolation, and once having all my cloths burned. It seems the Navy is not fond of the possibility of hepatitis running through the ranks.

Each time, on further investigation and medical consideration, those diagnoses were proven a bit pre-mature.

As we were leaving the doctor's office that day, I had one more question for the Doc and went back in. I went into his office and asked outright, *"So, Doc, how long do I have?"*

He equivocated a little but finally came out with, *"One to two years, without a transplant."*

I suppose at some point the doctors are going to get it right. I mean, even a blind sow finds an acorn now and then. I don't mean that in any disrespectful way. It's just my way of coping with what I would consider a very serious prognosis. *Some things in life are so serious if you don't laugh at them you will go crazy.*

As a young man I remember making kamikaze hits on much larger, faster and stronger football players or went back into a game after a hit that left me wondering where I was and unable to remember the play I just called.

I spent twenty years flying, sometimes with students who were intent on trying to kill me, or having to take-off a few hours after some very close friend had not returned. Or, maybe flying into the teeth of a typhoon or close to the edge of some easily angered foreign land where not long before one of our aircraft had been shot down. Then there was the time I was in a 60 degree angle of bank in the clouds over Chiang Kai-shek's palace watching pine-cones just off my left wing.

A pilot could lose his wings if he *"exhibited no apparent fear of death."* Yet we often defied death every day. If that rule were liberally enforced there would be few pilots left in the Navy.

So pardon me if I didn't take the pronouncement of my imminent demise too seriously. Besides, only one entity knows when you are going to leave this earth and He is being very quiet about it.

I visited with the transplant doctor in San Antonio a couple of times. He reviewed all my health records and drew about a gallon of blood. He reiterated the medical fact that, while modern medicine has made great strides, there remains a 40% mortality rate from complications associated with a bone marrow transplant.

A transplant is a high-risk, high reward procedure. Right now, I have a fair amount of energy, not as much as a few years ago but I'm 65, the autumn of my life.

A bone marrow transplant is about a two year commitment. First, they kill all your bone marrow with chemo and radiation. This takes you right up to the edge of death. They then roll the dice that the transplanted marrow will like its new home and eventually bring you back from the brink. While they have made great medical strides, there still remains an almost infinite number of things that can go wrong. When they kill your marrow they kill your white cells resulting in a great risk of infection, which can be fatal.

There is a difference today from all that has occurred in the past; that is, my family. My wife was there with me when I received the news and she understands how I feel and her support is magnificent.

But the greatest dread I have is breaking the news to my daughters. I suppose I can lean on my wife to break it to our oldest, Stacey. But it will be on my shoulders to find a way to tell Lauren, the youngest. She lost her mother at 14 and now she will have to deal with this, ten years later at age 24.

Lauren is a strong young woman, as is Stacey, and they will be fine. But still, there remains so much of their lives that I would like to see.

Some of the greatest joys of my life have included being an observer of the great things my wife and daughters have accomplished. While I have no plans to leave anytime soon, I suppose it is prudent to plan for the worse and hope for the best.

While we are making the necessary arrangements for a transplant, we are not rushing into something that is so fraught with danger. In the meantime, life goes on and I intend to live every moment that makes up my future as full as those moments in the past.

Death is indeed a part of life; albeit, the last part. But when my time comes I hope it is a time of celebration, certainly not a time for anger, guilt or regret. I like the idea of a New Orleans funeral where they are solemn going out, but rejoicing and happy on the way back.

It's easy to be angry when you lose someone close to you. It just doesn't seem fair. But the truth is, you can go to God in anger or you can go to Him for comfort and support, it's your choice. Either way *He* has big shoulders and understands if you are angry and is always prepared to offer his comfort when you are ready. So, why waste your time avoiding the comfort and the peace *He* offers?

As I face the uncertainty, I marvel at the wonderful life I have been given. I have played the cards I have been dealt to the best of my ability. If I have hurt anyone, I think it was unintentional. Either way, I did it all the best way I knew how. If I am judged, I hope that carries some weight.

I have come through the crucible and now there is at least one more test for me. I will face it the way I have faced all obstacles in my path and the only way I know, military power. It is out of my hands so I bless those who have blessed me and lovingly pray for those who don't…that is my blessing to them.

Psalm 31 - *In Thee, O Lord I have taken refuge. In thy righteousness, deliver me…for my life is spent and my body has wasted away…Into thy hand I commit my spirit…thou hast ransomed me, O Lord God of truth. Be strong and let your heart take courage, all you who dwell in the Lord.*

Regrets? *I have a few, but then again, too few to mention.* Yes, I like to think *I did it my way, but I hope I did it God's way!*

Larry J. Nevels, (born October 20, 1945), M.A., Commander, United States Navy (retired), Graduate-Texas Lutheran University (BA) (1968), U.S. Navy Pilot (1968-1988), Economic Developer (1990-2004), Teacher, Bed & Breakfast Owner (1990-present), Rancher, Community Volunteer, Poet, Author:'Course Corrections' (2011). Larry resides in Fredericksburg,Texas where he raises Texas Longhorns along with his wife, Linda. They have two daughters; Stacey (New York City) and Lauren (Dallas, Texas).

Made in the USA
Lexington, KY
28 October 2015